WILLIAM BLAKE AND GENDER

WILLIAM BLAKE AND GENDER

Magnus Ankarsjö

McFarland & Company, Inc., Publishers
Jefferson, North Carolina, and London

LIBRARY OF CONGRESS CATALOGUING-IN-PUBLICATION DATA

Ankarsjö, Magnus.
   William Blake and gender / Magnus Ankarsjö.
      p.   cm.
   Includes bibliographical references and index.

   ISBN 0-7864-2341-2 (softcover : 50# alkaline paper)

   1. Blake, William, 1757–1827—Political and social views.
2. Man-woman relationships in literature.   3. Sex discrimination
in literature.   4. Sex role in literature.   5. Utopias in literature.
6. Sexism in literature.   7. Women in literature.   I. Title.
   PR4148.P6A55   2006
   821'.7—dc22   2005022638

British Library cataloguing data are available

©2006 Magnus Ankarsjö. All rights reserved

*No part of this book may be reproduced or transmitted in any form
or by any means, electronic or mechanical, including photocopying
or recording, or by any information storage and retrieval system,
without permission in writing from the publisher.*

Cover image ©2005 Pictures Now

Manufactured in the United States of America

*McFarland & Company, Inc., Publishers
  Box 611, Jefferson, North Carolina 28640
  www.mcfarlandpub.com*

For Helena

Acknowledgements

My work with the poetry of William Blake began at the University of Gothenburg, Sweden, where I took several courses in English over many years. As it turned out, I actually took virtually every course there was in the English department, after many years' labor emerging as a doctor of English literature with a dissertation on Blake. Naturally, a lot of the research for this book was done in those years and at that place. Therefore my sincerest thanks go to the people at my alma mater who have helped and inspired me in many different ways: My supervisors, Docent Hans Löfgren, Docent Ronald Paul and Professor Emeritus Lennart Björk, who have provided advice and support of my work in its various stages. I owe particular gratitude to Lennart, who urged me to apply for a two-year scholarship at the Knut and Alice Wallenberg Foundation, which enabled me to move on with my work at a crucial point and do a great deal of the research for this project, as well as for the thesis. Thanks are also due to the foundation itself for financial support. I would further like to thank Lars Malmsten for helpful assistance of editing my material.

In recent years I have benefited to an increasing degree from my good international scholarly contacts. Most of these are concentrated to England, mainly London. My deepest thanks here go to the person who so kindly volunteered to be the external examiner of my dissertation, Professor David Worrall. He has gradually ushered me into the truly Blakean context. David never fails to inspire and encourage his colleagues, and I have benefited from many fruitful discussions with these in the last few years, often at the British Library. In particular I am thinking of Keri Davies, Mei Sung, Bill Goldman and Will Easton. I am also grateful to David for enrolling me as a visiting fellow at the Nottingham Trent University. Further, in the United States I would like to thank Professor Emeritus Morton Paley and Professor Josephine A. McQuail.

But my most heartfelt thanks go to the person who in her position as the director of studies at the University College of Borås had faith in me as a university teacher seven years ago. She has kept faith in me, and I in her, since that day. I owe her more gratitude than can be expressed in words—Helena Bergmann.

Contents

Introduction	1
1—Apocalypse, Utopia and Gender	9
2—Blake's Radical Context	40
3—The Gender Utopia of *The Four Zoas*	60
4—The Gender Utopia of *Milton*	122
5—The Gender Utopia of *Jerusalem*	158
Afterword	191
Bibliography	197
Index	205

Introduction

When William Blake composed his three epic prophetic poems *The Four Zoas*, *Milton* and *Jerusalem* he had, we must assume, no notion at all of feminism. Nonetheless, these majestic poems are in many respects expressions of a feminist line of thought. Provided with the right sort of keys, it is difficult not to read them as, if not responses to, then at least moving within the same discourse as the one emerging among new radical women writers of that time like Mary Wollstonecraft and Mary Hays. Or—why not?—even as being part and parcel of that discourse.

In spite of this, Blake has over the years frequently been regarded as a sexist or a misogynist, and critics have read his female symbols as manifestations of anti-feminism. Most commonly, female characters in Blake's poetry have been understood as considerably weaker and less active than their male counterparts. In essays that have by now become near classics to Blake studies, Anne Mellor and Alicia Ostriker, among others, have proposed that Blake's female characters are to be placed at the extremes of a paradigm of passive and weak on the one end, and active and evil on the other.[1]

In the 1804 epic poem *Milton* it is Ololon, one of Blake's allegedly strong female characters, and not her counterpart male character Milton, who is taking the initiative to descend into the mundane to actively search for and be reconciled with her partner. Her activity pays off positively when the two are reunited before apocalypse in the final plates.

---

[1] See Mellor, "Blake's Portrayal of Women," and Ostriker, "Desire Gratified and Ungratified: William Blake and Sexuality." These two are probably the most well-known essays, but there are numerous examples of comments in a similar fashion; therefore see also Bruder pp. 1–32 for an exhaustive outline of recent feminist criticism on Blake, as well as Blake criticism in general.

In the earlier *The Four Zoas* it is another female character, Enion, who initiates the apocalypse by acting as a harbinger of apocalypse and utopia. The positive ramifications of female activity are even more obvious in the concluding epic *Jerusalem*, where the eponymous character, another of Blake's strong females, manages to arouse her symbolic consort Albion from his slumber, and the reunited couple together go through the apocalypse and enter the afterworld of Blake's highest Eden at the end of the poem.

Already on the title page of *The Four Zoas*, where he has scribbled "The Torments of Love & Jealousy" (Brit. Mus. Add. MS. 39764 1), Blake implies that the struggle between the sexes is the main theme of this poem and the two subsequent ones. Although unfinished, *The Four Zoas* is a very important poem in Blake's overall production; it is of special significance since it embodies all his basic utopian ideas. Here, for the first time Blake, tries to create a complete mythological system by establishing a structure of opposed and interactive male and female characters. Since he uses this system throughout the three major epics, my argument is that in these epic prophecies Blake presents a gender utopia with a vision of complete equality between the sexes.[2]

One of my aims in this book is to demonstrate the hitherto unacknowledged significance of Blake's female characters in greater detail. Through my analysis I will dismantle the claims that define Blake as condescending towards the female sex. When feminist critics comment on the activity of Blake's characters, they almost exclusively regard male activity as positive and female activity as negative. In stark opposition to this view, I maintain that in his three major epic poems *The Four Zoas*, *Milton* and *Jerusalem*, Blake emerges as an advocate of a utopian existence with complete gender equality. Accordingly, my discussion does not follow the main current within Blake criticism; the central difference between my view and other studies of Blake's gender utopia

---

[2] *Blake's poems are not generally recognized as utopian, and to my knowledge few studies have approached Blake from this angle. Some commentators indicate, merely in passing, that there is a certain utopian quality in the poetry of Blake, for example A. L. Morton and Nicholas Williams. In his outline* The English Utopia, *Morton, as one of very few critics, spots the utopian dimension of Blake's poetry when he calls the Prophetic Books "utopian from end to end" (157). Stating the purpose of his study* Ideology and Utopia in the Work of William Blake, *Nicholas Williams writes: "Given the central position which a utopian vision holds in Blake's work—the apocalypse to which his poetry always points and occasionally reaches—part of my purpose will be to interrogate this position and see whether there is a utopia which is not mere wishful thinking" (14). Although it uses the apocalypse and utopia as central concepts, Williams's analysis focuses on the ideological and historical perspective from a Marxist angle, rather than on the issue of gender.*

lies in the interpretation of male and female activity in the epics. As I will show, Blake's notion of gender equality calls for an active female, as well as an active male, and consequently, for increased gender interactivity altogether.

Blake promotes a vision of gender utopia through a reconciliation between the male and female characters in the concluding apocalypses of the epics. Particularly the increased activity of the female leads to mutual gender interactivity in Blake's male and female characters, which is expressed in the symbolism of the poems. Because the poems are set in a post-lapsarian world, the male and female characters are separated already at the beginning, most notably in *The Four Zoas*, and are symbolically thrown into a fallen existence. The main urge of the characters is to search for their spiritual and corporeal counterparts in order to prepare for the apocalypse at the end of the poems. The apocalypse, Blake insists, can only be entered by man and woman together. Hence, a reconciliation between the male and female characters is the conclusion of *The Four Zoas, Milton* and *Jerusalem*.

The final gender utopian goal of complete equality between the sexes in Blake's poetry is expressed through tropes of male-female togetherness, and we may discern a clear line of development both from the early shorter poetry to the epics and within the three epic poems. Although sometimes executing successful representations of the female, Blake in the early poems is at pains to find an appropriate expression of the positive interactivity of man and woman. As he moves on to the great epics, he starts creating more complex symbolic representations. In *The Four Zoas* no explicit symbol of male-female togetherness exists besides the individual reunion of zoas and emanations. In *Milton*, Blake uses two of his characters, the male character Milton and the female character Ololon, to symbolize the male-female reunion in a more effective way, as they are reconciled in the penultimate plate. On the other hand, these two characters do not achieve the final stage of male-female togetherness. But eventually, in *Jerusalem*, Blake moves even one step further towards an appropriate representation of his poetic and philosophical ideal of gender utopia, when the universal man Albion is reunited in togetherness with his emanation Jerusalem at the end of the poem. Therefore, *The Four Zoas* and *Milton* express male-female *reunion*, the stage before and during apocalypse when male and female have revoked the fall and are ready to enter Blake's utopian level; *Jerusalem* expresses the more advanced stage of male-female *togetherness*, the post-apocalyptic stage where male and female together have finally entered the highest symbolical level of gender relations in Blake's poetry, the utopia of Eden, with complete gender equality as the norm.

Blake's later works to some degree mirror the relation between the sexes, the lack of gender equality and the onset of modern feminism at the end of the eighteenth century. The overall status of the female in Britain, and in Europe, at this time was gradually but slowly improving. Even though women were still dominated by men in a society with a patriarchal structure, the Enlightenment emphasis on the individual also had positive repercussions on the situation of the female. The complex intermediate and transitional nature of the period is shown in the way Blake portrays the female. While still passively locked up in a hierarchal class-system, his female characters strive for freedom and final reconciliation through activity and resistance. The paradoxical status of woman at this time is surely also one of the major reasons for many of the unsuccessful and generalizing interpretations of Blake's female metaphor.

In spite of not focusing their discussions on gender equality with an accompanying utopian society, a few of the feminist studies on Blake in recent years are in some aspects and to a certain degree related to the issue of the female and gender equality. Familiar to Blake scholars are the works of Susan Fox, Anne Mellor, Alicia Ostriker, Catherine Haigney, Diana Hume George, Brenda Webster, Irene Tayler and Helen Bruder, to mention the chief names of the most debated commentators. The impact of, for example, Fox's and Ostriker's new ideas on contemporary Blake studies cannot be overestimated, and Mellor's influential essay "Blake's Portrayal of Women" has probably been one of the most discussed by Blake critics in recent years.

The most useful support for the analytical purposes in my book is provided by Helen Bruder's challenging study *William Blake and the Daughters of Albion*, which investigates Blake's gender utopia in the light of contemporary feminist thinkers such as Mary Wollstonecraft and Mary Hays.[3] Like Blake, Mary Hays is a writer who regards female activity as positive, and as imperative for the improvement of gender

---

[3] *Bruder's* William Blake and the Daughters of Albion *is in my opinion one of the most significant and provocative works on Blake to appear in recent years. Also Nicholas Williams's* Ideology and Utopia in the Poetry of William Blake *deserves to be mentioned in connection with Bruder. Like Bruder, Williams makes an effective analytical parallel reading of Blake's* Visions of the Daughters of Albion *and Wollstonecraft's* Vindication of the Rights of Woman. *Using different approaches, both Williams and Bruder provide valid commentary on Blake's utopia. Their methods differ considerably, however: Williams's investigation is socio-historic-political, while Bruder calls her study a "feminist historicist work" (177).*

equality. In the light of those feminist writers and the sexual politics of the time, one can read Blake as a feminist, according to Bruder:

> Blake is of value to feminism not because he maintained an exemplary and unwavering feminist commitment but rather because he took sexual power seriously and engaged with many of the contemporary discourses and contexts in which it was being exercised or resisted [36].

A further similarity between Blake, Hays and Wollstonecraft is that they were natural members of the radical discourse that flourished in the London of the 1790s, with Joseph Johnson's print- and bookshop famously one of the most important gathering-points for the small crowd supporting such ideas. The radical literary coterie around Johnson was one of the vital contextual milieus that contributed to Blake's progressive view of the female and gender relations in general, as displayed in his later works. Not least was this intellectually stimulating environment important to Blake as a developmental platform for his ideas of religion and sexuality. It was here that he met Mary Wollstonecraft, pioneer feminist; Mary Hays, feminist and Unitarian; and Joseph Priestley, Unitarian minister and colonial explorer, to mention the most crucial influences on Blake's thinking.

More generally, my book aims at giving a good insight into Blake's conception of gender issues, and particularly his view of the female. Since his attitude to women is regarded by most scholars as a negative component, the representation of the female has become something many regard as a flaw in Blake's otherwise highly valued artistic output. I do not regard it so. At first represented by childlike innocent characters like Lyca of the *Songs* and Thel of the early minor prophecies, the female becomes a more mature, developed and complex character, experienced as it were, in the three long epics—all in line with Blake's more refined mythology. The initial offshoot of this momentous change can be seen in Oothoon, the heroine of *Visions of the Daughters of Albion*, Blake's first fully developed strong female character. But must a strong female character be, as most commentators so reassuringly insist, a negation? Does that strength not rather come with the enhanced life-experience as we grow older and respond to increasingly complex situations in an often negative everyday environment?

Already in his earlier short poems and minor illuminated books Blake shows an awareness of issues of gender and sexuality. *The Book of Thel* and *Visions of the Daughters of Albion* are of course the two shorter illuminated works most conspicuously dealing with the subject, but for instance a Song like "My Pretty Rose Tree" unveils a theme of illicit sexuality. In this condensed poem, the "Rose turned away with jealousy / And her thorns were [the] only delight" available for the potentially unfaithful speaker of the poem, who had been offered another flower, in spite of having "passed the sweet flower over" (Erdman 25).[4] This seems to have been an obsessive idea to Blake at this time, and we find it repeated in several of the note-book poems, for instance "To my Mirtle," "The Wild Flowers Song," "Soft Snow," and the scorching "My Spectre Around me Night & Day." In the more sophisticated "I Saw a Chapel all of Gold" Blake pushes this theme to its extreme, where the phallic "serpent rise[s] between / The white pillars of the door," and in a violent act foreboding Bromion's rape of the innocent Oothoon in *Visions,* "Down the golden hinges tore" of the prohibited chapel. The serpent eventually "vomit[s] his poison out" and, in contrast to the unaffected Bromion, in shame lies "down among the swine" (E 467–68).

Many accomplished studies of Blake's shorter poetry, particularly of the *Songs,* have already been written and therefore it is not my ambition to discuss these poems in this book. Even though arguably not many of these studies deal with gender issues, and though such an exploration would be a welcome addition to the unceasing augmentation of the corpus of Blake criticism, I have found it more rewarding for my purposes to concentrate my analytical effort on the longer epic works.

My reading endeavors exclusively to focus on the whole poems as utopias aiming at improved gender equality. In line with this view, John B. Pierce in *Flexible Design: Revisionary Poetics in Blake's* Vala, *or* The Four Zoas explains, "It is clear that the larger meaning of Blake's canon arises from the component parts of his text and the interdependence of these parts. In Blake's canon, the whole can accommodate itself to the particular no matter how unusual the part may at first seem" (22). However, it must also be underscored that my claim is not that Blake wrote *The Four Zoas, Milton* and *Jerusalem* intentionally as utopian poems, rather that this is one possible way to read them. Through this reading it will become clear that Blake shows an awareness of such acute radical issues as feminism and the aim for improved gender equality. But inevitably the concepts of utopia and apocalypse are fundamental for my inquiry into Blake's conception of gender and his gradually coming to grips with his single-minded idea finally to be expressed in *Jerusalem.*

---

[4]*All references to Blake's poetry in the text are from Erdman, ed.,* The Complete Poetry and Prose of William Blake, *hereafter indicated by E.*

In particular it is to the biblical notion of these terms that Blake adheres, and therefore it is essential to incorporate, for instance, the creation, the fall, the millennium and the impact of the Jesus-figure with the forgiveness of sins into such a discussion.

In the first chapter I will begin by discussing a few of the basic concepts that will enlighten and support my analysis of gender utopia in the three epics: apocalypse, utopia, and gender. In the second chapter I give an outline of the radical context that Blake was part of by the end of the eighteenth century: the tradition of Dissent, English Jacobinism and early feminism. Subsequently, the first analytical chapter is an examination of *The Four Zoas* as a gender utopian poem. The gender vision of *The Four Zoas* is incomplete, however, so Blake revises and improves this unfinished gender utopia in his second epic poem, *Milton*, and his final epic, *Jerusalem*, the latter forming a conclusion to Blake's vision of gender utopia. In the fourth and fifth chapter, respectively, I will therefore consider these two poems as a development of and response to the gender utopia of *The Four Zoas*, showing how Blake finally arrives at his desired goal of gender equality.

1
Apocalypse, Utopia and Gender

Blake and Apocalypse

Utopia and apocalypse are crucial concepts for the understanding of Blake's vision of gender equality in the three major prophecies. The utopian existence of equality in Eden which Blake visualizes is the aftermath of the apocalyptic conclusions of the poems. In *Apocalypse and Millennium* Morton Paley ties the two concepts together through the related term, the millennium: "Apocalypse, a revelation of the meaning of history typically accompanied by vast destruction, is succeeded by millennium, a period of social perfection upon an earth often pictured as regenerate in all its life. The meaning of each term can be defined only in relation to the other" (9). That the concepts "utopia" and "millennium" are roughly interchangeable becomes evident as we continue to follow Paley's line of argumentation. Paley underscores the natural place of apocalypse, millennium and utopia in Blake and in Romantic poetry in general. These concepts are central in Blake's poetry from the mid 1790s onwards, and particularly so in the three great epics (1).

The term apocalypse is somewhat ambiguous and not only used in the established connotation of revelation. In this context the term can also be used to denote a literary genre, and Blake's prophecies, which are epic poems with a rich framework of otherworldly mythological characters, could be placed in this category. However, adhering to the biblical use of the term, apocalypse is primarily and most commonly understood as "revelation," and in connection with Blake's prophecies this is surely the most relevant application. Apocalypse reveals the two extremes of redemption and damnation, as Paley suggests: "[I]t is important to stress that the whole conception of apocalypse has to do with a revelation of ultimate truths. There may be colossal disasters without any revelation preceding or ensuing, but an apocalypse involves, as the *OED*'s primary definition states, uncovering or disclosure" (*Apocalypse* 2).

Blake is a descendant of earlier revelatory writers such as the biblical scribes Isaiah, Ezekiel, Daniel and John. This is conspicuously shown in the structure and imagery of the three epics. The similarity between Blake and the biblical prophets is shown in Blake's use of symbolism in the great epics. For example, this is evident in the apocalypse of the final Night in *The Four Zoas*. The apocalyptic feast takes its beginning as the Eternal Man, Albion, awakes:

> The Eternal Man arose he welcomd them to the Feast
> The feast was spread in the bright South & the Eternal Man
> Sat at the feast rejoicing & the wine of Eternity
> Was servd round by the flames of Luvah all day & all the night
> [9:617–20, E 401]

We note here that although they are "rejoicing" and drinking "the wine of Eternity" in an apocalyptic festive mood, still "the flames" linger as a final reminder of the hell of the fallen world. This is a clear indication that the Blakean apocalypse is a vision of redemption. Kathryn Freeman, for one, has endorsed the view that to Blake "[t]he apocalypse is therefore not the destruction of the world at the end of time, but the continuous annihilation and inevitable building of the dualistic world and its infinite variations" (157). In Revelation the negative images are pre-dominant: "When he opened the sixth seal, I looked, and there came a great earthquake; the sun became black as sackcloth, the full moon became like blood" (6:12–13, 2317–18). Likewise, we encounter negations in the version of the apocalypse in Isaiah: "For the stars of the heavens and their constellations will not give their light; the sun will be dark at its rising, and the moon will not shed its light.... Therefore I will make the heavens tremble, and the earth will be shaken out of its place" (13:10–13, 1032).

In her analysis of the structure of *The Four Zoas* Freeman uses the term nostalgia. She suggests that "[n]ostalgia ... lies in idealizing past ignorance" (154). Blake often recounts the story of the fall and the peaceful existence that preceded it, something which is particularly frequent in *The Four Zoas*, with its turbulent narration. Thus, it is a significant feature of Blake's three great epics that their characters cast glances at a utopian existence, either, most commonly, nostalgic glances backward to the state of original innocence in pre-lapsarian Eden, or forward to a future state of eternal bliss. "In futurity / I prophetic see," Blake writes in "The Little Girl Lost," a poem originally included in *Songs of Innocence* but, significantly, transferred in many of the copies to *Songs of Experience* by Blake himself. This early poem is a good example of Blake's use of a satirical technique with nostalgic glances from one state to the other. In *Songs of Innocence* the state of experience is satirized through these glances, and in the three great epics Blake retains this satirical technique, but on a grander scale.

These nostalgic and satirical glances are part of Blake's familiar dualistic technique. *Songs of Innocence and of Experience* is maybe the most evident example of Blake's use of a dualistic/dialectical structure in his poetry where he pursues his dualistic manifesto from *The Marriage of Heaven and Hell*, "without Contraries is no progression," (3:6, E 34). However, this structure is substantive not only in the short lyrical poems of the *Songs*, but is just as pregnant in the longer poems, although not so easily detected in them. In the three major epics a visualized utopian existence stands opposed to the fallen world in which the poems are set.

The dualistic satirical technique has lent a sometimes fragmentary and disruptive character to the epic poems. In *Poetic Form in Blake's Milton*, Susan Fox convincingly outlines the parallel and dualistic structure of that poem. A parallel or dualistic structure is also the basic framework of *The Four Zoas* and *Jerusalem*. Blake's approach to the gender issue is clearly dualistic, and he juxtaposes the basic binary male–masculine and female–feminine with a dialectical sublation as the conclusion in the utopia of Eden where man and woman are finally reunited.

This male-female reunion is the most important stage in Blake's utopian writing since it is Blake's threshold to eternity. In Blake's poetry man and woman symbolically begin in pre-lapsarian unity, are divided in the fall, and then reunited in his utopia of Eden in which a kind of original paradise is regained. According to Blake's vision, man and woman have then been redeemed from the sins of the fall and from that moment go on to live in eternal harmonious togetherness. The biblical idea of the "Millennium," professed in Revelation, where, after the second coming of Messiah, peace will reign on earth for a period of a thousand years is close to the harmony of Blake's utopia which is manifested in the two components, the active Eden and the passive Beulah. "They came to life and reigned with Christ a thousand years…. This is the first resurrection," as the last book of the Bible tells us (Revelation 20:4–5, 2334). Keeping Paley's view in mind, the approximate relation of utopia, apocalypse and millennium is evident.

Blake and Utopia

In English literature there is a long-standing tradition of utopian works, which saw its beginning in Sir Thomas More's momentous *Utopia* from 1516. But in spite of the fact that Blake's poetry fulfils some of the criteria of the literary utopian genre, as much as the criteria of apocalyptic literature, it is difficult to read his poems primarily as literary utopias. Although conceived at a spiritual and personal level, they certainly depict both some kind of ideal society and the realization of that society so frequently advocated by utopian literature, but we cannot claim that Blake deliberately wrote them according to the utopian literary tradition. Blake is not generally recognized as a utopian writer, even if there are examples of commentators doing so in Nicholas Williams and A. L. Morton. Morton rightly emphasizes the utopian quality of Blake's major prophetic books. But there are unmistakable utopian components already in the minor prophecies: *Visions of the Daughters of Albion, Europe, America, The Song of Los, The Book of Los, The Book of Ahania, The First Book of Urizen*. We can find characters and ideas that appear later in the major prophecies, but compared to the long poems the minor prophecies inevitably look like sketchy and unfinished forerunners.

As early as in *The First Book of Urizen* from 1794 Blake presents an embryo of his form of gender utopia. In the dark fallen everyday existence Urizen longs for a better future world:

> From all the depths of dark solitude, From
> The eternal abode in my holiness,
> Hidden, set apart, in my stern counsels,
> Reserv'd for the days of futurity,
> I have sought for a joy without pain,
> For a solid without fluctuation.
> Why will you die, O Eternals?
> Why live in unquenchable burnings?
> [4:6–13, E 71]

Some of the characteristics of Blake's gender utopia can be found already in this poem. To start with, the representation of Blake's utopian world in his later writing is "Eden." This level is sometimes referred to as "Eternity," and in this early poem he labels his utopia "the eternal abode." As we can see here, the symbolism of his early poetry was not as sophisticated as that of his later long epic poems and was thus not sufficiently developed. Already here, though, Blake in a prophetic way envisions "the days of futurity" in a utopian existence. The human characters in this utopian world, "Eternals," will live in an eternal post-apocalyptic existence. A few of his recurring utopian characters are also introduced in this poem, so *The Book of Urizen* offers an introduction to Blake's world of mythology. The great negation Urizen is the speaker of the above passage and later in the poem Los, Enitharmon and Orc all appear. In the first epic *The Four Zoas* Blake adds a few new key characters: Vala, Luvah, Tharmas and Enion. From *America* he imports the character Urthona, and from *The Book of Ahania* the eponymous character, in order to complete his structure with four zoas and four emanations.

It seems that it was in the early years of the 1790s that utopian ideas began to take form in Blake's mind, and we can even go back to the earlier minor prophecy *America* from 1793 to find indications of utopian thinking in his poetry. For one thing, Urizen, Enitharmon and Orc participate already in this poem. In plate 8 Orc announces the imminent advent of apocalypse: "The times are ended; shadows pass, the morning 'gins to break" (8:2, E 54). Even though Blake's poetry in those post-revolutionary years of the early 1790s was more explicitly political, of which his unfinished poem *The French Revolution* is one good example, he situates his writing in an apocalyptic timeless context characteristic of his later utopia. In the major prophecies Blake's unconventional use of time is even more pronounced, and it is one of the devices used to describe his perception of a utopian world.

These early specimens of Blake's utopia indicate the future direction of his poetry. But it is only in *The Four Zoas*, begun in 1795, that for the first time he finds more appropriate symbols to describe his utopian ideas, through a considerable extension of his mythological landscape. In *The Four Zoas* Blake thoroughly develops the early ideas from the minor prophecies from the immediately preceding years. Then in the two following epics, *Milton* and *Jerusalem*, Blake develops these ideas even further. *The Four Zoas* is important in a gender utopian context, since it is the first to include the basic concepts and symbols of gender utopia, but *Milton* and *Jerusalem* are also crucial poems in Blake's development towards the final revision of gender equality in the last poem.

Biblical Apocalypse and Spiritual Utopia

As a theoretical, philosophical and religious concept utopia has much broader implications, and it is primarily in this respect that it is possible to speak of Blake's major epics as prophetic, visionary or utopian. Following a wider utopian notion, we can even go a step further back in time than Plato, whose *Republic* is regarded as the original work of the genre by many commentators, to the biblical texts. In the Bible we find a pervasive prophetic utopian tradition, from Genesis to Revelation. Certainly, one must regard the apocalyptic prophetic books of Ezekiel, Daniel, Isaiah and Revelation as having a clear utopian dimension in their proclamation of a peaceful millennium. The Christian prophetic notion of an ideal paradisiac existence in a regained Eden of the millennium following the apocalypse and the resurrection of Christ underpins a whole number of the Bible books, not merely the more conspicuously apocalyptical ones. The millennial desire for a peaceful Christian utopia is in fact a prerequisite of the apocalypse, a moment when sin will be expiated in a fallen existence in order for man to be finally redeemed and avoid eternal damnation.

The mental redemption in a post-lapsarian world is the dominant theme in most of Blake's poetry. The Christian prophetic form of utopia is fundamental to Blake's development of utopian ideas in his poetry, with the forgiveness of sins in the brotherhood of man, which becomes a predominant concept in *Jerusalem,* as the only conceivable way to accomplish the complete gender equality visualized as the goal of the utopia that Blake called Eden. Already in *The Marriage of Heaven and Hell* we can detect the great influence of the prophetic biblical writers, where in the first of several sections called "A Memorable Fancy" the poet Blake dines with the two prophets Isaiah and Ezekiel (Plate 12). Other early examples are the two early illustrated poems "All Religions Are One" and "There Is no Natural Religion."

The long epic poems of Blake are often referred to as prophecies, so the sub-genre of prophetic or visionary utopia is a category to which Blake's poetry almost by definition belongs. Whether one accepts this label or not, Blake, in a visionary prophetic fashion, proposes a future utopian realm. Blake continuously moves towards, what Saree Makdisi calls "the eternal, a state in which thought and life, body and mind, are unified and coextensive, strengthening and reaffirming each other" (262). Anticipation of an improved society is one of the main features of utopia, and in *The Four Zoas* Blake describes a movement towards that existence:

> For when he came to where a Vortex ceasd to operate
> Nor down nor up remaind then if he turnd & lookd back
> From whence he came 'twas upward all & if he turnd and viewd
> The unpassd void upward was still his mighty wandring
> The midst between an Equilibrium grey of air serene
> Where he might live in peace & where his life might meet repose.
> [6:190–95, E 349]

Here then, anticipation of the utopian society is described as an "upward," and forward progressive movement. Typically, it is through the symbolic interactivity of the male and female characters that *The Four Zoas* moves forward towards its conclusion in apocalypse and reunion.

Prophecy may be defined as a kind of visionary anticipation, or prediction, of an event, which is often religiously related. According to the biblical definition prophecy is also related to inspiration, but in Blake it is clearly a forward-directed anticipatory and visionary concept. Originally, prophecy was associated with certain books in the Bible and unquestionably prophecy is a theme that pervades the Bible. If we consider its overall structure with a division into two parts, the Old and the New Testament, the respective prophecies envision two different advents: first of Christ, then the apocalypse of Messiah's second coming with the ensuing peaceful millennium. However, not only the recognized apocalyptic books are prophetic, and if we apply a wider definition of the term as signifying a foreboding of events to come in a more general sense, or simply the prophecy of the Word, many other Bible books to some degree fit the definition. Morton Paley singles out Joel 2:28–32, 2 Peter 3:10–13 and the so-called little apocalypse of Matthew 24:29–30 as the most frequently echoed (*Apocalypse* 8).

Still, the most evident prophetic books in the Bible are the ones commonly referred to as apocalyptic: Isaiah, Ezekiel, Daniel and Revelation. D. S. Russell points out the close connection between apocalypse and prophecy: "The scholarly consensus sees a strong link between the apocalypse and biblical prophecy, and regards such writings as Ezekiel

38–39, Isaiah 24–27 ... if not as apocalypses per se then as forerunners to them" (34). There is little doubt about Daniel and Revelation, though, and according to Russell these are the two great apocalypses in the Bible.

In the Bible, then, there are four overtly apocalyptic books. Each of these works predicts an apocalyptic upheaval that will terminate mankind's earthly existence. Particularly The Book of Revelation is a prototype work closely associated with apocalypse. The major biblical apocalypses were also the most important ones to Blake when he visualized his own apocalypse and utopia, and he imported some pivotal symbols into his own epic poems, above all from Revelation. It is mainly the biblical visionary tradition that Blake conforms to in his three major epic poems, and it has almost become a commonplace among Blake commentators to call them prophecies.

Isaiah is chronologically the first of the apocalyptical books in the Bible. The book is composed by several authors and normally divided into the first, second and third Isaiah. The apocalypse of Isaiah is the longest in the Bible, stretching over four chapters. In length the apocalypse of Isaiah is rivalled by the apocalypse in *The Four Zoas*, which is longer than the compressed one in *Jerusalem*. In Isaiah we do not find many of the symbols that we normally associate with apocalypse, but there are clear predictions of the shakings and eventual disintegration of the earth on the day of resurrection: "And it shall come to pass in that day, that the great trumpet shall be blown, and they shall come which were ready to perish" (27:13, 715). There are many passages in *The Four Zoas* where Blake alludes to the apocalypse in Isaiah, so it is clear that this Bible book provided him with valuable literary material.

The author of Ezekiel is said to have been both a priest and a prophet, and this book contains one of Blake's most pertinent symbols, the wheel within a wheel: "and their appearance and their work was as it were a wheel in the middle of a wheel" (2:16, 820). Blake contrasts this image, which denotes spiritual unity, with its opposite "wheel without wheel," a symbol that signifies the spiritual degeneration of Western society, mainly manifested in corrupt state religion. Further, in Ezekiel the female Jerusalem appears as God's adulterous wife, an idea that Blake transformed into the complex eponymous symbol of his last epic poem. The day of judgement is also significant in the prophecy of "the day whereof I have spoken" (39:8, 864).

Isaiah and Ezekiel are typical apocalyptic books, and so is the book of Daniel, though in a somewhat different way. Although recognized by commentators as an apocalypse, it differs from the other two books in being a vision seen in a dream by its unknown author: "In the first year of Belshazzar king of Babylon Daniel had a dream and visions of his head upon his bed: then he wrote the dream, and told the sum of the matters" (7:1, 887). Like the other three apocalyptic books, Daniel speaks of the end of times. This prophecy is the shortest of the four acknowledged apocalyptic Bible books.

Nevertheless, Daniel is the most conspicuously apocalyptic book in the Old Testament. Its importance lies particularly in its use of basic apocalyptic metaphors. In Daniel the author uses the images "four winds of the heaven" and "four great beasts" (7:2–3, 887). The four horsemen of the Apocalypse are also well known. The figure four is echoed in *The Four Zoas* with the four zoas and their four emanations, and also in *Milton* where it occurs significantly in several places like the fourfold union Bard/Blake/Milton/Los. And *Jerusalem* consists of four chapters. Furthermore, it is easy to detect the correspondence to the fourfold mythological world of Blake with its four levels: Ulro, Generation, Beulah and Eden.

However, it is The Book of Revelation that is Blake's chief source of apocalyptic symbols. "Flashes of lightning, rumblings, peals of thunder, an earthquake, and heavy hail" (11:19, *Study Bible* 2323) are only a few of the well-known images. Written by an unknown author named John, Revelation is without doubt the most explicitly apocalyptic book in the Bible. Nowhere in the other three books do we find equally colourful passages, abundant with cataclysmic symbols: "The first angel sounded, and there followed hail and fire mingled with blood, and they were cast upon the earth: and the third part of trees was burnt up, and all green grass was burnt up" (8:7, 1223).

In Revelation Blake unquestionably found some of the fundamentals of his utopia. It is quite clear that Revelation is a God-given prophecy of the future, as is emphasized in the *New Dictionary of Biblical Theology:* "From chapter 4 onwards it points towards the future, describing in sobering yet magnificent language both the judgments and the blessings which God has ordained" (710). Thus indicating the double-edged vision of Revelation, the forward-directedness of prophecy as a concept is underscored.

Most importantly, Blake imported the concept of the double function of Jerusalem as both a city and a woman from Revelation. Firstly, it gave him the model of his utopian city: "I will write upon him the name of my God, and the name of the city of my God, which is new

Jerusalem, which cometh down out of heaven from my God" (3:12, 1220). Some chapters later Jerusalem is identified as a woman, and this image, which is also found in Ezekiel, probably gave Blake the idea of Jerusalem as the consort of Jesus: "And I John saw the holy city, new Jerusalem, coming down from God out of heaven, prepared as a bride adorned for her husband" (21:2, 1234).

In Revelation the number seven is significant, and Blake follows this apocalyptic tradition. For one thing, this number is an important trope for a pertinent description of the advent of the Apocalypse. "The number *seven* (used fifty-seven times in Revelation) symbolizes the divine pattern evident in both the universe and history," the commentary to Revelation 1:4 explains (2310). For example, one verse in Revelation depicts God's angels about to initiate the apocalypse with their trumpets: "And I saw the seven angels which stood before God; and to them were given seven trumpets" (8:2, 1223). Moreover, as Morton Paley informs us: "The conception of the Seven Eyes of God was one of the additions to *Vala* which changed it into *The Four Zoas*" (135) and contributed towards making it an apocalyptic poem.

In line with this biblical symbolism, Blake, in the fourth Night of *The Four Zoas*, gives us a view of the suffering in the seven ages of God. After the seven ages had passed over,

> The Council of God on high watching over the Body
> Of Man clothd in Luvahs robes of blood saw & wept
> Descending over Beulahs mild moon coverd regions
> The daughters of Beulah saw the Divine Vision they were comforted
> And as a Double female form loveliness & perfection of beauty
> They bowd the head & worshipped & with mild voice spoke these words
> Lord. Saviour if thou hadst been here our brother had not died
> And now we know that whatsoever thou wilt ask of God
> He will give it thee for we are weak women & dare not lift
> Our eyes to the Divine pavilions.
> [4:247–57, E 337]

The passage of the seven ages is used again in *Milton*, but it was already employed in *The First Book of Urizen*. David Worrall enlightens the issue further in the introduction to the Tate Publishing edition of the latter poem: "There are seven ages in this Urizenic version of creation. These not only correspond to the days of the Biblical creation but also parody Paine's goal of a single Age of Reason, a visionary myopia which Blake economically criticizes" (22).

Blake and the Fall of Man

The foundation of Blake's depiction of utopia, apocalypse and gender, and the mythological structure in general of the three major epic poems is Blake's notion of the fall of man. Blake's view of the fall is close to the orthodox Christian version but differs somewhat from it. In a few important details the difference is significant. The predominant impression of traditional biblical exegesis of the version of the fall in the Bible is that woman carries the entire blame for the ensuing division of the sexes. Blake rather sees woman as something of a catalyst of the sin implied in Genesis. This view is important in that it gives us the background and framework of the four levels of existence which is the basis of the actions of all the characters in Blake's poems, and provides the underpinning of his female characters.

Hence Blake does not put the blame wholly on woman, a view which Blake criticism in general has endorsed since the pioneering work of Northrop Frye. Blake rather sees the fall as a burden equally shared between woman and man, a mutual responsibility that has to be accepted by both parties. Man and woman must of course actively do their best to redeem the fall by improving their everyday situation. This position is evident throughout Blake's poetry through the interactivity of the characters which results in a movement towards complete gender equality in a post-apocalyptic existence of a utopian Eden. In this metaphorical utopian level the pre-lapsarian world is fully recovered, and even improved with new hard-won human experience.

Blake believes that the fall is mainly a mental state of aberration and therefore one has to interpret his view of the fall metaphorically. As a consequence the apocalypse also takes place in the mind of individual man, which is a radical divergence from the orthodox reading of the Bible. According to Blake the fall has never actually taken place and is only a mental state. The fall is a fall in man's consciousness, and therefore we first have to recover the paradise of Eden on the mental level. However, since we live in a fallen reality, consequently the negations of our everyday world have also to be extinguished.

To a great extent Blake's view follows the narration of the fall in the Bible, where one could also interpret certain passages more to the advantage of woman. For one thing, woman was deceived into tasting the fruit by the serpent: "And the woman said, The serpent beguiled me, and I did eat" (3:13, 3). Further, the equality between man and woman is suggested in an early passage from Genesis by the use of the word "helper": "Helper does not indicate a servant relation but a true partnership. Similarly, the making of woman from man's rib suggests their equality and kinship, not her subordination" (Genesis 2:20, commentary in *Study Bible* 8).

In Blake, but also in the Bible, the issue of guilt is not uncomplicated and both man and woman are severely punished and forced to live and work in a fallen world. Even though woman was the instigator, both the responsibility and punishment are after all mutual, which is indicated in the Bible commentary: "Woman's historical subordination to man is a consequence of human events, not an ideal in its own right. Responsibilities of procreation will compromise the autonomy of both sexes" (Genesis, commentary 3:16, 9). The responsibility should be equally shared, but it seems that, as in Blake, woman becomes something of a catalyst for sin. Since the Bible is one of Blake's main sources, this may be one of the reasons why Blake's female characters are sometimes tinged with a negative anti-feminist aura.

Blake and the Patriarchal Legacy

Another major reason for Blake's ostensibly sexist portrayal of women is of course the patriarchal legacy of the age that he lived and worked in, something which is frequently used by commentators as one plausible explanation for this. The fact that he was caught up in a language for centuries ingrained by a dominant patriarchal system made it difficult for him to give his ideas of gender equality a relevant representation in his poetry. The inevitable immersion in the long-standing patriarchal tradition helps to explain why many of Blake's symbols and images can be interpreted as conservative from a gender-political perspective. Blake's persistent use of the Bible as a main source underscores a patriarchal influence in his poetry. Diana Hume George points to Blake's difficulties in finding an appropriate position outside the norms of the gender-specific language of his age:

> Blake's problems with portrayal of sexuality and of women, as I see it, are problems of symbol formation that express themselves in limitations of language. If, as Blake posits, consciousness is itself sexual, dialectic, and gender-specific, then the development of language will also be gendered; and this is, of course, the case. Blake's vision of the human form and his idea of the value of being human was constantly

rendered problematic by language. He had to speak the literary unspeakable [199].

In the last few decades a similar discussion has been conducted by leading feminist theoreticians. These theorists have exhaustively questioned the penetrating influence of an inevitably gendered patriarchal language. The members of the French school of *l'écriture féminine,* Luce Irigaray, Julia Kristeva and Hélène Cixous, have, in different ways, outlined the patriarchal linguistic dominance. In line with this, the Australian feminist critic Rita Felski speaks of "the linguistic conventions of a phallocentric symbolic order," (4) while the American gender theorist and political commentator Judith Butler calls the patriarchal system and its language "a masculinist signifying economy" (*Gender Trouble* 13). Most pertinently for my discussion of Blake's linguistic strategies and symbol formation, particularly his female metaphor, Butler writes:

> Within a language pervasively masculinist, a phallogocentric language, women constitute the unrepresentable. In other words, women represent the sex that cannot be thought, a linguistic absence and opacity. Within a language that rests on univocal signification, the female sex constitutes the unconstrainable and undesignatable [*Gender Trouble* 9].

Correspondingly, Luce Irigaray has notably called the female the "sex which is not one." What Butler calls the undesignatability of the female sex is one major reason for Blake's difficulties in creating representative female characters, a fact which is commonly acknowledged by Blake critics. In particular the feminist critics of later years are scorching in their critique of Blake's female symbols. Anne Mellor, predominantly, in "Blake's Portrayal of Women" reads Blake's female symbols negatively and argues that Blake is a sexist in his portrayal of women (148). But also Leopold Damrosch recognizes Blake's problem:

> I agree, of course, that Blake should not be held responsible for the prejudices of his age.... But I would argue that the status of the female in his myth is significant in betraying the same philosophical difficulties that surround the whole problem of dualism. We cannot salvage the integrity of the myth merely by imagining some alternative metaphor to take the place of the female. The metaphor is more than metaphor: it is a fundamental concept, and participates in Blake's conceptual dilemma [181].

Blake's conceptual or linguistic dilemma is not all that remarkable, since in a phallo(go)centric language, indeed in any language, it is an impossible task to appropriate an outside position, as Butler suggests: "To enter into the repetitive practices of this terrain of signification is not a choice, for the 'I' that might enter is always already inside: there is no possibility of agency or reality outside the discursive practices that give these terms the intelligibility that they have" (*Gender Trouble* 148). In opposition to Butler's position, Luce Irigaray has maintained that feminist discourse must find a place of articulation outside the already existing signifying system of patriarchy. From this outside vantage-point feminism could subvert patriarchy. However, this is an impossible position according to Butler, and she directs a harsh critique at the views of Irigaray.

Certainly, one could question why the subject should exclusively be granted linguistic agency. In Blake's language woman attains agency through sexual power. Woman, as Damrosch writes, "is both the victim of temptation and its agent" (225). Woman becomes a catalyst of the expressions of the corrupt sexuality, in Blake's terminology called "Sexual Religion," which from the moment of the fall spreads like a plague over the world. It is symbolically manifested through negative institutions such as legal marriage, prostitution, industrialization and materialism which, as we know, Blake condemns in his art and poetry.

Hence Blake's linguistic problem is shared by contemporary feminists and post-structuralists. For both Blake and feminists/post-structuralists the difficulty is to find a linguistic foundation for the "outside" position of language. Concomitantly, this difficulty can also be read as a critique of the "elsewhere" of language that Luce Irigaray proposes. Where is this elsewhere of language, and on what foundation is it built? It appears that feminists and post-structuralists/deconstructionists still have difficulties in solving this linguistic dilemma. This is also Blake's problem: to articulate something previously unrepresented by patriarchal language and to express his ideas of the utopia of Eden. Blake's problem is analogous to the problem that Butler points at in her critique of Irigaray: "And there will be no way finally to delimit the elsewhere of Irigaray's elsewhere, for every oppositional discourse will produce its outside, an outside that risks becoming installed as its non-signifying inscriptional space" (*Bodies That Matter* 52). Thus, it seems, no matter how radically innovative and original a language Blake managed to create, his "outside" language would inevitably be caught up by the governing patriarchal language, only to become "inside" again.

The aim for an outside of a future horizon to what from the writing position inside looks like an impossible task of signification, to write the inexpressible, characterizes the writing of Blake. He tries to find ways to express his utopian ideal of gender equality through the apocalypses in *The Four Zoas* and *Jerusalem* with its aftermath of post-apocalyptic utopian existence, formerly unknown to mankind and thus inexpressible. Helen Bruder points out this great linguistic dilemma for Blake:

> (W)orking with 'the social stock of available signs' placed restraints upon what Blake could actually do with language. He was not free to say or even think whatever he wanted, hence perhaps all the fury and repetition in his works, because he could not empty words of other people's intentions and meanings [3].

Particularly *The Four Zoas*, with its often chaotic structure, is a repetitive poem. This difficulty of precise linguistic expression places Blake in a position close to feminism with its aspiration towards both a practical and linguistic expression of gender equality.

The urgent need for new ways of expression to represent the fluctuations between the two sexes is obvious in Blake's poetry. That is also the case with the ideas of Judith Butler, who provocatively interrogates the predominant use of biological sex as well as different gender roles as identity-determining factors. Most crucially, Butler points to the necessity to create new vocabulary and symbols, in relation to the sex/gender distinction:

> If gender is not tied to sex, either causally or expressively, then gender is a kind of action that can potentially proliferate beyond the binary limits imposed by the apparent binary of sex. Indeed, gender would be a kind of cultural/ corporeal action that requires a new vocabulary that institutes and proliferates present participles of various kinds, resignifiable and expansive categories that resist both the binary and substantializing grammatical restrictions on gender. But how would such a project become culturally conceivable and avoid the fate of an impossible and vain utopian project? [*Gender Trouble* 112].

If society could transcend, at least symbolically, the binary of sex with its coerced limits, it would have access to the prolific domain where the male-female distinction is theoretically dissolved. To Butler, the category of gender is the manifestation of this domain. Blake, through provocative interrogation of the concept, goes one step further by projecting an imaginary utopian world where gender does not even exist and all binaries are dissolved into harmony and male-female togetherness. As Butler argues, to describe something formerly unknown, symbols with new a meaning and a new vocabulary must be invented. Consistent with such a conception, Blake, as we know, created a whole mythology with a wide array of new symbols to represent his characters and his ideal of male-female togetherness.

Blake's Mythological System

Many commentators have emphasized the need to interpret Blake's poetry metaphorically, for example Frye and Damrosch. The metaphoricity of Blake's poetry is of course closely related to Blake's extensive use of mythological symbols. As we know, he imported a wide selection of symbols, terms and concepts from a number of sources: the Bible, Milton, Jacob Boehme and most likely also symbols of antinomian religious origin. In most cases, Blake adopted the symbols, changed them somewhat in names and connotations, and thus developed his own new radical symbolism, his "new vocabulary." In this way, Blake's mythological system was created: "I must Create a System. Or be enslav'd by another Mans / I will not Reason & compare: my business is to Create" (10:20–21) as he famously states in *Jerusalem*.

The basic structural foundation for Blake's epic poems can be traced to his use of four levels of existence: Ulro, Generation, Beulah and Eden. In *Fearful Symmetry* Northrop Frye helpfully explains the significance of the respective levels:

> We have said that there are at least three levels of imagination. The lowest is that of the isolated individual reflecting on his memories of perception and evolving generalizations and abstract ideas.... Blake calls this world Ulro; it is his hell, and his symbols for it are symbols of sterility, chiefly rocks and sand. Above it is the ordinary world we live in, a double world of subject and object, of organism and environment, which Blake calls Generation. Above it is the imaginative world, and Blake divides this into an upper and a lower part, so that the three worlds expand into four [48–49].

The last two worlds are Eden and Beulah, respectively. If we, as some critics do, follow the basic binary thinking in Blake, a further distinction into a negative side consisting of Ulro and Generation, and a positive with Beulah and Eden can be made. In plate 69 of *Jerusalem* we find a good summary of this contradiction, where Blake contrasts Generation with Beulah and Eden, a level he frequently calls Jerusalem in this poem:

> Drawing the free loves of Jerusalem into infernal bondage
> That they might be born in contentions of Chastity & in
> Deadly Hate
> ....
> Till they refuse liberty to the Male, & not like Beulah
> Where every Female delights to give her maiden to her husband:
> The Female searches sea & land for gratifications to the
> Male Genius, who in return clothes her in gems & gold
> And feeds her with the food of Eden; hence all her beauty beams.
> She Creates at her will a little moony night & silence
> With Spaces of sweet gardens & a tent of elegant beauty,
> Closed in by a sandy desart & a night of stars shining
> And a little tender moon & hovering angels on the wing;
> And the Male gives a Time & Revolution to her Space
> Till the time of love is passed in ever varying delights.
> [69:9–11; 14–24, E 223]

Even though the images belong to a patriarchal tradition, here with a possible touch of Blakean irony, this is still a significant example of the juxtaposed positive gender interactivity in Jerusalem/Beulah/Eden and the stalemate enchained passivity of fallen Generation. Many commentators on Blake seem to miss this point: that Blake includes, and indeed must include, the negations of a fallen existence as a contradiction to the positive innocent and utopian images. These negations must exist until they are revoked by the positive contraries at the moment of revelation. As we know, this is the basic premiss of all Blake's art. In other words, "the free loves of Jerusalem" are opposed to the "infernal bondage" expressed through "Chastity" and "Deadly Hate" in Generation.

Some time during the composition of *The Four Zoas* the basic structure of Blake's mythology was fundamentally changed, and Blake went from a binary mythology to a fourfold mythology. In *Flexible Design*, John B. Pierce has explained this alteration very aptly:

> The introduction of figures as important as Tharmas and Urthona
> (through his Spectre) brought a change in the mythic structure of the

poem. It represents a move away from the duality of the Urizen–Orc, Urizen–Luvah struggle towards a fourfold struggle between reason and passion and also imagination and raging despair. We cannot say exactly when Blake saw the potential in this fourfold myth, but its effects on the manuscript seem wide-ranging [123].

This new structure implies a dramatic break with the earlier twofold structure, which made Blake rename the poem first entitled *Vala* and gave him the definite symbolic organization centered around four male and four female characters. Taking Blake's religious background and great interest in the Bible into account, it seems natural that he adopted the emphasis of the fourfold from for instance Ezekiel and Revelation.

As for the specific symbols in the three great epics, the origin can be found in the basic prototypical character, the universal man, Albion. This symbol is one of the most multi-faceted in Blake's mythology. Albion at the same time symbolizes collective mankind and the nation of England, or Great Britain. It is from this unified symbol that all other characters emanate. Thus, in *The Four Zoas* this structure is obvious in the fall of man, which encompasses all characters, symbolized by the universal man Albion. To completely revoke the fall, all characters must be reconciled for Albion to wake up again and enter the higher utopian state.

The individual characters in *The Four Zoas*, then, are called zoas and emanations. The male zoas all have a specific corresponding female emanation. Zoas and emanations are what in Blake's mythological system would be labelled contraries. In the symbolism of *The Four Zoas* Blake also dualistically posits the negations of the positive characters. The negative character related to the male zoa is the spectre, while the negation of the emanation is the female will.

THE EMANATION VERSUS THE FEMALE WILL

While the almost unanimous view among critics has been that female activity in Blake's poetry is negative and passivity is more positive, there is more disagreement about the view of Blake's representation of female activity, the female will, and female passivity, the emanation. In fact, it frequently seems that commentators confuse the main characteristics of these two basic symbols. Even an observant critic as Leopold Damrosch somewhat distorts the issue. To begin with, he places the emanation in Blake's highest level, the utopia of Eden, as the female part of the reunited man: "The Emanation is the female aspect of the androgynous self, which should never exist at all in separation" (182). In spite of this, he inappropriately goes on to argue that, after all, the emanation is a representation of the fallen female in the poems themselves: "Whatever the Emanation may be in eternity, in the world of the poems it is a symptom of the fall" (183). This is not quite the case, since Blake's ultimate representation of the fallen female is the female will. The female will is the opposite of the emanation in Blake and not, as Damrosch proposes, a subcategory of the emanation (182). If Damrosch's interpretation appears reductive, Harold Bloom's definition of the foremost function of the emanation is even more questionable: "The function of the Emanation is to become what Shelley called 'a soul out of my soul,' a creative achievement, the form of what a man loves through creation" (285–86). In this remarkably discordant interpretation Bloom fails to take any form of balanced outlook on gender, something which feminist studies on Blake in the last two decades have fortunately been able to remedy to a great extent.

However, one certainly has to agree that the emanation and the female will are notoriously complicated concepts in Blake. Damrosch's generalisations do little to clarify the issue, when he for instance claims: "Henceforth the active Emanation will be a tyrannical Female Will, the passive a 'disorganized' and 'evanescent shade' as Jerusalem is when severed from Albion (J 78:28)" (183). The implications of activity and passivity in both male and female characters, for one thing, are much more complex than this, as I show in this study.

The emanation as a construction of Blake's mythos, then, is almost exclusively positive. It is at least a positive symbol in the context of Blake's utopian androgynous level Eden. Since Blake regards activity as mainly positive, activity is more frequently linked to the emanation than is generally believed. After all, continuous intellectual activity is one of the basic foundations of the utopia that Blake postulates in Eden.

Epistemologically, one might derive Blake's theory of the emanation from Plato, Neoplatonism, Jacob Boehme and the Jewish Kabbalah. That Blake read and absorbed ideas and concepts from Boehme which he developed we have documented evidence of. What has been more puzzling for Blake criticism is the etymological explanation of the word. Since emanation roughly means "outflow" many commentators have taken that as a pretext to argue that Blake visualizes the emanation as the subordinate and inferior outflow of the male zoa. Northrop Frye, for one, writes: "In the fallen states the Emanation ... becomes the source of a continuously tantalizing and elusive torment. In imaginative states it is united with and emanates from the man" (73). Even more surprisingly, he claims that "[t]hese emanations are not very clearly distinguished in *The Four Zoas*, being shadowy creatures who do practically nothing but wail, and seem to have chiefly a symmetrical function" (277). Again, this is a good example of a reductive reading. To be sure, the *Zoas* is a complex poem with sometimes rather shadowy characters, but the emanations have many other and more important functions than wailing.

Harold Bloom, on the other hand, explains that "[a]n emanation is literally what comes into being from a process of creation in which a series of effluxes flow from a creator" (195). As a construction this is of course true insofar as, through his adherence to the biblical version of creation, Blake sees the female as something of an outflow of the male. However, Blake in no way regards the female as inferior as a human being. "My Emanation, Alas! will become / My Contrary," Blake states in *Jerusalem* (17:38–39, E 162). He further claims that in Beulah Contrarities are equally True (Milton 30:1, E 129)," so from these two statements we can deduce that Blake in fact saw woman as man's equal, at least in an ideal gender utopia. In eternity the emanation is the positive and active counterpart and companion of the male.

In the fallen world the emanation turns into the female negation that Blake calls the female will. In *The Four Zoas*, and sometimes elsewhere, Blake calls this character the Shadowy Female. In the *Zoas* it is mainly the eponymous character of the earlier version of the poem, Vala, who assumes this name. In *Jerusalem* the female will is split into several characters: Tirzah, Rahab, Gwendolen, and also Vala.

This negative female character has been frequently portrayed by poets over the years. An earlier version of the female will is to be found in the character Beatrice in Dante's *Divine Comedy*. Since Dante is one of Blake's major inspirations this might of course have influenced Blake's conception of female characters, as Damrosch suggests: "Blake takes over Dante's symbols and reinterprets them to show that Beatrice ... is actually an embodiment of the Female Will" (186). Certainly, love is depicted as a negative force in the *Divine Comedy:*

> Cupidity! Which so pulls mortals down
> Under its surface, that no one has strength
> To get his eyes out clear above the waves
>   [*Paradiso* XXVII:121–23]

A relevant and related discussion focuses on the reason why the positive emanation is transformed, or transforms herself into the negative female will.

Beulah versus Eden

As we have learnt from Northrop Frye among others, Blake postulates four different levels in his mythological system: Ulro, Generation, Beulah and Eden. The first two belong to a fallen existence and are, as it were, negative while the other two are positive and belong to a utopian post-apocalyptic existence. We immediately notice that, as with the structure of the characters in *The Four Zoas*, the positive and negative sides are evenly balanced, with two levels on each side. Consequently, the two pairs of levels are often textually associated, although not interchangeable. The two fallen levels are loosely correlated, with Generation representing the world we inhabit. Below this level is Ulro representing the biblical conception of Hell, or Purgatory, if we follow Dante. More tightly connected are the positive pair, Beulah and Eden. As with Ulro, Beulah is a subexistence to the paradise in Eden, and the proximity of the two levels is so close that the inhabitants of each can move back and forth between the two.

Beulah is Blake's term for the lower level of his version of paradise, connected with the spiritually active eternal level of Eden. Beulah is said to be a "feminine" realm, which offers an opportunity to relax from the continuous activity of Eden:

> There is from Great Eternity a mild & pleasant rest
> Namd Beulah a Soft Moony Universe feminine lovely
> Pure mild & Gentle given in Mercy to those who sleep
> [1:94–96, E 303]

The fullest account of Beulah in Blake's poetry is to be found at the very beginning of the second Book of *Milton:*

> There is a place where Contrarities are equally True:
> This place is called Beulah. It is a pleasant lovely Shadow
> Where no dispute can come, Because of those who Sleep.
> ....
> Beulah is evermore Created around Eternity, appearing
> To the Inhabitants of Eden around them on all sides.
> But Beulah to its Inhabitants appears within each district

> As the beloved infant in his mother's bosom round incircled
> With arms of love & pity & sweet compassion. But to
> The Sons of Eden the moony habitations of Beulah
> Are from Great Eternity a mild & pleasant Rest.
>   [30:1–3, 8–14, E 129]

Although describing a feminine place of love that offers "a mild & pleasant Rest" to "[t]he Sons of Eden," it seems that Blake in this passage also visualizes some ideal of gender equality since in Beulah "Contrarities are equally True." Male versus female is the most fundamental of these polarities.

The sun, for one thing, is a very significant symbol in the final two Nights of *The Four Zoas* in the preparation for and in the workings of the apocalypse. Furthermore, in the symbolism of the passage from *Milton* above we can notice that, somewhat paradoxically, Blake's Beulah, with its emphasis on repose and harmony, is clearly closer to the traditional biblical Eden than Blake's Eden, as Frye points out: "In the account of 'Eden' in Genesis, the unfallen state of man is presented solely in terms of Beulah: nothing is left of the flaming city of the sun which Eden must have been" (231). The intimate relation between Blake's Beulah and the Eden of the Bible suggests that it is in fact closer to a pastoral utopia than Blake's Eden. The foremost example of this in *The Four Zoas* is the passage commonly called "Vala's Garden" in the final Night.

"Vala's Garden" is written in a pastoral mood and is a significant illustration of the natural bucolic setting of Beulah. Such reflections of nature occur mainly in the flashbacks where the characters glance from their fallen existence back to the lost Paradise and, not as frequently, towards the anticipated bliss of a future Edenic utopia. In the second Night, for example, Vala looks back to the innocent days of bliss: "In joy she heard his howlings & forgot he was her Luvah, / With whom she walk'd in bliss in times of innocence & youth" (2:78–9, E 317). As always in Blake, the major reason for the loss of innocence is the gender division that occurred at the fall. In the form of a repressive arising desire this split affects all the characters of the poem: "And Los & Enitharmon were drawn down by their desires, / Descending sweet upon the wind among soft harps & voices" (2:287–8, E 322). Once having been confronted with and experienced sexual desire, the divided Los and Enitharmon are, like Adam and Eve, expelled from Eden with its "soft harps & voices" to be inflicted with the evil expressions of sexuality in a fallen world. Desire in this world, as we know, is in turn the cause of jealousy:

> I saw that Luvah & Vala
> Went down the Human Heart, where Paradise & its joys abandoned
> In jealous fears, in fury & rage, & flames roll'd round their ferrid feet
> And the vast form of Nature like a Serpent play'd before them
> [3:94–7, E 328]

Blake here alludes to the Bible and, as we are told in Genesis, through the deceptive strategies of the serpent, man and woman have to leave Paradise.

A few Nights later the scene is changed into a display of nature's beauty, showing the all-encompassing character of Blake's conception of nature in Beulah:

> But the soft pipe the flute the viol organ harp & cymbal
> And the sweet sound of silver voices calm the weary couch
> Of Enitharmon but her groans drown the immortal harps
> Loud & more loud the living music floats upon the air
> Faint & more faint the daylight wanes.
> [5:23–7, E 339]

The images here amplify the simple pastoral beauty into representations of utopia through traditional bucolic symbolism: "[T]he soft pipe the flute the viol organ harp & cymbal," "the sweet sound of silver voices," and in particular "the immortal harps." Also the omnipoetical association between Beulah and the bucolic reinforces the significance of these images.

The serene beauty is disturbed and ruined at the end of the same Night, as Blake contrasts the lost harmony of the Garden of Eden with the fallen state that dominates the poem:

> My fountains once the haunt of Swans now breed the scaly tortoise
> The houses of my harpers are become a haunt of crows
> The gardens of wisdom are become a field of horrid graves
> And on the bones I drop my tears & water them in vain
> Once how I walked from my palace in gardens of delight
> The sons of wisdom stood around the harpers followed with harps
> Nine virgins clothd in light composd the song to their immortal voices
> And at my banquets of new wine my head was crownd with joy
> [5:194–201, E 343]

Thus, instead of the utopian positive images "fountains," "harpers," "new wine," and "immortal voices" of "[t]he gardens of wisdom," and a "palace in" the "gardens of delight" we have the fallen negative images "the scaly tortoise," "a haunt of crows," "and "a field of horrid graves" with "bones" in them.

Blake's Eden has traditionally been equated with eternal intellectual and spiritual activity. Damrosch, for instance, suggests this kind of activity: "It is essential to stress that Blake's Eden differs decisively from the traditional heaven by reason of its continuous activity" (234). This is of course a correct picture, but I believe there are inevitably elements of harmony in Blake's Eden. It is after all Blake's version of the post-apocalyptic level at which all opposites have been reconciled and all contradictions harmoniously resolved. At the same time, it is a utopian existence which can be reached with stern effort in this world, as Damon stresses: "In Eden, however, which is the ideal life *on this earth*, the male and female, when reconciled, cooperate" (Damon, 121). Thus, man and woman must work together in the fallen world to regain and elevate Paradise.

It might be appropriate to compare Blake's Eden with the City of St. Augustine, described in his lengthy theological treatise the *City of God*. Augustine's City of God actually consists of two different cities, as John O'Meara explains in his introduction to the Penguin Classics edition of Augustine's work: "The concept of the City of God, or rather of the two cities—the heavenly and the terrestrial cities—receives its fullest treatment in the last twelve books of Augustine's great work" (xxix). O'Meara goes on to state that they "are spiritual or mystical cities" (xxx). Augustine himself writes: "We see then that the two cities were created by two kinds of love: the earthly city was created by self-love reaching the point of contempt for God, the Heavenly City by the love of God carried as far as contempt of self" (Book XIV:28). Augustine's two cities roughly correspond respectively to Blake's earthly level of Generation and heavenly level of Eden. These two are opposed, both in Blake and St. Augustine, and it is of course the heavenly city that corresponds to Blake's Eden, or at times to Beulah.

It is also obvious that this is a utopian, and partly post-apocalyptic, existence, similar to Blake's Eden: "These cities existed before earthly created nature and will exist when it is no more" (xxx). Like Blake in his great epics, Augustine refers back to the lost paradise and follows the apocalyptic books of the Bible in envisioning a millennial Christian utopian existence.

Moreover, Blake appears to have found inspiration for the communal life of his Eden in Augustine. As St. Augustine writes in the *City of God:* "[A]nd he bound them together in one fellowship, which we call the Holy and Heavenly City, in which God himself is for those spirits the means of their life and their felicity, is, as it were, their common life and food" (Book XXII:1, 1022). Blake calls his collective fellowship the Brotherhood of Man. This is not a very significant concept in *The Four Zoas* but it becomes central in *Jerusalem,* where forgiveness of sins in the brotherhood of man is the foremost principle of society.

Eden is the most mysterious of Blake's levels. In *The Four Zoas* Blake frequently calls this level Eternity. For instance, in Night Seven as the apocalypse draws closer:

> this delightful Tree
> Is given us for a Shelter from the tempests of Void & Solid,
> Till once again the morn of ages shall renew upon us,
> To reunite in those mild fields of happy Eternity
> [7a:267–70, E 359]

Obviously, "Eternity" here signifies the utopia Blake postulates in Eden after the apocalypse, and the two signifiers are thus interchangeable. All the same, the world of Eden is how Blake imagines his ideal utopian existence. It is a difficult task Blake tries to undertake in that it is a form of existence impossible to describe fully, since we have no previous knowledge of it.

What is most mysterious about Eden is Blake's representation of its sexuality. According to Damrosch, Blake by giving in to a dualist impulse makes a major mistake in dispensing with sexuality as we know it for the level of Eden. In a somewhat self-contradictory way Damrosch goes on to write: "The role of the Emanations in Eden—of the female in a realm where sex is not—must similarly be understood as a mystical attempt to keep what we have and yet transform it utterly" (240).[5] Since the post-apocalyptic level of the utopian Eden is a state that we at present know nothing about, how can we know anything about the way in which sexuality is expressed in this after-world? In spite of this, perhaps Damrosch is right in writing that Blake does not use a traditional male-female heterosexual model of sexuality as he describes Eden.

---

[5] *Ironically the phrase "A realm where sex is not" is a paraphrase of Luce Irigaray, who, with her deconstructive analyses of patriarchal discourse, has been one of the sharpest critics of male hegemony in recent years.*

We would be seriously mistaken if we took for granted that Blake dispenses with sexuality altogether in his Eden. It is merely sexual lust, and all its accompanying destructive negations, which he envisions as being excluded in his utopian level. It seems that Blake here adopts some of St. Augustine's ideas of this issue in the *City of God*: "For my part, I feel that theirs is the more sensible opinion who have no doubt that there will be both sexes in the resurrection. For in that life there will be no sexual lust, which is the cause of shame" (Book XXII:17, 1057). One might read Augustine as an early advocate, if not precisely of gender equality, then at least of the Blakean kind of male-female union. This becomes even more evident when he writes: "The woman, then, is the creation of God, just as the man; but her creation out of man emphasizes the idea of the unity between them" (Book XXII:17, 1057). An even earlier source is of course the Bible, more precisely Matthew: "For in the resurrection they neither marry, nor are given in marriage, but are as the angels of God in heaven" (22:30, 973). Blake has adopted this idea in *Jerusalem*, where Albion tells Vala that "[i]n Eternity they neither marry nor are given in marriage" (34:15). Significantly, in the *City of God* Augustine also refers to this passage in Matthew (Book XXII:17, 1058).

While Beulah is a "sexual" level, Eden is not, but is rather a level of "love." Fallen sexuality therefore has to be elevated into the love and compassion of male-female togetherness in Eden, as Bloom has suggested: "[G]enerative sexuality is raised to a more fulfilled level" (*Complete* 966). In Blake's utopian city, called Jerusalem already in *The Four Zoas*, man and woman reunited and together will live a peaceful life near God:

> Thus shall the male & female live the life of Eternity
> Because the Lamb of God Creates himself a bride & wife
> That we his Children evermore may live in Jerusalem
> Which now descendeth out of heaven a City yet a Woman
> [9:215–22, E 391]

Obviously, Blake aims to lift humanity one level higher from the level of fallen sexuality, but it is not quite clear what his utopia consists of. The most uncertain feature is the sexual/emotional life in this world. We cannot therefore with full conviction infer that there is no male-female "sexuality" in Blake's Eden. Minna Doskow is one of the few commentators to support this view: "The natural world is thus not exchanged for another, but *remains sexual*, generating but not generative, since it is now inhabited by imaginative man" (166, emphasis mine).

In *Jerusalem* love is expressed through "comminglings," which is one of Blake's most successful terms in this context. In line with this, Damrosch comments: "Who can say what that mysterious 'commingling' would be in which Blakean man escapes what Frosch calls the 'tyranny' of genital sexuality (p. 162)? For non–Blakeans, nongenital sexuality is nonhuman sexuality" (Damrosch 238). Who can really know what utopian "sexuality" is, one might wonder. I endorse the following statement by Leopold Damrosch, but not his overall idea that sexuality completely disappears from the level of Eden: "In some mysterious way the sexual act must be the entrance to an apocalypse in which fallen sexuality will be burned up and replaced by something else" (238). Fallen sexuality must be replaced, as Blake shows, but not necessarily "sexuality" as a whole.

Blake's Symbolic Gender Interactivity

In his three epic prophecies, Blake seeks to portray a balanced state of male-female togetherness through visionary glances at the desired state of utopia, similar to the satirical glances of the *Songs*. For this purpose Blake invents new symbols to represent this unknown ideal of unity. Already in *The Four Zoas* Blake attempts to represent the ideal of togetherness when the male zoas are joined by their respective emanations just before apocalypse.

Blake's most significant poetic strategy in the three major epics is to use the many characters of the poems in an interactive way. A. L. Morton, who is one of the few commentators to recognize Blake's poems as utopias, claims in *The English Utopia*: "So, for the first time, we have a utopia reached not by abstract speculation but by the transformation through struggle of what actually exists. This is shown most clearly in the complex interaction of Blake's symbolic figures " (161). This symbolic interaction is indeed complex and takes place on several different levels in Blake's poems. One example is the symbolic interaction in *Milton* of the four inspired characters Bard, Blake, Milton and Los. These characters at some points of the poem even merge into different combinations. Another more complex example is the gender interactivity of the male zoas and their female emanations in *The Four Zoas*.

The interactivity of the two sexes is the most important level of interaction in Blake's gender utopia. Since the male-female reunion is Blake's ultimate expression of gender equality, the fluctuating degree of interdependent activity is a determining factor in Blake's poetry for the symbolic advent of mankind's redeeming, and damning, apocalypse. Throughout his poems Blake tries to show the inevitably lost state of human affairs. If immediate practical action is not taken, the advent of apocalypse and utopia remains remote in a fallen world. The general view of society, particularly in the days of Blake, is that male activity and female passivity constitute a positive equation.

There is virtual consensus within Blake criticism that active female characters in Blake are negative, since they tend to dominate the male characters in an aggressive way. For example, Anne Mellor has claimed that "the poetic and visual metaphors that Blake develops and uses throughout the corpus of his work typically depict women as either passively dependent on men, or as aggressive and evil" ("Blake's Portrayal" 148). Susan Fox has argued that Blake portrays the female gender "as inferior and dependent ... or as unnaturally and disastrously dominant" ("The Female as Metaphor" 507). Further, in spite of being positive towards Blake's gender utopia as a whole, Nicholas Williams also interprets female activity negatively: "Clearly, Blake's equation of the feminine with the monstrously domineering threatens the status of his genderless sexual utopia" (72).

In contrast to these commentators I argue that female activity is not presented in a completely negative way. In my opinion there are several instances in Blake's poetry where female activity leads to a positive outcome. In fact, the final positive outcome of the three major epics in apocalypse or, as in *Milton*, pre-apocalypse, is accomplished much through the intervention of positive female activity.

It is not only female activity that is an important parameter in Blake's utopian poems. Consistent with the overall scheme of gender interactivity, the activity of the male characters is also crucial. Quite logically, there is an abundance of examples of active male characters in Blake's poetry. Activity and dominance are after all the norm for a Blakean male character and the sometimes conventional picture of the dominant male is an inevitable by-product of the largely patriarchal influence pervading the language of Blake's age.

Isolated male or female activity, on the other hand, is no sign of progress in Blake's poetry. To make any movement closer towards Blake's utopian goal Eden, man and woman must work actively together. Blake tries to show the exigency of movement and active male-female cooperation through the symbolic interaction of his male and female characters.

Blake's Female Symbols

In the wake of third-wave feminism there has, in the last few decades, emerged quite a number of feminist Blake critics who have brought invigorating and fresh ideas beneficial into Blake criticism and inspired it to take directions formerly unthought of. The feminist Blake scholars mainly concentrate their analytical efforts on Blake's use of language, and many of them approach the problem of Blake's linguistic strategies and symbol formation from a more advantageous critical position than the more conventional Blake criticism of earlier years.

Most of all, and quite naturally so, the feminist critics deal with the issue of Blake's female characters. The problem of the ambiguity in Blake's portrayal of women has led Blake critics to diverge into different directions, thereby causing something of a controversy within Blake criticism. Two opposing standpoints have thus emerged and as Karleen Middleton Murphy claims: "From the works we can make a case for Blake being either a feminist or an anti-feminist, since evidence exists for both sides" (272). This is of course also a comment on the status of Blake's gender politics. Consequently, the two categories among feminist and other critics on this dimension of Blake's poetry that have surfaced in recent years are either positive or negative to his ideas of gender equality.

The most extreme form of recent feminist Blake criticism sees Blake as a misogynist or as sexist. Anne Mellor, as we have already seen, is one of several commentators who reads Blake's female metaphor negatively. Brenda Webster, using pseudo–Freudian psychoanalysis, is another valid example of this critical category. She finds Blake's views on female sexuality hostile to women: "Finally, during the writing of *Jerusalem*, Blake begins to feel that female sexuality can be dispensed with altogether. He considers female sexuality inferior to the total body sensuality of the child, for the loss of which he holds women responsible" (222). In my opinion Webster's view is quite restricted since it only considers the position of Blake's female and states nothing about Blake's male or his idea of male-female togetherness. Not only does Blake believe that female sexuality can be dispensed with in his utopian level of Eden but, as we have seen in Damrosch, according to many critics he could dispense with sexuality altogether. Thus, it is my contention that Blake can be no misogynist, since he embraces a humanitarian utopian position which eliminates or, rather, transcends, *all* corrupt forms of sexuality in a future utopia, male as well as female.

Susan Fox, on the other hand, holds a neutral and more balanced position between the two extremes of Blake critics. She sees Blake as neither misogynist nor feminist. Instead she clearly positions Blake's difficulties at the socio-linguistic level. Fox goes deeper than does Webster's psychoanalysis, and penetrates Blake's linguistic dilemma to the core by pointing out the contradictory nature of his metaphor. Even though it is mainly a comment on Blake's contemporary society, Fox claims that his metaphor also tells us something about his art and mind. The paradox, then, is that in spite of being a stronger opponent to misogynist attitudes than any other contemporary male author, Blake was to some degree naturally a victim of those tendencies ("The Female As Metaphor" 519). So once again the linguistic double bind of Blake is indicated: no matter how unbiased the intentions of his gender politics were, there was little chance for him to express them.

At the other extreme of Blake criticism, however, there are a few more directly positive critical views on Blake's female metaphor. Helen Bruder's study is one such example. Another example is Rachel V. Billigheimer who in "Conflict and Conquest: Creation, the Emanation and the Female in William Blake's Mythology," in overall agreement with the present argument, states that the final outcome of Blake's poetry is a positive reunion between the male and female characters: "Though many critics have expounded on Blake's denigrating attitude towards the role of the female it is nevertheless shown that the ultimate union of the female Emanation with her male counterpart precipitates the vision of eternity" (94). Yet one more highly relevant example of a critic with a positive interpretation of Blake's female characters is to be found in the writings of Josephine A. McQuail. Taking her stance against the Freudian analysis of Brenda Webster, McQuail in "Passion and Mysticism in William Blake" discards psychoanalytical criticism as an effective interpretive tool of Blake's poetry. She argues: "In itself, of course, the condemnation of sexual repression is a message that went against traditional dogma. But, in other ways Blake advocates the rejection of a carnal doctrine that focuses on the female as primary bearer of the burden of guilt" (122–23). Further, K. D. Verma has claimed that the characters in Blake are mental states which only take place as projections in language: "In Blake's myth male and female are states and not characters and historical figures.... Surely, Blake does not say, as does Aristotle, that woman is biologically—and, hence, morally and spiritually—inferior to man, nor does Blake relegate woman to a secondary or inferior position" (208). I share Verma's view of the equal position of woman in Blake's overall mythological scheme, but in contradistinction to Verma I believe that Blake's symbols must also be read both as characters and historical figures. It would not be possible for us to interpret these characters, and concomitantly the whole oeuvre of Blake's poetry, if we did not see them in relation to history and literature both before and after Blake. Therefore, Blake's poems must be read both historically and allegorically. Read in that context, the male and female characters will emerge as representations of what Blake sees as the defects of the society of his time.

As this survey has shown, the bulk of critical impressions of Blake's female is negative. Nonetheless, I will maintain that the final outcome of Blake's writing, in the concluding chord of the gender utopia of *Jerusalem*, is positive. Although some passages and illustrations of that poem might, according to most of its commentators, be interpreted as hostile to the female sex, I will argue that this is not the case if we assess this poem, and Blake's work in general, as a single entity. We must read Blake's poetic oeuvre holistically, as one great unity, and that is particularly essential for the three major epics. It is with these precepts in mind that I will read Blake's visionary utopia of gender equality in the subsequent chapters.

2
Blake's Radical Context

Around the time of the revolutions in America and France a radical optimism flourished all over Britain. In the late 1780s and early 1790s artists, poets, artisans, petty merchants and other minority groups organized themselves in various radical societies. Particularly this was the case in London, and it was this environment of revolutionary utopian spirit that inspired Blake's most radical writing during the 1790s and provided the backbone of his subsequent epic poems.

Also religious life was influenced by the new ways of thinking. The radical Protestant tradition, and in particular the tradition of Dissent, emerged as a consequence of the new clerical regulations introduced by the Act of Uniformity in 1662 and the Act of Toleration in 1689, which legal measures led to the acceptance of deviant religious groups. Naturally, this resulted in a dramatic rise in the number of Dissenting affiliations during the eighteenth century. We have good reason to believe that Blake and his family somehow were among the people caught up in this new radical religious movement.

Significantly, modern feminism had its initiation in these years, and for the first time women also came to be at least partly embraced by the new ideals. In the writings of the first modern feminist Mary Wollstonecraft, for instance, one can discern a striving for complete equality between the two sexes. Blake's contact with Wollstonecraft and certain feminist circles were most likely a major influence on his attempt at creating a gender utopia in his three great epics.

Human responsibility is something of a motto for Blake's radical humanist thinking, and it is his belief that to redeem the fallen state of this world each individual human being has to take full active responsibility. The decisive step to realizing a gender utopia according to

Blake, is that man and woman assume equal responsibility and work actively together towards the mutual goal to revoke the fall. Blake must therefore be seen as a radical humanist following Christian ideals.

In the Romantic period there was an increasing interest in humanism, which found some manifestation in the new poetic doctrines of Blake, Wordsworth, Coleridge and Shelley, among others. As poetic manifestos like Wordsworth's "Preface" to *Lyrical Ballads* and Shelley's *Defence of Poetry* as well as the basic ideas of Blake's mythological system show, the core was located in the individual human being. The impact of the individual imagination was underscored both by Blake and Coleridge, who in *Biographia Literaria* divided the mental faculties in three parts: "fancy," "the primary imagination," and "the secondary imagination." In particular, the individual was the focus of the poetic scheme of Blake and, as in the philosophy of David Hume, the link between the imagination and humanism is obvious, as John Beer has explained in *Blake's Humanism*. In Blake there arises a view of the individual combining imaginative power with social pathos, which leads Beer to label him a "humanist visionary" rather than a "visionary humanist" (14–15).

Along with a greater belief in the individual and the imagination came a gradual secularization of religion during the eighteenth century, which was of great importance to the poets and artists of the early Romantic period. Indications of this had appeared as early as by the mid-century in the philosophical doctrines of David Hume. Instead of traditional faith in God the Romantics believed in the visionary moment of creation in which the poet encapsulated and equalled God.

In spite of the general influence from Enlightenment humanism, the greatest stimulus for Blake's gender utopia was exerted by a more explicitly radical ambience, with a considerably smaller, but dedicated, following. Specifically, this inspiration came from two radical factions. The first of these consisted of various artists around the London publisher and bookseller Joseph Johnson, while the other was to be found in the religious tradition of Dissent with its diverse congregations.

Out of a rather general humanist environment, then, emerged a number of more explicitly radical ideologies which found various expressions. It is without doubt that this radical ambience exerted a major influence on Blake in the 1780s and 90s, and even had a greater influence than the so frequently proposed mystical sources. But since the Bible is Blake's major source we must go even further back in time to trace the origin of Blake's unusual radical blend, to the reforms of the previous century, around the time of the so-called Glorious Revolution in the late seventeenth century.

The Dissenting Tradition

It is at the time after these clerical reforms that the strong Dissenting tradition first appears on a more noticeable basis. In a rather short time the influence of Dissent grows considerably and by the middle of the following century it is established as a major force in English religious life. This tradition came to be particularly important for the Romantic and revolutionary movement.

Since there are many different groups within the English tradition of Dissent, and since there until quite recently has been little substantial evidence of the connection of Blake and his family, the determination of Blake's exact religious affiliation has inevitably always been a bit speculative. That Blake was influenced by this tradition is without doubt, though. In his much-debated book *Witness Against the Beast* E.P. Thompson sets out to demonstrate the connection between Blake's ideas and antinomianism. Thompson's outline in this work stresses Blake's association with an antinomian context at the same time as it, like Mee's study *Dangerous Enthusiasm*, undermines the widespread notion of Blake as a mysticist. Instead Thompson traces the antinomian bonds of Blake's family, particularly his parents. The plausibility of his standpoint is accentuated by some biographical information in G.E. Bentley's *Blake Records*. For one thing, the marriage register tells us that "James Blake and Catherine Harmitage of St. James's, Westminster, were married in St. George's Chapel, just off Hanover Square, on Sunday, October 15th, 1752" (2). This small church was used by those who wanted to marry at short notice. Thompson goes on to suggest that Catherine Harmitage, through her first husband, already had a natural connection with one of the radical religious sects at the time, the Muggletonians (121). Keri Davies, on the other hand, does not accept this as determining evidence for any religious radicalism. "Marriage at Mayfair is certainly no evidence of leanings towards Dissent" (*William Blake in Contexts* 41), he concludes after convincingly demonstrating that marriages at Mayfair/St. George's chapel were actually following the Church of England ceremonies and the chapel was merely used to "get married in a hurry" in a more private manner (40–41).

In his biographical work, Bentley suggests that also Blake's elder brother James had some visionary qualities that would connect him with religious Dissenters: "He had, however, startling qualities that he shared with his younger brother. 'James—for the most part an humble matter-of-fact man—had his spiritual and visionary side too; would at times *talk Swedenborg*'" (2, qtd. in Gilchrist 48). Swedenborgianism is one of the antinomian religious sects that can most confidently be associated with Blake. This commonplace of Blake studies has its most obvious proof in the signatures of Blake and his wife to a document of the so-called New Church: "At the first session of the general conference of the New Church on April 13th, 1789 sixty or seventy readers of Swedenborg's writings met at a public house, and the first thing they did, as a prerequisite to attendance, was to sign the following paper.... Among the signatures to this manifesto were those of 'W. Blake' and his wife 'C. Blake'" (*Blake Records* 35). In fact, these are the only signature and evidence we have of Blake participating in a religious meeting of any kind, which David Worrall recently has verified by examining the original document.

How sincere, far-reaching and long-standing Blake's Swedenborg sympathies were has of course been much discussed. It is generally accepted that Blake was enthusiastic about Swedenborg in younger years but gradually grew sceptical, finally to renounce his ideas altogether. Bentley writes: "By the winter of 1788–9 Blake had become deeply interested in the New Jerusalem Church promised by Emanuel Swedenborg. He had bought copies of Swedenborg's *Heaven and Hell* (1784) and *Divine Love and Divine Wisdom* (1788)" (34–5). As we know, *Heaven and Hell* was satirized in *The Marriage of Heaven and Hell*, so it is probably with the publication of this illuminated book that the assumed "break" with Swedenborg occurs. Bentley points out that "[h]e soon became actively hostile to both Swedenborg and Swedenborgians. His notes to Swedenborg's *Wisdom of Angels*, concerning the Divine Providence, 1790 (p. 434), assert with some relish Swedenborg's 'Cursed Folly,' and in *The Marriage of Heaven and Hell*, partly written in 1790, he enthusiastically damned Swedenborg and his followers as arrogant spiritual predestinarians" (37–8). Nevertheless, Swedenborg left a lasting imprint on Blake's imagination, for one thing shown in Blake's use of a near Swedenborgian dualism throughout his work. Morton Paley has pointed this out in an early *Blake Quarterly* article: "Blake continued to retain the Swedenborgian notion of God's human form; and in general it can be said that Blake retained numerous Swedenborgian ideas even during the period in which he repudiated Swedenborgianism"

("A New Heaven" 88n26). Indeed, in *Heaven & Hell* Swedenborg himself writes: "Nothing exists without its opposite, and the nature of something can be known by looking at what is opposite to it" (120–21). As we easily understand, this is close to Blake's dualist core-belief where "Opposition is True Friendship" (*Marriage* 20:20, E 42).

Perhaps Swedenborg's influence on Blake was even more profound than that. Many of the unconventional principles on love and sexuality proposed by Swedenborg in *Conjugial Love* seem to be echoed, at least in an amended form, in Blake's poetry. Some commentators have detected a prototype of feminism in Swedenborg and regard him as something of the first feminist. In the foreword to *Conjugial Love*, for example, Alfred Acton writes: "Thus since a married couple in heaven embody good and truth, they must inevitably play an equal role in their marriage. The fundamental principle of equality was thus established by Swedenborg, long before it began to be asserted by the feminist movement" (X). Furthermore, there has in recent years been a debate within Swedenborgian circles on the nature and scope of feminism and gender politics in Swedenborg's work. In the December 2003 number of *Studia Swedenborgiana* several commentators have responded to an article by Kimberly Hinrichs, "Distinguishably One: Envisioning a Confluence of Swedenborgian and Feminist Theology," published in the previous issue of the journal. For instance, although endorsing the common view that Swedenborg, like Blake, in spite of advocating gender equality in some sense and to some degree, was biased from living in a patriarchal age and society, Wilma Wake in "Swedenborgian Feminism: The Next Steps" considers Hinrichs's article as a major breakthrough (27).

But E.P. Thompson has argued that it is another even less known religious sect, the Muggletonians, that exerted the greatest influence on Blake. This is the main argument of *Witness Against the Beast*, and he invests considerable effort in tracing the possible Muggletonian influence of Blake's family. It is his claim that Blake introduced the typical Muggletonian vocabulary of symbolism in a congenial and almost instinctive way into the images of his poetry.

Of particular significance to Blake's views was the belief in a singular God or Christ in the image of man. That part of the Muggletonian doctrine could well have suited Blake and his interpretation of the Bible is possible if we consider Thompson's definition of the central features of the sect: "Muggletonian doctrine concentrated upon three areas—the problem of the first creation of matter and of the origin of evil; *Genesis* and the Fall; and *Revelation*" (70). As we know, the fall and apocalypse are fundamental concepts in Blake.

Intriguingly, Blake could have found his radical idea of an uncommonly active female among the Muggletonians. Thompson writes: "One senses that there was an active feminine presence in the tiny Muggletonian church; many songs were written by women, and in the 1770s a dissident group (of both sexes) left the church under the leadership of Martha Collier, an aspirant visionary and prophetess" (81). In contradiction to this, somewhat paradoxically, through the doctrine of the Two Seeds, the Muggletonians embraced patriarchal as well as feminist principles.

The Muggletonians were a very secretive sect. They were based in London and their followers consisted mainly of artisans and a few artists. Thompson outlines a number of characteristics that remind us of Blake. Through the doctrine of the Two Seeds the Muggletonians used a Behmenist dialectic which Blake's contraries seem to echo, but the Two Seeds are more properly speaking what Blake would have called "negations," not principles of creative opposition. This was for instance manifested in the Satanic and divine principle within each man and woman struggling for dominance and the rejection of body/soul dualism. Like Blake, they felt great hostility to reason and therefore there was no priesthood in their congregation.

Thompson rounds off the discussion of the antinomian influence in Blake most appropriately by pointing to the similarity between Muggletonians and Swedenborgians: "But it is relevant to note now that the similarity of certain Muggletonian and Swedenborgian tenets was remarked upon by observers at the time" (102). This is underscored by the fact that Blake's brother James talked Swedenborg, but also saw visions of Abraham and Moses, which was not common to Swedenborgians at the time and, as Thompson implies, this rather points in the direction of the Muggletonians. Albeit speculative, one important outcome of Thompson's argumentation is that the antinomian connections of his family show the inevitable immersion of Blake in that tradition.

Keri Davies, by contrast, is sceptical about this evidence. "There is not a shred of evidence to suggest that Blake's parents were Muggletonians or even Dissenters of any kind," Davies argues, and continues: "The implication of the surviving documents is that the elder Blakes were more conventional in their religion and political beliefs than some scholars have romantically envisaged." He concludes with two pertinent questions: "Why has it been so unacceptable for Blake to have had very ordinary parents? Why can't his politics and religious views be a conscious divergence from the parental milieu?" (*Blake Journal* 67) Also Bentley is skeptical about Thompson's Muggletonian "evidence," but rather skillfully builds a case for the Dissenting tradition of Blake's family in *The Stranger from Paradise*: "Blake's parents raised their children in the Dissenting tradition of private devotion and private Bible reading rather than public catechism and public worship. But we do not know their church or creed" (7).

Indeed, in his most recent research, documented in his still unpublished dissertation *William Blake in Contexts,* Davies has found compelling evidence which make sure that Blake's mother had no connection to the Muggletonians at all. According to Davies, the incorrect speculative statements of Thompson all have their origin in a confusion of names. Although Catherine's first husband has long been known as Hermitage, or Harmitage, this has never been supported with any acceptable substantial evidence. Through a scrutiny of genealogical sources Davies has now presented evidence to forcefully refute this presumption, and has established that his real name instead was Thomas Armitage.

We can therefore now safely dismiss Thompson's speculative notion that Blake was influenced by Muggletoianism, at least what concerns his mother's family inheritance. "There is just no evidence whatsoever linking William Blake directly to known followers of Lodowicke Muggleton," as Davies writes (56). It is instead another religious orientation and congregation, the Moravians, which provided the family background on Blake's mother's side. With the help of an entry in the Marriage Register of the Mayfair Chapel for December 1746 Davies establishes that the maiden name of Blake's mother was Wright, and that she married Thomas Armitage (46). Through exploring the Moravian Church Archive, Keri Davies has managed to be the first to trace and establish the birthplace of Catherine Wright to the small north Nottinghamshire village Walkeringham. Here she was raised in a family with Moravian beliefs.

Then what were the main characteristics of this currently little known religious group; characteristics that make us more certain of having enacted a main influence and served as a source of inspiration to Blake's art, more conspicuous and closely tied than Muggletonianism, and even Swedenborgianism? "The position of this body in England during the eighteenth century was quite unusual ... they *were* and then again *were not* Dissenters," Davies writes, indicating the unsevered ties between the Moravians and the Church of England (284–85). Appearing in England at a crucial time in the mid-eighteenth century at the height of Enlightenment ideals and just before the revolutionary commotion of the final decades, the Moravian Church usurped a unique position in English religious life. Thus the Moravians became the leaders of the great Evangelical Revival, as E. R. Hassé has confirmed: "It not only stirred England to its very depths, but it shaped the course of our people at a most critical period" (XI).

The Moravian Church in England was formed by a small number of missionaries from Herrnhut in Saxony, who first arrived in 1722. In its turn this small group was a renewal of the next-to extinct Bohemian Brethren from the fifteenth century. The group soon acquired a small but dedicated following in London, and in 1738 the Fetter Lane Society was established, which saw the Wesley brothers John and Charles as early members, and came to heavily influence the ideas of the former. And as we have seen in the case of Blake's mother, the Moravians had already spread northwards in England, with Yorkshire as an early major congregation, and an affiliation in Nottingham.

Moravianism is rather a spirituality than a doctrine, a trait that certainly seems to have been one that suited Blake. Concomitantly they were no adherents of a state-dependent Church, dominated by priesthood and rules, a notion omniscient in Blake's work. Instead, like Blake, they emphasized the importance of Jesus and a Christian brotherhood of man. Reason was not believed to be the foundation of the faculties, but feeling and passion. Most intriguingly they professed the glory of sexuality, a significant role for the female, and to some extent even equality between the sexes. The most extreme expression of this was their strong accentuation of a common veneration of the sexual organs, the male as well as the female. They cherished the belief that since Jesus was born with a penis, this organ should be the beauty of the male body and not mentioned with shame; and since he was born through the female organ the same should go for that. We need only think of Blake's many illustrations including naked bodies to grasp the connection, the designs of *Jerusalem* to mention only one prominent example. Moreover, the male-female union in the form of marriage was another cornerstone in the Moravian creed and, remarkably, "married people ... were not looked upon as lawfully married, unless they performed the conjugal Duties in the Presence of the Elders" (Rimius, *Candid Narrative* 119). Not only does this remind us of Blake's early ideas of "free" love, a Wollstonecraftian notion paraphrased mainly in *Visions of the*

Daughters of Albion, but also the Swedenborgian tenets of "conjugial love."

Hence, how radical Blake's religious outlook in fact was is more uncertain than most commentators have previously believed, and therefore his biography, and even his poems, now has to be renegotiated. And as Davies concludes: "The social and political implications of what we know about Blake's parentage have to be amended in the light of these discoveries" (*William Blake in Context* 58).

The Dissenting connection also suggests an unusual perceptibility of unorthodox, not traditionally patriarchal Christian, beliefs of greater equality between the sexes. Most important, however, is the exceptional open-mindedness that surrounded Blake in his early years, which doubtlessly made him prone to take in new radical ideas, like feminism and gender equality, at a more mature age.

The English Jacobins

The antinomian religious tradition was not the only radical movement to influence Blake in the 1790s. The other major radical orientation, the English Jacobins, was overtly political. We know that a strong revolutionary current flourished in the London of the early 1790s, particularly among artists, intellectuals and artisans, and it was mainly associated with the support of the French revolution. However, the English Jacobins were not as unified a movement as may first be expected, and should not be considered merely as liberal supporters of the French revolution. One of the better known organizations was the London Corresponding Society, which was founded in 1792 and had 3000–5000 members at its climax in 1795. In the main it consisted of articulate artisans, small shopkeepers and lesser professionals such as medical men, law clerks, attorneys, publishers, printers, preachers and journalists. Throughout Britain there existed a large number of corresponding societies at that time. But there were also other not so well-known radical circles of a more common and proletarian nature in London at the time, something which could have informed the poetry of Blake. In *Radical Culture* David Worrall has taken great pains to map this rather undiscovered part of London society. In his essay "Blake and 1790s Plebeian Radical Culture" in the *Blake in the Nineties* compilation, Worrall claims that "in 1793 there is evidence to suggest the existence of a plebeian radical culture whose rhetorics are assimilated in

Blake's works" (194). In his recent book *William Blake and the Impossible History of the 1790s* Saree Makdisi uses the term "liberal radicalism" to denote the politically progressive ideas of the groups described in this section.

Nevertheless, there is little doubt that the early phases of the French revolution provided the decisive impetus for the English Jacobins. As violence grew to drastic proportions in France, however, the enthusiasm among the English Jacobins gradually died out. On the whole, the English Jacobins were peaceful and did not resort to violence. From the legacy of Enlightenment humanism they kept the belief that reason should be the guiding light in society.

Some of the artists and writers with revolutionary Jacobin inclinations were downright utopian in their thinking, among them Samuel Taylor Coleridge and Robert Southey. Most notably their radical doctrine found its expression in their advanced plans to found a utopian community called Pantisocracy. Their utopian ideas were formed around the same time as Blake's, namely in 1794 when Southey and Coleridge had just first met, as a visionary project related to the contemporary political environment. It was Coleridge who invented the name but also Southey entertained utopian ideas before meeting Coleridge. Les Tannenbaum informs us that Southey and Coleridge at the time envisioned an escape from the corrupt Europe to a pastoral exotic paradise. Coleridge even gave voice to this utopian fantasy in a poem called "Pantisocracy" (2–3).

Coleridge contemplated writing *The Book of Pantisocracy*, and in a letter to Southey he states that it "[w]ill of course be submitted to the improvements and approbation of each component member" (Aug. 29, 1794). The plan was to establish Pantisocracy in America, more specifically at the Susquehanna River in Pennsylvania. All property was to be common, with no specific religious or political beliefs. (Tannenbaum 3) The settlement of Joseph Priestley in Northumberland, Pennsylvania (also on the banks of the Susquehanna), provided an additional incentive to Coleridge. However, the two poets did not see eye to eye as regards the usefulness of the ideas outlined by William Godwin in *Political Justice*. This was only an initial albeit important discord, and even though Coleridge and Southey managed to recruit other people with utopian interests, the project soon met with some practical difficulties. The main problem concerned the social and sexual status of the women in the community. In line with Godwin's, Wollstonecraft's and, at a time, Blake's liberal view of sex, Coleridge wanted the women to be sexually shared, just like the goods of the society property. Southey's complete refusal of these ideas widened the breach between the two, and when Southey suggested that they bring slaves with them the end of the project was near. Coleridge was furious with this idea, and utopian Pantisocracy was abandoned. The seemingly eternal insurmountable obstacles race and gender had again proved too strong to eradicate. (Tannenbaum 4-5)

Significantly for the affinity between the more politically oriented radicalism of the Jacobins and the religious radicalism of the antinomian congregations, Coleridge's and Southey's utopian colonial project took some ideas from a Swedenborgian forerunner initiated by the two Swedes Carl Bernard Wadström and August Nordenskjöld. In 1789 they drew a plan to set up a utopian community entirely based on the Swedenborgian principle of conjugal love in Sierra Leone on the west coast of Africa.[6] Since it is an established fact that Blake met the two Swedes at the Swedenborg conference at Great Eastcheap the same year, and bearing in mind the similarity between his ideas of male-female relations and conjugial love, it is not an unfounded assumption that Blake took some basic values from this utopian scheme, and then possibly also from Pantisocracy.

The basic principle of *Conjugial Love* is the desire of the male and female to be joined, sexually and spiritually, into one: "Conjugial love is in essence nothing but two people wishing to be one, that is, wishing their two lives to be one" (X, 215:1,214). Although still being a male-dominated hierarchal system, it was at that time a remarkably egalitarian system which welcomed the female sex as an essential component in society. It is therefore not surprising that such a philanthropic personality as Wadström appropriated Swedenborg's notion of conjugial love and incorporated it in his and Nordenskjöld's utopian colony, but that the society was to be wholly based upon its principle is exceptional. The central tenet of the project is found in Wadström's *Plan for a Free Community*:

> The Conjugal [sic] Alliance of the Community, which is between the Sexes, or between the Understanding in the Man and the Will in the Woman; or, Man's Wisdom and Woman's Love, because upon this depends entirely the improvement of the very elements in all

---

[6]*In the introduction to* Conjugial Love *Alfred Acton explains Swedenborg's preference of the term "conjugial" to the frequently, and often wrongly, used "conjugal." Basically, in Swedenborg's use "conjugial" is a positive term, while "conjugal" is negatively charged.*

Communities, which are Marriages, or the Conjugal [sic] Unions, and not, either Man or Woman separately considered [29–30].

So, as David Worrall emphasizes in his comments of the project: "Wadström intended it to be a colony not based upon empire but upon the idealistic sexual and social compact of distinctively Swedenborgian conjugal [sic] love" ("Thel in Africa" 18).

However, for a number of reasons the Sierra Leone project was never accomplished. The major cause was probably the schism within the London Swedenborgians over some controversial components of the principles of conjugial love. For instance, they had the belief that the "virile potency" of the male was to govern the marital relations and under certain circumstances the man was allowed to take a concubine. The crisis led to the expulsion of some of the key-members of the Society, among them Wadström and Nordenskjöld. Wadstöm for a while pursued the African scheme and in 1794 issued a new project that tried to find shareholders to invest money for an expedition, and after that devoted his life to other philanthropic projects and ended his days in Paris. Nordenskjöld, on the other hand, eventually went to Africa in 1792, according to Worrall most likely in pursuit of the lost prophetic books of the Bible, but died of ill health in an expedition to the heart of Africa.

Blake, we know, went on to express opinions promoting an improved equality between the sexes. It is Worrall's, highly plausible, theory that Blake found the central Swedenborgian beliefs still too patriarchal and patronizing towards women and therefore opted out of this environment. Worrall claims that he incorporated some of the tenets and wrote *The Book of Thel* as a corrective to the ideas of conjugial love. And undeniably some of the principles of Wadström's *Plan* caught on with Blake. Most significantly his insistence on activity of both sexes and a mutual interactivity between them can be found expressed here: "This Government must exactly resemble a Marriage, which consists of two distinct Powers, the Active on the part of the Husband, and the Re-active on the part of the Wife" (20).

The most important Jacobin-oriented formation for Blake on a daily basis was the well-known circle around the London publisher Joseph Johnson. As has been frequently recounted, the members met regularly every Sunday afternoon in a room above Johnson's bookshop in St. Paul's churchyard for tea and discussions. Blake was, if not a regular member, a frequent guest at these gatherings. The circle comprised such famous radicals as Thomas Paine, Henry Fuseli and Joseph Priestley, and surely must have influenced Blake's art and poetry to a great extent in the 1790s.

Crucial for the conception of Blake's gender utopia was his encounter, through Johnson and his circle, with the leading feminist Mary Wollstonecraft, and probably other major feminists like Anna Barbauld and Mary Hays. We have substantial evidence of their co-operation in Wollstonecraft's *Original Stories from Real Life* and *Elements of Morality*, which Blake illustrated. Less obvious is the influence Wollstonecraft, and other feminists, might have exerted on the composition of certain poems. Many commentators have noticed the similarity between Wollstonecraft's *Vindication of the Rights of Woman* and Blake's *Visions of the Daughters of Albion*, both in title and basic ideas. This may be the most evident example, but there are also others, like the two poems from the *Pickering MS*, "Mary" and "William Bond" and possibly even parts of *The Four Zoas*.

Joseph Johnson may have been even more important to Blake as a shop-owner and publisher. As far as we know, Blake's poems were only printed once during his lifetime, not counting his self-printed illuminated books. The "publication," his juvenile collection of poems *Poetical Sketches*, was realized through the financial aid of some of his friends. A second work, however, part one of the poem *The French Revolution*, was due to be printed by Johnson's company. To our knowledge, this poem was never printed, but even so it is of great importance in adding circumstantial evidence to our limited knowledge of Blake's life. Together with the new discoveries of Keri Davies, Blake's intention to produce a more publicly accessible literary work might provide evidence of a previously unrecognized commercial potential in some of Blake's poetry. Peter Ackroyd has indicated this in his Blake biography: "He still wanted, or expected, to be an established poet. No doubt Johnson was happy to encourage him, especially since he was intent upon a theme of such topical interest" (161). Although *The French Revolution* was soon abandoned, Johnson was during a period of a few years in the early and mid–1790s prepared to give Blake the artistic and financial support he could offer through his rights of publication and the display of the works in his shop. As we know, this undertaking eventually failed, but in these years Johnson's commitment to the commercial value of Blake's art suggests a wider circulation and readership of his poetry than have formerly been recognized.

Naturally, Blake was a frequent visitor to Johnson's shop. For one thing, he bought, or maybe borrowed, his own copies of radical and other literature in the bookshop, such as Tom Paine's *The Rights of Man* and the works of Wollstonecraft. Secondly, and most noteworthy, he wanted to enquire about the sales of his own volumes. Although his total "publication" was restricted to only one volume, new evidence has recently emerged to suggest that also some of the illuminated books that Blake printed himself were probably displayed in Johnson's shop more often than previously believed. These are indeed significant findings that shed new light on certain matters in Blake criticism, as David Worrall rightly emphasizes:

> Keri Davies' crucial piece of evidence ... that works by Blake were available in Joseph Johnson's bookshop in late 1794, with their joint imprint four out of five copies of *For Children*, puts his output in the midst of the most progressive elements of London's contemporary radical intelligentsia ["Plebeian Radical Culture" 195].

Not only does this prove a wider circulation of Blake's works, but it also suggests the great influence Wollstonecraft had on Blake in the mid–1790s. Significantly, the book displayed is *For Children*, at a time when we know that Blake illustrated Wollstonecraft's children and conduct books. Jon Mee points in a similar direction when he claims that "*The Gates (of Paradise)* is stylistically very similar to the plates Johnson commissioned from Blake for Wollstonecraft's books, a detail which suggests that it would have fitted neatly on to the bookseller's shelves" (219).

Through the new crucial discoveries of Keri Davies we can verify not only that Blake actually had a bigger contemporary audience than formerly thought, but also that his works attracted a female audience to a large degree. By scrutinizing the correspondence between Francis Douce and Richard Twiss, Davies manages to undermine recent arguments about Blake's female readership: "Feminist assessment of Blake has grown increasingly skeptical over the past two decades, but attention to Rebecca Bliss and her milieu obliges us to reassess the appeal of his works to a contemporary female audience" ("Mrs Bliss" 212).

Davies has found the central evidence for the wider circulation of Blake's work in a letter from Twiss to Douce: "You will see several more of Blake's books at Johnson's in St. Ps Ch.yd" (216). Certainly, Davies makes a logical claim when he writes that "[n]ot only does Twiss's letter suggest *For Children* was on sale, it also suggests other works by

Blake were available at Johnson's shop in late 1794" (217). According to Davies, the Twiss-Douce letters further imply a greater commercial potential than formerly recognized for the works of Blake in Johnson's shop. Davies concludes his important essay with a final contradiction of the traditional argument for the small size of Blake's audience: "Taken together, these new pieces of evidence should compel a revision of the established assumption that Blake lacked any significant contemporary audience" (226).

Feminism

The situation for women in the late eighteenth century was in many respects paradoxical. On the one hand, there was a clear decline in patriarchal authority, in the wake of John Locke's educational and psychological theories on individualism. On the other hand, women were facing Evangelicalism's insistence on the home as the centre of religious and moral life. As Anna Clark explains: "By the early nineteenth century, however, a new ideology of gender as separate spheres had arisen, in which individual men joined together as equals to form the public sphere of politics, while keeping their wives in the private sphere of the home" (4). Women were basically still locked up in between these two extremes, and Barbara Caine points out that people counted on women to guide men morally, religiously and otherwise, while at the same time they were still inferior to men in all other respects. Through religious and moral inspiration in their family, women were supposed to bring this enhanced spirit out in society. Paradoxically and strikingly, they were not allowed to enter this social world, not according to political rights at least (43). In *The Struggle for the Breeches: Gender and the Making of the British Working Class* Clark develops the issue further:

> The late eighteenth and early nineteenth centuries witnessed significant changes in views of masculinity and femininity, the sexual division of labor, and sexual mores, and these changes were intimately intertwined with the evolution of class politics. This period saw a shift from a notion of gender as hierarchy to a notion of gender as separate, complementary spheres [4].

As can be understood from this, in spite of the gradual dissolution of the old hierarchical structures of society, the roles of women were still largely dependent on men. As Clark puts it: "Men ruled over women, who were seen as men's inferiors, just as gentry ruled over common people, householder over servants, and masters over apprentices and journeymen" (4). Even though women were becoming recognized as rational beings and had their rights as citizens, the male hegemony still governed vital areas of society: "It was impossible for women to demand the right to be seen as sexual subjects rather than as sexual objects, for example, and equally difficult for them to claim the capacity of genius," as Caine explains (43). It is significant that the first feminist, Mary Wollstonecraft, was never fully able to solve the dilemma of sexual difference. While having advanced liberal ideas of free sex, she retained the conservative view that a woman's proper place was in the home, thus subscribing to a natural labour division between the sexes. And as Caine aptly concludes: "The Rights of Man could never simply be claimed by women, since much of their meaning came from the fact that men alone were entitled to them" (51).

Though feminism as a term was not coined until the nineteenth century, it saw its first modern expression in the radical ideas of Mary Wollstonecraft. As we know, Wollstonecraft belonged to the Joseph Johnson circle, just like her friend the radical pamphleteer and writer Mary Hays and William Blake.[7] Faint evidence as that might be, Blake was most probably influenced by the radical feminist ideas of the two Marys, ideas that for some time he tried to express in his own way in his poetry.

Wollstonecraft's influence on Blake has of course been highlighted and examined by many critics before.[8] Helen Bruder, for instance, explores this relation in *William Blake and the Daughters of Albion*. She also indicates Blake's link with feminism:

> Blake is of value to feminism not because he maintained an exemplary and unwavering feminist commitment but rather because he took sexual power seriously and engaged with many of the contemporary

---

[7]*The inclusion of Hays is not frequently indicated by commentators, but through the correspondence of Mary Wollstonecraft we can assume that Hays was a rather regular visitor at Johnson's. For the last six years or so of Wollstonecraft's life Hays was a close friend, and in a letter to her in 1795 Wollstonecraft writes: "I have promised to dine with Mr Johnson to morrow, and he requested me to invite you" ("To Mary Hays" 328).*
[8]*See for example Michael Ackland's "The Embattled Sexes: Blake's Debt to Wollstonecraft in* The Four Zoas," *in which he sets out to prove, sometimes on rather weak evidence, Blake's use and development of Wollstonecraft's ideas in* The Four Zoas: "[T]he full and lasting extent of her influence shows itself not in direct echoes or explicit allusions, but in broad and significant areas of conceptual agreement" (175). See also Mellor, "Sex, Violence, and Slavery: Blake and Wollstonecraft."*

> discourses and contexts in which it was being exercised or resisted. Moreover, and perhaps more important still, Blake's real "feminist" gesture is that he constructs a notion of femininity centered upon the concept of dissent. He allows disputatious female voices into his texts in a truly revolutionary way and this polyphonic liberty can be historically located... [36].

From this it is of course doubtful whether we can define Blake as a feminist, but it is possible to read his poems as expressions of the need for increased gender equality.

In *Ideology and Utopia in the Poetry of William Blake* Nicholas Williams outlines the utopia of Blake's poetry through an ideological socio-political reading. In one of the chapters he juxtaposes the gender utopian agendas of Wollstonecraft and Blake in a parallel reading of *Vindication of the Rights of Woman* and *Visions of the Daughters of Albion*. To begin with, Williams argues for Wollstonecraft as a utopian thinker: "Her thought does thrust itself toward the future in a manner which can only be described as utopian" (84). However much Wollstonecraft resembles Blake in being a utopian thinker, her future utopia nonetheless differs from Blake's on closer examination, as Williams goes on to point out: "In distinction to Wollstonecraft, the progress to utopia in Blake is not effected by the elimination of any element of the fallen world, whether sexuality, labor, or war, but instead by the 'copula' which will join fallen signifiers to their utopian meanings" (88).

While Williams argues for the need to read Blake historically in an ideological and socio-political context, Helen Bruder historicizes and contextualizes Blake in line with feminist thinking. About *Visions of the Daughters of Albion* she argues that, "[h]ere Blake attempts to find a place for the unfettered expression of women's desires at a historical moment when the controlling discourses of patriarchy were attempting, with much more effectiveness, to silence the voices of female eroticism" (57). Bruder goes on to claim that Blake as a whole does not succeed in this venture. On the contrary, as I argue, Blake was in fact successful in this difficult task.

The gender utopias of Blake and Wollstonecraft have many similarities as well as many differences. In spite of significant points of disagreement, for instance her greater emphasis on the importance of reason, Wollstonecraft's feminist utopia is a vital component of the radical context that Blake was a part of. As we have already seen, it is at least possible to find indications of a gender utopia in Wollstonecraft, and, as Mary Lyndon Shanley comments, "'Wollstonecraft's dilemma' is a dilemma for those living between an oppressive past of sexual inequality, and a hoped-for future of sexual equality whose institutions and social practices can only at present be imagined" (167). As we know, in the 1780s and 90s the Enlightenment values of a puritan sexual morality still remained the standard of society.

Mary Hays is not so well-known and in no way the monumental feminist figure as is Wollstonecraft. "Mary Hays had started her career as a journalist committed to questions of religious dissent," Helena Bergmann explains. (3) Interestingly, her religious orientation puts her in the same antinomian environment as Blake. Hays's two novels, *The Memoirs of Emma Courtney* from 1796 and *The Victim of Prejudice* from 1799, read in the light of modern feminism, can certainly be considered as even more innovative and, particularly, more radical than most of Wollstonecraft's works.

With her radical attempts to reconcile reason and passion, it is perfectly possible that Hays provided an even stronger link with Blake in the radical milieu of London in the 1790s. Consistent with the idea of utopian gender equality proclaimed by Blake, as Bergmann points out, "in her literary works and in her *Appeal to the Men of Great Britain in Behalf of Women* (1798) Hays propagated a deeper understanding between the sexes, voicing an ideal of friendship" (5). For example, in her second novel *The Victim of Prejudice* she states about the two main characters Mary and William that they were "[a]nimated but by one heart and one mind" (11), which seems similar to the male-female togetherness that is outlined as the final utopian goal of mankind by Blake in his long prophecies. After the gender reunion in *Jerusalem*, for instance, the emanations "stand both Male and Female at the Gates of each Humanity" (88:11, E 246).

In her novels, particularly *Emma Courtney*, Hays, much in agreement with the basic notions of Blake, questions the governing paradigm of Enlightenment reason by trying to reconcile it with its supposed opposite, passion. According to Hays, and to a lesser degree Wollstonecraft, these two forces need not exclude one another, and, like David Hume before her, she tries to resolve the dichotomy. As Sandra Sherman claims: "Hays's ultimate view that reason is ideologically freighted, and hence aligned with the disruptive potential of emotion, distinguishes her epistemology from Wollstonecraft's. While the war between reason and emotion is the common coin of late eighteenth-century women's texts, Hays complicates this dichotomy" (166n10).

For a woman in the late eighteenth century it was a brave step to challenge the social controlling principle of male-governed patriarchal authoritative reason so strongly. In doing so both Wollstonecraft and Hays assumed a more radical position than other female writers, for instance the more conservative Bluestockings like Hannah More, Hester Thrale Piozzi, Anna Leatitia Barbauld and Fanny Burney. The most consistent radical opposition is found in Hays, who invented a powerful metaphor, "the magic circle," to denote the female sex's imaginary refuge from patriarchy's repression, "a room of one's own," as it were.[9] In *Victim of Prejudice* the "heroine" Mary declares: "I felt grounded as by a talisman, encompassed in a magic circle, through which neither danger could assail nor sorrow pierce me" (122). This symbol is central to Hays's programme of gender equality, but it is also possible to interpret Maria's imprisonment in Wollstonecraft's *Wrongs of Woman* in line with this concept (114).

While the close ideological connection between Blake and Wollstonecraft has been much documented, the even more important relation between Blake and Hays has not yet been recognized by literary commentators. However, Helena Bergmann in her work has recently recognized the similarities in themes, language use, compositional techniques and basic tenets of gender equality between Hays and the male Romantic poets: "Mary Hays's use of the epistolary form, mainly inspired by Rousseau's *La Nouvelle Héloïse* (1761), was close to the writings of the Romantic poets" (5). Although without specifically pointing out Blake among the Romantic poets, it is a well-known fact that Blake emphasizes the importance of the intuitive faculties of passion and desire as a counterbalance to reason, and this also seems to be the case with Hays. As Tilottama Rajan puts it in "Autonarration and Genotext in Mary Hays' *Memoirs of Emma Courtney*," indicating the crucial link between Hays and Blake:

> If reason is originally the elaboration of passion in a series of general principles, the outward circumference of energy as Blake would say, then passion remains vitally necessary to the reconsideration of what would otherwise congeal into law. For Emma's passion causes her to rethink the social structures that condemn that passion as outrageous, and thus if her passion is not initially political, it becomes the site of her emergence as political subject [157].

[9] *The protected female space promoted by Hays, and at times also by Wollstonecraft, seems to anticipate the basic idea of Virginia Woolf's feminist classic* A Room of One's Own.

In this way inaugurating a discourse of passion, Hays's main character Emma cannot wholly condone its great power and succumbs to its force after having tried to apply doctrines of reason by rationalizing passion. Ensconced from a conservative and uncomprehending patriarchal society in her "magic circle," the forces of passion are to no avail. Thus Emma creates a barrier of odd and alienating incidents and is never fully united with her male object of desire, Augustus Harley. As we shall see, how to portray the active endeavour of the female characters to reunite with their male counterparts is also one of the major dilemmas in the poetry of William Blake. However, while a reconciliation of characters representing male reason and female passion is ultimately thwarted in the novels of Hays, Blake, in a few crucial key passages of the major epics, is more successful in reuniting male and female characters.

3
The Gender Utopia of *The Four Zoas*

Most commentators on Blake have found that his articulation of sexual issues expresses a male view of male sexuality. Still almost unrecognized, though, is the way he describes female sexuality. Critics have often considered Blake's female characters as passive but this is not always the case. An example of an active female character is Oothoon in *Visions of the Daughters of Albion* who Eaves, Essick and Viscomi have in fact recognized as "[a] forerunner of modern feminism" (233). A comparison can be made with Emma Courtney in Hays's novel, who gradually acquires a male-dominated language through her voracious reading. This makes her more active and ready to assume a radical discursive position. That she gains power in its turn makes the men close to her ineffective, as Eleanor Ty suggests (51).

However Blake came to be acquainted with the emerging feminist ideas in the early 1790s, there is surely a development, an improvement, in his thinking of typical feminist issues around that time. In his poetry we can notice a gradual appropriation of such radical views, most significantly an insistence on greater equality between man and woman. It is then his female characters become more complex, inherent with good as well as bad qualities, in order to better correspond to the already more developed male characters.

In *Europe: A Prophecy* from 1793 we find some premature components of a "feminist" Blake. Important new female characters are introduced. Enitharmon is consistently participating in *Europe,* and both Leutha and Oothoon are mentioned, later to be used in *Milton*. The other female characters have little known names like "lovely jealous

Ocalythron" (8:7, E 62) and "Ethinthus, queen of waters" (14:1, E 65), so it is obvious that Blake's mythological world is not yet completed. Most clear this is in the character who is soon to become Vala, here simply labelled "the nameless shadowy female" (1:1, E 60). Blake's view of the fall and how to share its burden of guilt as equally as possible between male and female also finds one of its first expressions in this poem.

The years Blake lived in "lovely Lambeth," between 1790 and 1800, were from his perspective relatively prosperous and certainly very productive. It is therefore something of a surprise to find that he did not produce a single illuminated book from *The Marrriage of Heaven and Hell* in 1790 until *Visions of the Daughters of Albion* appeared in 1793. Why did he not? Given the scarce biographical facts on Blake, we can of course only speculate. But it was in these years that the meetings at Joseph Johnson's bookshop supposedly were at its most intense, in the enthusiasm of the early phases of the French Revolution. At no other time in his life was Blake more open for and confronted with new feminist ideas and a desire for a more egalitarian society. Probably he met and was influenced by Mary Hays and, certainly, by Mary Wollstonecraft. Significantly, one of the first illuminated books Blake produced in 1793 was his co-operation with Wollstonecraft, *The Gates of Paradise.*

Anyway, in 1793–94 Blake's poetry takes a new direction with a stress on greater gender equality, partly manifested and brought on by the improved richer female characters in his poetry. Many commentators have pointed to a break in Blake's writing sometime around 1795. Correctly so, but Blake's views of the female sex does not become more conservative and disillusioned, which has been the general opinion. On the contrary, we see an artist more at leisure and in better command in creating fully drawn characters, male as well as female.

For the first time we can see this new Blakean poetic authority on display in the abortive master work *The Four Zoas*. But already in *Visions of the Daughters of Albion* from 1793, at least two years before Blake began *The Four Zoas*, he applied a few central tenets from Wollstonecraft, and it may from a gender utopian perspective be read as a precursor to the later poem. In this poem we find some of Blake's ideas of female sexuality and liberation, the much debated concept of "free" love, and equality expressed for the first time in his poetry.

However, already in the earlier illuminated poem *The Book of Thel* from 1789 Blake deals with "feminist" issues through the use of a female lead character. This poem describes the transition from innocence to experience of the main protagonist Thel. But while Oothoon in *Visions*, although her newly acquired experience is hard-won and disastrous, succeeds in this rite-de-passage, Thel utterly fails and relapses back to childhood. Hence, while Oothoon is a strong character at the conclusion of the poem, Thel is ultimately weak. This is one compelling reason not to see *The Book of Thel* as a forerunner to *The Four Zoas* of the same dignity as *Visions;* another reason is the proximity of date of creation to the *Zoas*.

Visions of the Daughters of Albion *as a Forerunner of* The Four Zoas

In *Visions* the female character Oothoon persists in her promotion of free love. Close to the end, in something of a climax of the poem, she exclaims: "I cry, Love! Love! Love! happy happy Love! free as the mountain wind!" (7:16, 260, E 50) But however persistent she is, the experiences of the poem have ultimately taught her to be more reserved: "Can that be Love, that drinks another as a sponge drinks water?" (7:17, 260, E 50) Oothoon seems here to have learnt the hard lesson that love which is restricted by the negative expressions of a fallen world is ultimately drained of all energy.

What many commentators have considered as an argument for a far more liberal view of sexuality, or "free" love, can, they believe, be derived from Blake's supposed acquaintance with Mary Wollstonecraft. On the mere linguistic level, as the three editors of the Tate edition of *Visions* point out, the title *Visions of Daughters of Albion* echoes *A Vindication of the Rights of Woman* in syntax and rhythm (231). It is specifically this famous treatise that is singled out as the main influence of *Visions*, for instance in Williams's and Bruder's comments on and juxtapositions of the two texts.

Wollstonecraft's idea of sexuality may have been more liberal in younger years, and in the *Vindication* she in fact voices a more traditional view, with the rational powers of the mind as a foundation. In its female emancipatory message of gender equality, however, *Vindication* is sharply radical, as Wollstonecraft challenges Rousseau's staunchly patriarchal notion of gender roles. "[I] have thrown down my gauntlet, and deny the existence of sexual virtues.... For man and woman ... must be the same," she writes in a polemic style, suggesting equality between the sexes in a revolutionary gesture. Moreover, her discourse undeniably stands out as an extremely radical exception in the context of her contemporaries of the 1790s. Her use of terms is sometimes quite original, and one can in fact only compare them to a modern twentieth-century discourse. For instance, in *Vindication* she most radically writes about (female) "sexual desire," a very frank way of putting it in that century.

Thus, placed in their contemporary context both the *Vindication* and *Visions* are very radical texts. With their utopian messages of gender equality, they belong to the revolutionary, or radical, discourse of the 1790s. A key passage in *Visions* serves to indicate the textual link between the works:

> Till she who burns with youth, and knows no fixed lot; is bound
> In spells of law to one she loaths: and must she drag the chain
> Of life, in weary lust!
> [8:21–23, 256, E 49]

This is indeed close to the ideas of the *Vindication*, and as the Tate editors of *Visions* comment, it is "a criticism of marriage as a form of slavery from the woman's perspective, perhaps influenced by Wollstonecraft" (277n). If one continues a few lines further the pattern becomes even more intricate with a rape that produces a child which in its turn leads to enchainment in marriage:

> Must chilling murderous thoughts, obscure
> The clear heaven of her eternal spring! To bear the wintry rage
> Of a harsh terror driv'n to madness, bound to hold a rod
> Over her shrinking shoulders all day; & all the night
> To turn the wheel of false desire: and longings that wake her womb
> To the abhorred birth of cherubs in the human form
> That live a pestilence & die a meteor & are no more.
> [8:23–29, 256, E 49]

The outcome of this is disastrous and implies a three-fold suffering of the three protagonists of the poem, Oothoon, Bromion and Theotormon.

Visions of the Daughters of Albion, then, is the story of its sexually innocent main female character, the virgin Oothoon, who loves and longs for one of the poem's two male protagonists, Theotormon:

> I loved Theotormon
> And I was not ashamed
> I trembled in my virgin fears
> And I hid in Leutha's vale!
>   [3:1–4, 246, E 45]

In her innocent state she cannot understand but that love should be free for all to take and share. Therefore she plucks the flower of sexual experience, only then to understand that love in the world of experience is not free but rather enchained. The story turns into a triangular drama when she is raped by the other male protagonist, Bromion, who is the negation of this poem:

> I pluck'd Leutha's flower,
> And I rose up from the vale;
> But the terrible thunders tore
> My virgin mantle in twain.
>   [3:5–8, 246, E 45]

Having been raped, Oothoon spends the rest of the poem chained back to back to Bromion, and not even her beloved Theotormon shows any inclination to liberate her. In other words, this could be traditionally interpreted as a classic female depiction of the repressive norms of patriarchy with its twisted view of sexuality. Although she has to succumb to male power and never wins her freedom, Oothoon is certainly the strongest character of the poem. Most of all she is already from the beginning strikingly active. At the opening of the poem, before her fall into experience, her activity is sexual, as she sets out with no hesitation to procure the object of her strong emotions. Hence, as the male in the shape of Theotormon here is the object, Oothoon as a female acts as a subject/agent—a very radical idea at the end of the eighteenth century, particularly since the author is a man.

It is precisely in this that *Visions* deviates from the *Vindication* and proves to be the more radical of the two works. One has to agree with the editors of *Visions,* who claim that "[f]or Wollstonecraft, women must free themselves from social and sexual bondage by developing their rational powers. *Visions* implicitly replies that liberation requires the recognition and expression of sexual passion, not its suppression" (231–2).

However far-reaching one considers Wollstonecraft to be in this respect, the insistence on passion is one of the indications that the female author of the 1790s closest to Blake's radical project of gender equality is in fact Mary Hays who in her writings never wholly suppresses female passion, as is exemplified in *Emma Courtney*. The similarity between *Emma Courtney* and *Visions* from a gender equality perspective is in fact striking. As in *Visions*, the female protagonist in *Emma Courtney* is the subject and the male protagonist, Augustus Harley, is the object of Emma's quest for emotional and sexual fulfilment.

The gist of *Visions of the Daughters of Albion* is described in a condensed form, similar to *The Four Zoas*, in "The Argument," and the poem proper consists of retrospective narration. As in *The Four Zoas* there is no real "action" in the poem; it is instead told in the flashbacks of the main characters. Not only from a gender equality perspective, then, is *Visions* a harbinger of the later poem, but also through its innovative narrative strategies, something which is another major feature of Blake's gender utopia.

Since the male activity of Bromion and Theotormon is negative, the outcome of the poem is still deadlock. However much Oothoon attempts in an active female manner, either through the mental activity of complaining, or through the concrete physical action of trying to break her chains, to undermine the patriarchal structures of society, she remains a captive and there is no progress made in gender equality. As both male and female positive activity, in Blake's view, are needed to transcend the gender barriers, the poem ends with the reflecting echoes of Oothoon's sighs from her fellow sisters, the Daughters of Albion:

> Thus every morning wails Oothoon. But Theotormon sits
> Upon the margind ocean conversing with shadows dire,
> The Daughters of Albion hear her woes, & eccho back her sighs.
> [8:11–13, 262, E 51]

The Four Zoas *as a Gender Utopian Poem*

In *Visions of the Daughters of Albion* Blake does not find a poetic or linguistic strategy to describe a state of complete gender equality. The male remains the standard as Oothoon's "revolution in female (sexual) manners" fails, and she finally succumbs to the patriarchal repression of Bromion and Theotormon. Admittedly, it was not Blake's purpose to convey a picture of male-female equality in this poem; it seems rather that one of his interests was to describe an unusually strong female character, possibly with his feminist friend Mary Wollstonecraft in mind.

Having accomplished this, Blake, in the next few years, went on to develop his writing by trying to create a more complex form of poem. It is in these years that his ideas mature and he begins to outline his own mythology. His poems start moving closer to the epic genre and he prints many of the so-called minor prophecies. *Visions* was printed in 1793 and is the first of Blake's "Lambeth-books." Between 1793 and 1795 the rest of the books in this series were produced: *America, Europe, The Song of Los, The First Book of Urizen, The Book of Ahania* and *The Book of Los.*

At this time Blake had launched many of his characters and, as we already know, some time between 1795 and 1797, he begins his first long epic poem *The Four Zoas*. While the preceding Lambeth poems are mere fragmentary sketches of Blake's radical ideas, in *The Four Zoas* for the first time he finds a suitable form for his gender utopia. There are of course several reasons for this development, but the radical context of the early 1790s London environment certainly exercised a major influence on the formation of Blake's gender utopia, maybe particularly the early feminist ideas of Wollstonecraft and Hays.

Closely linked to, and more or less determining, the relation between reason and passion is the concept of desire. This is especially significant in Hays's *Memoirs of Emma Courtney*. Since Emma does not succeed in balancing passion with reason, she does not transcend the opposition, and desire therefore works negatively. In Blake's view—and that of traditional Christianity—desire arose from the male-female division in the fall. However, Blake believes that *both* man and woman desire their respective counterpart, in contrast with what had traditionally been the biblical view. In *The Four Zoas* desire is described as the result of the fall of the characters, here represented by Los and his emanation Enitharmon: "And Los & Enitharmon were drawn down by their desires / Descending sweet upon the wind among soft harps & voices" (2:287–88, E 322). Sexual desire eventually brings the characters down to the level where fallen sexuality sets the norm of society. On this level love is a negation, and desire therefore only breeds jealousy. This in turn sets up obstacles, in Blake's poetry represented by corrupt or legalised forms of sexuality such as prostitution and marriage. A highly relevant example of this in Blake's earlier work is of course the poem "London" in which "the youthful Harlots curse / Blasts the new-born Infants tear / And blights with plagues the Marriage hearse" (*Experience*, E 27).

Vala is the representation of female desire in Blake's later poetry. However, the issue of gender interactivity in Blake's poetry is quite complex. For one thing I believe, in contradistinction to the view of most commentators, that Vala is not the only female character who represents female desire, if we are somewhat simplistically to call it that. The most negative of Blake's female creations in *The Four Zoas* is in fact Enitharmon.

Blake moves one step further than most critics have considered when, to begin with, he portrays female desire and activity as positive. Next, to transcend the binary opposition of gender Blake posits a dialectical poetic model in which, ultimately, man and woman have to be reconciled in order to revoke and transcend the negations of the fallen world. Therefore the utmost goal of Blake's radical utopian poetry is the reunion of male and female. However, before man and woman can be reunited and repass the gates there is a long and demanding way to go. In fact, it takes a poem of more than a hundred pages until the reunion can be realized at the end of *The Four Zoas*. In these pages the numerous troubles of gender struggle are related in Blake's repetitive diction, intermingled with depictions of the delightful, innocent state of the still undivided genders in pre-lapsarian Eden. By juxtaposing these two contradictory states, Blake strongly enhances the contrastive effect of the pre-lapsarian and the fallen world.

Since the fallen world in Blake's view is a mental construction in the first place it can only be redeemed by an equally strongly raised consciousness in man and woman. Mutual work of course also has to be carried out on the daily practical level if any progress in gender relations is to be made and if we are to achieve an equal society. Quite naturally activity is the prerequisite of this labour for gender equality, and according to Blake both sexes have to participate to the same extent in this labour through active co-operation. Inevitably then, the activities of man and woman are equally important, which Blake is sometimes at pains to describe.

Does it follow, then, that male and female activity are equally strong and equally positive? It is a difficult question, but there are, as it were, intimations of increasing positive female activity in Blake's three major prophecies. Once the development in portrayal of the female characters in these poems is established, we can also assume that female activity is more positive, and more important for the conclusion, in each poem.

The Characters of The Four Zoas

The characters in *The Four Zoas* are at a superficial level structured according to a rather symmetrical pattern. The basic division is organized into eight main characters, four male zoas and four female emanations. Each male character is linked to a specific female character, a coalition quite crucial to the gender perspective of the poem and its eventual outcome in the apocalypse of the final Night.

If we go beneath the surface, the structure and outline of characters in *The Four Zoas* immediately become quite complicated, which corresponds to the great complexity of the poem as a whole. To start with, the zoas and the emanations represent the positive aspect of universal man. In contrast to these positive characters, Blake posits the negative aspect of man in the form of a male character, the spectre, and a female character, the already discussed female will. The spectre and the female will are the fallen, negated forms of man who appear when the positive zoa was separated from his likewise positive counterpart, the emanation. Since this division occurs already at the fall at the beginning of *The Four Zoas*, both the male and the female characters appear in their negated forms throughout the poem until the apocalypse at the very end.

Moreover, in line with Blake's dialectical structure the characters often act or work in pairs. Broadly speaking, among the male characters, Tharmas and Los/Urthona might be classified as positive while Urizen and Luvah/Orc are negative. According to Ostriker, one can divide the four emanations into two couples, with Enion and Ahania as positive and Vala and Enitharmon as negative. She considers Ahania and Enion to be good and passive characters, and Enitharmon and Vala active and evil (162). Although I agree that the four emanations could be grouped in the suggested couples, no single character is only good or evil, passive or active. To grasp the complex symbolism of *The Four Zoas* one must understand how the various characters interact with one another, both the male zoas and the female emanations.

As a consequence of this structure, in *The Four Zoas* the basic division of the female characters is a most pertinent distinction for interpreting Blake's gender utopia. As long as male and female are undivided in unity the world is in an ideal, perfect state and accordingly the emanation is the positive female character in Blake, since the emanation and her consort the zoa represent the undivided aspect of man. But once man has fallen, the emanation is lost to the male. When *The Four Zoas* begins, the fall has already occurred:

> Lost! Lost! Lost! are my Emanations Enion O Enion
> We are become a Victim to the Living We hide in secret
> [1:23–4, E 301]

The speaker here is the male character Tharmas, whose emanation is Enion. Not only the emanation of Tharmas is lost, but actually all four emanations are fallen and "lost" to their respective zoas and to the innocent existence in the paradise of Eden. As explained elsewhere in the poem, the emanation of Los, Enitharmon, has captured and hidden the other three female characters. The emanations from then on become destructive female wills with delusive negative strategies.

Vala: Absent Active Character

As the pronunciation of the name indicates, Vala is associated with the word "veil." In *The Four Zoas* Vala may be perceived as essentially a negative character, which is underscored by this connotation since clothing in Blake is generally negative, hiding, or veiling, as it were, the true spiritual and divine state. Alicia Ostriker has a number of further suggestions about the interpretation of Vala's name: "Her name means 'vale' as in 'valley,' and as Nature she is the valley of the shadow of death, the declivity of the female genitals, and the membranous 'veil' which preserves virginity, as well as the 'veil' covering the tabernacle of the Old Testament" (160). She continues to suggest that "she is Fortuna, Babylon, the Great Whore, enemy of Jerusalem. Where Enitharmon is a tease and a betrayer, Vala is the 'Female Will' incarnate as killer" (160). In these critical judgements Ostriker conveys a negative picture of Vala. Many commentators have supported this negative view. However, after her reappearance in the final Night, Vala, through great activity, ends the poem as a more positive character. Through the gender interactivity with her corresponding zoa, Luvah, she is the most important character at the inception of the apocalypse.

Vala is in fact absent for most of *The Four Zoas* and does not return until the end of the poem, in Night Nine. Therefore her degree of participation and activity in the poem is quite dubious. It may seem very strange that such an important character should be absent from the action for the major part of the poem, and all the more strange that Blake first named the poem after her.[10] Until the concluding pages of the poem we only get to know of her fate through the indirect narration of the other characters. The characters seem constantly to call on Vala for aid. It appears that Vala is the first of the Emanations to be cast out: "Luvah and Vala woke & flew up from the Human Heart / Into the Brain; from thence upon the pillow Vala slumber'd" (1:266–67, E 305). As Urizen, Blake's representation of destructive reason, says to his own Emanation, Ahania, in an outburst: "Art thou also become like Vala. thus I cast thee out" (3:113, E 328). One might infer from this that Vala has been in exile for some time when Ahania is cast out. In Night One all four Emanations are cast out, divided and driven away from the zoas as the post-lapsarian world arrives:

> Why does thou weep as Vala? & wet thy veil with dewy tears,
> In slumbers of my night-repose, infusing a false morning?
> Driving the Female Emanations all away from Los
> I have refusd to look upon the Universal Vision
> And wilt thou slay with death him who devotes himself to thee
> Once born for the sport & amusement of Man now born to drink
>   up all his Powers
> I heard the sounding sea; I heard the voice weaker and weaker;
> The voice came & went like a dream, I awoke in my sweet bliss.
>   [1:273–80, E 305–6]

This passage is indicative of a story that occurred, probably in innocence, before the fall of man into sexual delusion, and in a narrative perspective before *The Four Zoas*, thus unknown to the reader. Since the narration of *The Four Zoas* starts quite abruptly, in *medias res*, and the reader is thrown into the already fallen world of Generation, with Blake not providing much guidance, we lack information in the poem about Vala as a character. In spite of this, or perhaps because of this, the character Vala provides us with a narrative frame to the whole poem. *The Four Zoas* starts with Vala and, significantly, she reappears in Night Nine when Blake through his narration gathers up all the forces of the poem in preparation for the impending apocalypse.

---

[10]*Through the poetic device of the absent Vala, woman becomes an absent signifier for part of the poem. What does this absence of woman signify, then? Woman is of course always absent in a masculinist signifying economy, as Judith Butler calls it. The female has no position of power in this system and is therefore more or less absent from the hierarchies created by it. In* The Four Zoas, *however, Vala is a powerful female character, fully able through her negation the Shadowy Female to execute her sexual powers, in a way that is quite possible to transfer to modern twentieth century culture, with its wide range of sexual expressions.*

Vala, then, is the paradox of *The Four Zoas*. For one thing, she is present through the original title of the poem. On the other hand, she is absent from almost the whole poem. Whereas the other three emanations Enion, Ahania, and Enitharmon describe full circles of presence-absence-presence, Vala disrupts that circle, and her cycle in *The Four Zoas* only consists of absence-presence. Possibly Vala's paradox of absence and presence in the poem is mirrored in real life in the female/feminine paradox of dependence and power. Damon has suggested that Vala is the main cause of Albion's fall (428). From the very outset of *The Four Zoas* Vala is a fallen character who is delusive in her sexual strategies, tempting the defenceless Albion. In Night Seven Blake relates what happened when the Eternal Man, Albion, first encountered the delusive Vala who tempts him into sin, thereby causing Albion to become Fallen Man:

> Among the Flowers of Beulah walkd the Eternal Man & Saw
> Vala the lilly of the desert. melting in high noon
> Upon her bosom in sweet bliss he fainted Wonder seizd
> All heaven they saw him dark. they built a golden wall
> Round Beulah There he reveld in delight among the Flowers
> Vala was pregnant & brought forth Urizen Prince of Light
> First born of Generation. Then behold a wonder to the Eyes
> Of the now fallen Man a double form Vala appeard. A Male
> And female shuddring pale the Fallen Man recoild
> From the Enormity & calld them Luvah & Vala.
> [7:239–48, E 358]

The double form that appears is Man, long since divided into male and female, in this case Luvah and Vala. The zoa has lost contact with his female part, the emanation. Therefore, in Vala's absence throughout most of the poem, her fallen form, the Shadowy Female, appears instead. Only in the final night does the real character Vala eventually reappear, together with her zoa Luvah, summoned to take part in the apocalypse by the Eternal Man: "Luvah & Vala henceforth you are Servants obey & live / You shall forget your former state return O Love in peace / Into your place the place of seed not in the brain or heart" (9:363–65, E 395). The other three emanations also reappear at this crucial point of the poem, in order to resume their original form as emanations, thus complementing their male zoas in the post-apocalyptic bliss of togetherness after the male-female reunion. But while the other emanations reappear, the character Vala appears for the first time in the poem.

Accordingly, the apocalyptic reunion is a crucial state in Blake's utopia and differs from the pre-lapsarian unity between male and female in the paradisiac state that reigned in the original existence of the biblical Eden. At the post-apocalyptic level where male and female together have re-entered Eden both have gone through the tribulations of the fallen worldly existence of Generation, and from that existence gained hard-won and invaluable experience, thus reaching an even higher level of being compared to the original Eden. Innocence has thus become experience and thereby a higher, or organized, form of innocence. Unity has become separation, which has become reconciled togetherness. Hence, Blake says, a world with a dominant male only must inevitably be deficient. Only when the female reappears in time for the apocalypse is the world approaching an ideal state, finally to be reached in the male-female togetherness of the post-apocalyptic utopia in Eden.

Enitharmon: Blake's Eve

Of the four emanations Enitharmon is the most consistent, and possibly also the strongest. Clearly, she is the most active since she is the only one participating in virtually the whole poem. She is considerably more active than the other three emanations. That Enitharmon is a more forceful character than Vala might be one reason why Blake renamed the poem. In contrast to Vala, there is foundation in Ostriker's statement that Enitharmon is an evil character. At least she is certainly the most persistently evil of the four female characters.

Enitharmon's strategy is to tease the male characters of *The Four Zoas*. Not surprisingly Enitharmon is the female agent of the fall, Blake's Eve tasting the fruit, as it were. To begin with her male companion Los, here in the shape of the Spectre of Urthona, discovers her in the Garden:

> The Spectre of Urthona saw the Shadow of Enitharmon
> Beneath the Tree of Mystery among the leaves & fruit
> Reddning the Demon Strong prepared the poison of sweet Love
> [7:217–19, E 358]

Significantly, it is the negated male, the Spectre, that appears at this vital moment in order to substitute for the still unfallen Urthona, and Enitharmon's Shadow, her negation or female will. In the following passage Enitharmon has obviously already tasted the fruit:

> Intoxicated with
> The fruit of this delightful tree. I cannot flee away
> From thy embrace else be assurd so horrible a form
> Should never in my arms repose. Now listen I will tell
> Thee secrets of Eternity which neer before unlockd
> [7:233-37, E 358]

Since Enitharmon is the female tease of the poem, the final step is to make also Los taste the fruit through her alluring strategies:

> Eat thou also of
> The fruit & give me proof of life Eternal or I die
> Then Los pluckd the fruit & Eat & sat down in Despair
> And must have given himself to death Eternal
> [7:393-96, E 369]

The story of Enitharmon, however, begins in the first Night with her marriage to Los. Since we know that legal marriage is one of the institutions that Blake condemns as belonging to a fallen world, this is surely one of the most ironic passages of the poem: "And Los & Enitharmon sat in discontent & scorn / The Nuptial Song arose from all the thousand thousand spirits" (1:374-75, E 308). After the seemingly joyful nuptial feast of Los and Enitharmon, the newly betrothed are separated. Since Albion's original pre-lapsarian emanation, named Jerusalem in Blake's mythology, "is become a ruin" (1:545, E 312), the division of Albion's separate parts, the zoas from their female counterparts, the emanations, is now completed:

> The Daughters of Beulah beheld the Emanation they pitied
> They wept before the Inner gates of Enitharmons bosom
> And of her fine wrought brain & of her bowels within her loins
> Three gates within Glorious & bright open into Beulah
> From Enitharmons inward parts but the bright female terror
> Refusd to open the bright gates she closd and barrd them fast
> Lest Los should enter into Beulah thro her beautiful gates
> [1:560-6, E 313]

In the now fallen world gratified sexual desire is no longer freely accessible. Enitharmon opens three bright gates to tease and tempt the male, her former zoa Los, only to immediately shut them and refuse entry into the sexual realm of Beulah. The gates are three in number because, for one thing, Beulah is Blake's third, and sexual, level.

However, already before the nuptial feast there are references to Enitharmon's negative activity. The first time she is mentioned she sings the death song of Vala: "Hear! I will sing a Song of Death! It is a Song of Vala! / The Fallen Man takes his repose Urizen sleeps in the porch" (1:260–61, E 305). The world of Vala, as we know, is a fallen world. This becomes conspicuous in the following lines, at the first encounter in this poem of Enitharmon and her male counterpart Los. By her allusion to Vala's fallen world we can assume that Enitharmon already at this early point of the poem is, like Vala, a fallen character. As the fallen Eternal Man replies to Enitharmon, this becomes even more obvious:

> Why does thou weep as Vala? & wet thy veil with dewy tears,
> In slumbers of my night-repose, infusing a false morning?
> Driving the Female Emanations all away from Los
> I have refusd to look upon the Universal Vision
> And wilt thou slay with death him who devotes himself to thee
> Once born for the sport & amusement of Man now born to drink up all his Powers
>
> [1:271–78, E 306]

The last line, to be repeated later in the poem, manifests Enitharmon's status as an evil female character early on in the poem. Accordingly, she has demonstrated her own negative power by hiding her three fellow emanations from her consort. Los reacts instantly with violence: "Then Los smote her upon the Earth twas long eer she revivd" (1:281, E 306). However, Los soon understands that he has acted wrongly and regrets what he has done:

> Los saw the wound of his blow he saw he pitied he wept
> Los now repented that he had smitten Enitharmon he felt love
> Arise in all his Veins he threw his arms around her loins
> To heal the wound of his smiting
>
> [1:351–54, E 307]

If Blake could be considered to be traditional in the above sequence, this impression changes with the unfolding of the second Night. Also traditional is the Christian idea that these male and female reactions are the result of the fall, which is indicated in Night Two:

> And Los & Enitharmon were drawn down by their desires
> Descending sweet upon the wind among soft harps & voices

> To plant divisions in the soul of Urizen & Ahania
> To conduct the Voice of Enion to Ahanias midnight pillow
> [2:287–90, E 322]

Clearly, Los and Enitharmon descend from the innocence of Paradise with its "soft harps & voices" to a fallen world where desire and jealousy is the sexual norm. Interestingly, however, they are both equally afflicted by desire and drawn down together. It seems that they are also to collaborate in the evil scheme to separate the two still unfallen couples Urizen/Ahania and Tharmas/Enion. Vala, as we have seen, is at the very start of the poem a fallen character and consequently divided from her zoa, Luvah.

Even more remarkable is Enitharmon's reversal of traditional gender roles as she proclaims that Los is her slave and, most strikingly, that he is created for her will. This is a strong female reaction to his infidelity with Ahania:

> Wherefore didst thou throw thine arms around
> Ahanias image I decievd thee & will still decieve
> Urizen saw thy sin & hid his beams in darkning Clouds
> I still keep watch altho I tremble & wither across the heavens
> In strong vibrations of fierce jealousy for thou art mine
> Created for my will my slave tho strong I am weak
> Farewell the God calls me away I depart in my sweet bliss
> [2:227–33, E 323]

By emphasizing the strength of the female reaction in jealousy Blake indicates her powerful sexual position. Although she disappears from the poem for some time, Enitharmon gives more proof of her powerful position before she departs:

> The joy of Woman is the Death of her most beloved
> Who dies for Love of her
> In torments of fierce jealousy & pangs of adoration.
> The Lovers night bears on my song
> And the nine Spheres rejoice beneath my powerful controll
> [2:349–53, E 324]

This is one of the passages most commented on in *The Four Zoas* and, interestingly, it is one of the most frequently used in support of Blake's supposed sexism. Blake can hardly be a sexist here, though, since Enitharmon has no control over the rejoicing, as she continues to point out: "The birds & beasts rejoice & play / And every one seeks for his mate to prove his inmost joy" (2:357–58, E 324). So in spite of being an "evil" character, Enitharmon sees the necessity for male and female co-operation to retrieve the lost state of innocence in a future gender utopia. Before departing from the poem she therefore contradicts the negations of the fallen world with a positive echo from *The Marriage of Heaven and Hell*:

> Arise you little glancing wings & sing your infant joy
> Arise & drink your bliss
> For every thing that lives is holy
> [2:364–66, E 324]

The third Night is one of two in which Enitharmon does not take part. In the fourth Night she returns as Tharmas "saw Los & Enitharmon Emerge / In strength & brightness from the Abyss" (4:2–3, E 331). Los, or rather the Spectre of Urthona, gives an account of the creation of woman:

> Still beholding how the piteous form
> Dividing & dividing from my loins a weak & piteous
> Soft cloud of snow a female pale & weak I soft embracd
> My counter part & calld it Love I named her Enitharmon
> [4:97–100, E 333]

Blake here again emphasizes that the creation and the fall occurred at the same moment. While the above passage seems to describe the creation of Enitharmon, or Eve, out of the body of Los, or Adam, the male-female split is instantaneous: "I issued into the air divided from Enitharmon" (4:106, E 334).

The negative activity of Enitharmon is in fact not very significant from Night Three up to Night Six. In the fifth Night she gives birth to her and Los's son Orc, who is an important character in Blake's early prophetic poems and again in both *Milton* and *Jerusalem*, but in *The Four Zoas* mainly participates through his eternal name, Luvah. In the sixth Night Enitharmon is again altogether absent. Her presence and activity are all the more important in the crucial Night Seven. It is in this Night that Enitharmon tells us how first she and then Los taste the fruit in the Garden. When Los again encountered Enitharmon he therefore soon "felt the cold disease" (7:182, E 357) of jealousy and exclaimed: "Why can I not Enjoy thy beauty Lovely Enitharmon"

(7:184, E 357). In this the most fallen of the Nights of *The Four Zoas* in which the male-female split appears most irrevocable Enitharmon is of course referred to negatively as Tharmas looks ahead to a future improved utopian existence with the negations annihilated:

> But Tharmas most rejoicd in hope of Enions return
> For he beheld new Female forms born forth upon the air
> Who wove soft silken veils of covering in sweet rapturd trance
> Mortal & not as Enitharmon, without a covering veil
> [7:486–89, E 371]

As we have seen in Vala, the veil is a negative symbol restraining sexual activity, but in transcendent utopian Eden woman is significantly "without a covering veil."

In the final two Nights the activities of Enitharmon acquire symbolic functions. In Night Eight, to begin with, she is erecting looms. "In these Looms she wove the Spectres" (8:36, E 372), which is a negative activity since the Spectres are the fallen forms of man and of the male characters in *The Four Zoas*. This activity is not entirely negative, though, since the looms are used in the apocalypse to weave the eternal forms of man, as we shall shortly see.

The most important symbolic activity occurs at the end of the eighth Night when Los and Enitharmon take down the crucified body of Christ from the cross at the onset of the resurrection of man. It is essential to notice here that Los and Enitharmon, man and woman, do this together. Hence, male-female co-operation is again the key, and at the beginning of Night Nine Los and Enitharmon together start building the City of God, Jerusalem, or Eden. Through this they launch the apocalypse of the concluding Night and they finish the poem by entering Eden in complete togetherness as a final symbol of united man and woman.

Los and Enitharmon are the last couple to be reconciled in *The Four Zoas* in the very last lines of this monumental poem. Significantly so, since these two characters are the Adam and Eve of Blake's poem. They initiated the fall and it is also their duty to conclude it.[11]

---

[11]*Alicia Ostriker apparently fails to see this connection as she claims that Tharmas and Enion are the final couple to reunite in the poem: "Finally Tharmas and Enion, first pair to be seen in collapse and last to be seen regenerate, also undergo a double transformation" (160). It is no doubt a kind of double transformation that these two characters undergo, but since Ostriker, like most of the commentators on* The Four Zoas, *does not distinguish between the two steps of gender reconciliation in the poem, reunion and togetherness, she distorts the issue.*

Enion: Female Harbinger of Utopia

Enion and Tharmas are the first of the couples of *The Four Zoas* to illustrate the fall of man. In the first few lines, Tharmas is divided from his emanation Enion. In the fallen world Tharmas desires all females and therefore Enion hides the other three emanations:

> The Men have received their death wounds & their Emanations are fled
> To me for refuge & I cannot turn them out for Pitys sake
> Enion said—Thy fear has made me tremble terrors have surrounded me
> All Love is lost Terror succeeds & Hatred instead of Love
> [1:33–36, E 301]

Love is no longer the "pure" love of Eden, and in this negated existence the negative gender interactivity has put both Tharmas, and, most notably here, Enion into a state of jealousy.

The fallen state of man is accentuated in Enion's many inquisitive remarks throughout the first Night. After understanding that she lives in a fallen state where "Love is changd to deadly Hate" (1:111, E 303), she questions her sense of loneliness after the division at the fall: "What am I? Wherefore was I put forth on these rocks / Among the Clouds to tremble in the wind in solitude?" (1:137–38).[12] In a fallen existence all individuals are by definition lonely. The more specific cause of Enion's loneliness is the jealousy of fallen love, and the act it has made her commit: "I thought Tharmas a Sinner & I murderd his Emanations / His secret loves & Graces Ah me wretched What have I done" (1:163–64, E 304). Having gained this hardwon experience of the fallen world, Enion disappears from the poem until the eighth Night. She has already announced her departure somewhat earlier in the poem: "Enion said Farewell I die I hide from thy searching eyes" (1:68, E 302). Now, on her own initiative Enion also joins the other three emanations, whom she had hidden in jealousy from the sight of Tharmas at the start of *The Four Zoas*. She thereby definitely textually manifests the negative and secretive status of love in the fallen world of the poem.

Thus driven away and more or less banished by Blake from the poem's central action, Enion is held in exile for most of the remaining poem. She is isolated in the dark realm of Entuthon Benithon: "Enion

---

[12] *These lines are not included in Erdman's edition.*

blind & age bent / Plungd into the cold billows living a life in midst of waters / In terms she witherd away to Entuthon Benithon / A world of deep darkness where all things in horrors are rooted" (3:178–81, E 330). She reappears in Night Eight where in a dialogue with Ahania she tries to encourage the people of the fallen earth to awaken by professing their visions of the imminent future utopia:

> Fear not O poor forsaken one O land of briars & thorns
> Where once the Olive flourishd & the Cedar spread his wings
> Once I waild desolate like thee my fallow fields in fear
> Cried to the Churchyards & the Earthworm came in dismal state
> I found him in my bosom & I said the time of Love
> Appears upon the rocks & hills in silent shades but soon
> A voice came in the night a midnight cry upon the mountains
> Awake the bridegroom cometh I awoke to sleep no more
>   [8:534–41, E 384]

As a harbinger of the apocalypse Enion envisions a second coming with all-embracing love for all to share. It is also significant of Blake's apocalypse that the regeneration encompasses all living matter. Thus the personified "furrowd field" replies Enion:

> Behold the time approaches fast that thou shalt be as a thing
> Forgotten when one speaks of thee he will not be believd
> When the man gently fades away in his immortality
> When the mortal disappears in improved knowledge cast away
> The former things so shall the Mortal gently fade away
> And so become invisible to those who still remain
> Listen I will tell thee what is done in the caverns of the grave
> The Lamb has rent the Veil of Mystery soon to return
> In Clouds & Fires around the rock & the Mysterious tree
>   [8:549–57, E 384–85]

Conspicuous here are also the many images characteristic of the utopian literary genre. The narration is clearly forward-directed in anticipation of a future utopia: "[T]he time approaches fast"; it relates to something improbable: "[W]ill not be believd" and "immortality"; it describes an improved existence: "[I]mproved knowledge cast away / The former things." Noteworthy here are also the apocalyptic images: "rent the Veil of Mystery," "Clouds" and "Fires." In accordance with the genre of spiritual utopia, the Second Coming is near and this becomes even more evident as Enion, through the reply from the furrowd field, concludes:

> And in the cries of birth & in the groans of death his voice
> Is heard throughout the Universe whereever a grass grows
> Or a leaf buds The Eternal Man is seen is heard is felt
> And all his Sorrows till he reassumes his ancient bliss
> [8:580–83, E 385]

This elucidative and noteworthy passage is significant of the eighth Night, which is probably the Night most heavily influenced by the Bible. Appropriately, Blake concludes this Night by the clearest reference in *The Four Zoas* to the Book of Revelation: "John Saw these things Reveald in Heaven / On Patmos Isle & heard the Souls cry out to be deliverd" (8:600–01, E 385).

In Night Nine Enion first enters indirectly through the mourning and longing of Tharmas who entreats her to return. It is only after Vala calls on her in heaven that she fully materializes, at a point in the somewhat mysterious episode in Vala's Garden, as a child together with Tharmas. As Urizen, after the intimation of innocence in this dreamlike sequence, heralds the end of times Enion is truly regenerated and arisen:

> O Dreams of Death the human form dissolving companied
> By beasts & worms & creeping things & darkness & despair
> The clouds fall off from my wet brow the dust from my cold
>   limbs
> Into the Sea of Tharmas Soon renewd a Golden Moth
> I shall cast off my death clothes & Embrace Tharmas again
> [9:595–98, E 401]

Finally then, Enion is reconciled with her zoa Tharmas, in his natural element the sea, as the penultimate couple reunite in *The Four Zoas*. Symbolically she casts off the negation of the clothes she wore in the fallen state.

AHANIA: THE SCAPEGOAT OF *THE FOUR ZOAS*

Ahania and Enion are the two emanations with most in common, and to a great extent they both undergo the same experiences. For one thing, Ahania is like Enion exiled from most of the poem. She is first mentioned in the second Night, in a mutual gender interchange with her zoa Urizen: "He drave the Male Spirits all away from Ahania / And she drave all the Females from him away" (2:209–10, E 320). Again Blake emphasizes that gender activity should take the form of interactivity and here, we notice, jealousy works both ways. In this Night Ahania plays the role of scapegoat, and also this is the result of mutual gender activity of the wily schemes of Los and Enitharmon whose intent it is "[t]o plant divisions in the Soul of Urizen and Ahania" (2:239, E 322). This line, repeated some lines further on, is crucial to the development of this Night as is the image of Ahania as scapegoat. Enitharmon takes advantage of the tiny seed of jealousy she has planted in the breast of Los as she accuses him of having sinned with Ahania: "Wherefore didst thou throw thine arms around / Ahanias Image" (2:327–28, E 323). As Enitharmon thus disrupts the natural gender balance, she and her counterpart are thrown into the afflictions of a fallen world.

Ahania is the last emanation to appear "physically" in the poem, and then as a humble and obedient royal servant of her zoa:

> Now sat the King of Light on high upon his starry throne
> And bright Ahania bow'd herself before his splendid feet
> O Urizen look on Me. Like a mournful stream
> I Embrace round thy knees & wet My bright hair with my tears:
> Why sighs my Lord! Are not the morning stars thy obedient
>   Sons
> Do they not bow their bright heads at thy voice? At thy
>   command
> Do they not fly into their stations & return their light to thee?
>   [3:1–7, E 326]

Here Ahania is a significant representation of a passive woman in a fallen existence. A subservient attitude seems natural to her, and she finds it difficult to understand why the stars do not obey the commands of her "Lord" Urizen. The Shakespearean diction of this passage only helps to stress the naturally lower rank of women.

That woman is not always wholly passive is obvious in a scene earlier in the poem where Ahania brings happiness and positive spirits to her male counterpart, Urizen:

> Astonished & Confounded he beheld
> Her shadowy form now Separate he shudderd & was silent
> Till her caresses & her tears revivd him to life & joy
> Two wills they had two intellects & not as in times of old
>   [2:203–6, E 320]

It is all the more significant since this incident occurs after the division was finally achieved through the banishment of Ahania, if we are to follow the relative chronological narrative sequence of *The Four Zoas*. Urizen and Ahania now live in the state of fallen Generation and not in the old times of innocent Eden. Ahania and Urizen are therefore divided, with wills and intellects of their own.

The first time she appears Ahania is apparently not yet a fallen character, since in her innocent state she cannot understand Urizen's stern attitude: "Why wilt thou look upon futurity darkning present joy" (3:10, E326). She even begs him to heed her warnings about the impending disaster of his fallen state:

> Leave all futurity to him Resume thy fields of Light
> Why didst thou listen to the voice of Luvah that dread morn
> To give the immortal steeds of light to his deceitful hands
> ....
> They call thy lions to the fields of blood, they rowze thy tygers
> Out of the halls of justice, till these dens thy wisdom framd
> Golden & beautiful but O how unlike those sweet fields of bliss
> Where liberty was justice & eternal science was mercy
> Then O my dear lord listen to Ahania, listen to the vision
> The vision of Ahania in the slumbers of Urizen
>   [3:30-32; 37-42, E 326-27]

Here Ahania casts glances back to the state of original innocence in "those sweet fields of bliss" and, most interestingly, "Where liberty was justice & eternal science was mercy." This is a clearer expression of the "sweet science" of Eternity that reigns as *The Four Zoas* closes. "Science" is of course the problematic word here since it is used quite ambiguously in Blake's work, and in this place does not at all imply the more frequent negative associations with the growing industrial progress in society.

But, alas, Ahania's visions are just visions, and in a fallen world Urizen does not heed her call. Instead he loses his temper and cannot bear to have his dominance questioned: "Am I not God said Urizen. Who is Equal to me" (3:106, E 328). As we have noticed so many times already, this means that the relation between male and female is turbulent and cannot hold together, as first expressed in Urizen's violent outburst: "To cast Ahania to the Earth he seizd her by the hair / And threw her from the steps of ice that froze around his throne" (3:111-12, E 328). The final step for Urizen is to throw Ahania out into the fallen world through words that sound like a parody or satire of a typical male reaction to unexpected female power threatening the patriarchal hierarchies:

> Art thou also become like Vala. Thus I cast thee out
> Shall the feminine indolent bliss. The indulgent self of weariness
> The passive idle sleep the enormous night & darkness of Death
> Set herself up to give her laws to the active masculine virtue
> Thou little dimunitive portion that darst be a counterpart
> Thy passivity thy laws of obedience & insincerity
> Are my abhorrence. Wherefore hast thou taken that fair form
> Whence is this power given to thee!
> [3:113–20, E 328–29]

This intriguing and provocative passage is one of the most frequently used by commentators to imply that Blake was a misogynist. Indeed, Blake makes use here of a number of stereotypical clichés of a patriarchal economy of the most obdurate and rigid kind: "feminine indolent bliss," "indulgent self of weariness," "passive idle sleep," "passivity," "insincerity" and "that fair form" to describe the female negatively, as opposed to "the active masculine virtue" to describe the male in a positive way. However, as I indicated above, this passage should certainly be read ironically and, moreover, we must read these lines in the context of the whole poem. If we do, the inevitable outcome is that Urizen harshly rejects his emanation and, significantly, the key line is repeated: "And art thou also become like Vala thus I cast thee out" (3:130, E 329). Finally, then, Ahania must experience the same fate as Enion:

> Where Enion, blind & age bent wanderd Ahania wanders now
> She wanders in eternal fear of falling into the indefinite
> For her bright eyes behold the Abyss.
> [3:207–09, E 331]

Ahania is cast out into the afflictions of the fallen world and, like Enion, she almost disappears from the poem, only to return in time for the upheaval of the apocalypse. She reappears, as we have already seen, in Night Eight together with Enion. Ahania, in a visionary state, clearly sees the terrible condition of fallen man and again, she sees it as her duty to warn mankind of the dire consequences should this state prevail:

> But listen to Ahania O ye sons of the Murderd one
> Listen to her whose memory beholds your ancient days
> Listen to her whose eyes behold the dark body of corruptible death
> Looking for Urizen in vain. In vain I seek for morning

> The Eternal Man sleeps in the Earth nor feels the vigorous sun
> Nor silent moon nor all the hosts of heaven move in his body
>
> ....
>
> Man who lays upon the shores leaning his faded head
> Upon the Oozy rock inwrapped with the weeds of death
> His eyes sink hollow in his head his flesh coverd with slime
> And shrunk up to the bones alas that Man should come to this
> His strong bones beat with snows & hid within the caves of night
> Marrowless bloodless falling into dust driven by the winds
> O how the horrors of Eternal Death take hold on Man
>
> ....
>
> And the pale horse seeks for the pool to lie him down & die
> But finds the pools filled with serpents devouring one another
> He droops his head & trembling stands & his bright eyes decay
> These are the Visions of My Eyes the Visions of Ahania
>   [8:503–08; 13–19; 29–32, E 383–84]

Through the effective symbolism of this ominous passage it is obvious that even though Ahania is in possession of visionary powers the world is still in a fallen state. "Weeds of death," "slime," "caves of night" and "serpents" are only some of the negative images used here to indicate that. As a whole the passage gives a forceful impression of imminent catastrophic death. Interestingly, "The Ancient of Days" is the title of one of Blake's most well-known paintings, the frontispiece of *Europe*, and the meaning of this term is, befittingly, God.

Ahania still therefore looks "for Urizen in vain" and also in vain for the utopian new morning. It is only in the final Night that she is to encounter both of these. Possessing visionary powers, Ahania is significantly the first emanation to reunite with her zoa. Ahania rises with unselfish joy for her counterpart which, somewhat oddly, becomes too much for her and she drops dead from emotional excess. But with the second coming and as the heavenly city Jerusalem descends, all life is regenerated and Ahania revives to finally "cast off her death clothes" (9:344, E 394), in order to take "her seat by Urizen in songs & joy" (9:353, E 395).

In the male-female interaction, outlined by Blake in *The Four Zoas* as a means of attaining the reunion in togetherness of the post-apocalyptic utopia of Eden, also the activity of the male characters is important. However, it is not a controversial statement that male activity in Blake is positive. But as is the case with the female characters, the emanation and the female will, the male ones appear in their positive manifestations as "zoa," while their negation is the "spectre." But compared to the female character division, the split of the male into zoa and spectre is not as consequently done, and can sometimes even be bewildering.

The word "zoa" is derived from Ezekiel (1:5etc.) and Revelation (4:6 etc.), where it is translated as "beasts." Damon identifies them as the four evangelists and "the Four disastrous Riders of the Apocalypse" (458), an identification that fits the main characters of *The Four Zoas* very well. Frye further explains: "Blake, very sensibly, takes *Zwa* as a singular and forms from it the English plural 'Zoas'" (273).

As the most significant characters of the poem, something that we can already conjecture from the title, the zoas are individual characters who are all different aspects of the universal man Albion, who was divided after the fall. At first this construction is difficult to grasp, as for instance also Damrosch has pointed out: "A consequence of Blake's myth of the Universal Man is that it is hard to understand, within the symbolic structure of his myth, what the status of individual men and women might be" (149). The four zoas are the characters who carry the action forward, as far as it is possible to speak of a forward direction, or of action at all, since the narration frequently takes a backward leap in time through Blake's retrospective method.

Each of the four zoas has a fixed position to begin with. Blake establishes these positions in Night Six of *The Four Zoas*:

> But in Eternal times the Seat of Urizen is in the South
> Urthona in the North Luvah in East Tharmas in West
> [6:279–80, E 351]

These are quite important points of reference in Blake's poetry, but as the poems fluctuate the zoas at times change places in accordance with the action. However, since Blake repeats the positions of the four zoas in plate 59 of *Jerusalem* there can be little doubt of the importance of the four zoas as characters in his poetry and as vital components in his mythological system.

Consequently, the interrelatedness between the individual zoas is incorporated within Blake's concept of the four zoas. Each zoa operates in connection with the two zoas positioned next to him, thereby proving the complexity of Blake's scheme and his awareness of the complexity of human nature. For instance, being positioned in the east, Luvah is related to Urizen who is positioned in the south.

Tharmas: Solitary God of the Waters

It is natural to start by examining Tharmas, who, together with his emanation Enion, is the main protagonist of the First Night. This beginning is also textually established as an inauguration of the fallen existence of *The Four Zoas*: "Begin with Tharmas, Parent power, dark-ning in the West" (1:24, E 301). As we know, *The Four Zoas* begins in *medias res* and male and female are already divided:

> Lost! Lost! Lost! are my Emanations Enion O Enion
> We are become a Victim to the Living We hide in secret
> I have hidden Jerusalem in Silent Contrition O Pity Me
> I will build thee a Labyrinth also: O pity me. O Enion
> Why hast thou taken sweet Jerusalem from my inmost Soul?
> Let her Lay secret in the soft recess of darkness & silence.
> It is not Love I bear to Enitharmon. It is Pity.
> She hath taken refuge in my bosom & I cannot cast her out.
> [1:25–32, E 301]

This passage provides us with a difficult start to a difficult poem. It seems that already at this early phase of the poem Tharmas' emanation Enion suffers from jealousy with some justification. The reason is that Tharmas has been deluded by what Alicia Ostriker has labelled "La Belle Dame sans Merci"[13] of the poem, Enitharmon (159). Somewhat desperately he tries to legitimize his behaviour, but in vain, since Enion has hidden "sweet Jerusalem," here mainly a symbol of female delight, and consequently the other emanations are lost to Tharmas. The negative male-female interaction in this fallen world causes Tharmas in turn to threaten to build Enion "a Labyrinth" for her to become lost in that existence. This is indeed what happens in the poem, as we have already seen.

The emanations are fled from Tharmas, and Enion responds from her fallen perspective:

> Once thou wast to Me the loveliest son of heaven—But now
> Why art thou terrible? And yet I love thee in thy terror till
> I am almost Extinct & soon shall be a shadow in Oblivion
> Unless some way can be found that I may look upon thee & live.
> Hide me some shadowy semblance, secret whispring in my Ear

---

[13] See John Keats's poem about a similar negative sexual strategy conducted by a female character with a lot in common with Enitharmon. *Poetical Works* 350–51.

> In secret of soft wings, in mazes of delusive beauty.
> I have lookd into the secret soul of him I lovd
> And in the Dark recesses found Sin & cannot return.
> [1:38–45, E 301]

Although, as Enion finds here, love has turned into its negation and Tharmas is "terrible" instead of "the loveliest son of heaven," there is no alternative but to nurture these strong feelings, "unless," as Enion states, "some way can be found that I may look upon thee & live." Indeed, this is the main question of the poem, and we will shortly return to Blake's solution. What is definite at this point is that sin is discovered and that there is no way back to the innocence of the original Paradise. We must look ahead to a future utopia instead, with an improved existence that has elevated the original level to what in Blake can be labelled "radical innocence."

In the fallen existence governing *The Four Zoas*, however, Tharmas confesses that he is also to blame:

> Yea I know
> That I have sinnd & that my Emanations are become harlots
> I am already distraced at their deeds & if I look
> Upon them more Despair will bring self murder on my soul.
> [1:53–56, E 302]

Completing their separation, Enion then departs and hides from the sight of Tharmas who, since he is the ruler of the waters, returns to his element in bitterness. They both find it hard to accept their solitude and spend most of the remaining first Night raising questions and calling out to each other. The negative portion of Tharmas, his Spectre, eventually responds:

> Thou sinful Woman was it thy desire
> That I should hide thee with my power & delight thee with my
>   beauty?
> And now thou dark'nest in my presence; never from my sight
> Shalt thou depart to weep in secret. In my jealous wings
> I evermore will hold thee, when thou goest out or comest in
> Tis thou hast darken'd all My World, O Woman, lovely bane.
> [1:173–78][14]

---

[14] *For reasons unknown to me this strong passage is not included in Erdman's edition.*

As we can understand, Tharmas's Spectre lays the whole blame for the male-female division on woman. We must remember here, though, that the Spectre is the negative aspect and therefore represents the opposite of Blake's idea of Edenic utopia.

Tharmas and Enion, then, are the two characters used by Blake in the first Night to illustrate the negative outcome of the fall of man. Significantly, Tharmas also takes part in Night Four when he manifests his power as God of the waters. To begin with, he is still hovering on the brink of desperation, having lost Enion: "Wherefore do I feel such love & pity / Ah Enion Ah Enion Ah lovely lovely Enion / How is this All my hope is gone for ever fled" (4:7–9, E 331). Apparently, the separation has made him confused and he cannot keep his feelings apart: "And cannot those who once have lovd. Ever forget their Love? / Are love & rage the same passion? They are the same in me" (4:17–18, E 331). However, there is no escape from the torment of unrequited love: "When dark despair comes over (me) can I not / Flow down into the sea & slumber in oblivion. Ah Enion / Deformd I see these lineaments of ungratified Desire" (4:22–24, E 331–32). The reason why Enion does not reciprocate Tharmas's love is that they both belong to a fallen world where love is never mutual. Instead true love is hidden; therefore Enion and the other emanations were already hidden at the beginning of *The Four Zoas*. Now the turn has come to Tharmas to hide in his own element, the sea.

In the fallen world man must at least keep a faint hope of the final salvation, Blake indicates, in a somewhat chaotic interchange between Tharmas and Los, whom Tharmas calls his son. Initially, Tharmas tells him: "[R]enew thou I will destroy / Perhaps Enion may resume some little semblance / To ease my pangs of heart & to restore some peace to Tharmas" (4:31–33, E 332). Los appropriately retorts by forcefully seizing the power now that Urizen is fallen: "And Los remains God over all. Weak father of worms & clay / I know I was Urthona keeper of the gates of heaven / But now I am all powerful Los & Urthona is but my shadow" (4:41–43, E 332). By proclaiming himself to be Los, the fallen state of the world is further cemented. Both of them feel estranged in such an existence, and most remarkable is the change of Tharmas, whose unfallen form Los remembers in a characteristic glance back to innocence:

> Tharmas I know thee. How are we alterd our beauty decayd
> But still I know thee tho in this horrible ruin whelmd

> Thou Once the mildest son of heaven art now become a Rage
> A terror to all living things.
> [4:79–82, E 333]

In this existence Tharmas cannot silently accept the usurpation of Los and in a horrible act of vengeance rapes Los's emanation Enitharmon:

> What Sovereign Architect said Tharmas dare my will controll
> For if I will I urge these waters. If I will they sleep
> In peace beneath my awful frown my will shall be my Law
> So Saying in a Wave he rap'd bright Enitharmon far
> Apart from Los
> [4:53–56, E 332]

In spite of the understandable complaints of Los, Tharmas urges him on to positive labour: "Go forth said Tharmas works of joy are thine obey & live" (4:67, E 333). Most of all Tharmas implores Los to find joy in Enitharmon: "[T]ake Enitharmon for thy sweet reward while I / In vain am driven on false hope" (4:122–23, E 334). Tharmas is certainly a crucial character in this section since "Now all comes into the power of Tharmas ... Tharmas / Is God" (4:129–32, E 334). Tharmas acts with Godlike powers, usurping the position of an omniscient Jahwe/Elohim God-figure. It is also important that Tharmas rules the waters. At the same time as Tharmas encourages Los he seems, somewhat paradoxically, to doubt his own powers:

> Is this to be A God far rather would I be a Man
> To know sweet Science & to do with simple companions
> Sitting beneath a tent & viewing sheepfolds & soft pastures
> Take thou the hammer of Urthona rebuild these furnaces
> [4:146–49, E 334–35]

In a future utopia every single being is "a Man" who knows "sweet Science" with "sheepfolds & soft pastures." Urthona must therefore seize his hammer to "rebuild these furnaces" to create a new and better world. This is but a simple choice, according to Tharmas: "Death choose or life thou strugglest in my waters, now choose life" (4:152, E 335). Having relinquished his authority to Los/Urthona, Tharmas can now leave the poem:

> So saying Tharmas on his furious chariots of the Deep
> Departed far into the Unknown & left a wondrous void
> Round Los
>
> [4:157–59, E 335]

After a brief exchange with Urizen in Night six, Tharmas does not re-emerge until the final Night. Tharmas and Enion are the couple in *The Four Zoas* symbolizing hopeless and desperate solitude far more than the other three couples; hence the rage of Tharmas. Significantly, Vala sees Tharmas in a mournful state quite late in the concluding Night as the apocalypse is already going on:

> And as she rose her Eyes were opend to the world of waters
> She saw Tharmas sitting upon the rocks beside the wavy sea
> He strokd the water from his beard & mournd faint thro the
>   summer vales
> And Vala stood on the rocks of Tharmas & heard his mournful
>   voice
> O Enion my weary head is in the bed of death
> For weeds of death have wrapd around my limbs in the hoary
>   deeps
> I sit in the place of shells & mourn & thou art closd in clouds
> When will the time of Clouds be past & the dismal night of
>   Tharmas
> Arise O Enion Arise & smile upon my head
> As thou dost smile upon the barren mountains and they rejoice
> When wilt thou smile on Tharmas O thou bringer of Golden Day
> Arise O Enion arise for Lo I have calmd my seas
>
> [9:483–94, E 398]

Even though by now Tharmas has been reconciled with himself and significantly has calmed his seas, he cannot yet be reconciled with his female counterpart since the apocalyptic work is not quite completed. Therefore Enion again vanishes from his sight and, as we have seen, it is only when Vala calls her back that she returns in Vala's vision of Enion and Tharmas in innocent childhood. It is as if Blake wants to announce the imminent approach of the apocalypse.

Through this nostalgic detour, Tharmas and Enion are now ready to reunite in order to meet a future higher innocence:

> Joy thrilled thro all the Furious form of Tharmas humanizing
> Mild he embracd her whom he sought he raisd her thro the
>   heavens

> Sounding his trumpet to awake the dead on high he soard
> Over the ruind world the smoking tomb of the Eternal Prophet
> [9:613–16, E 401]

As the penultimate couple Tharmas and Enion are welcomed to the apocalyptic Golden feast. In a concluding demonstration of his powers "Tharmas takes the Storms. He turns the whirlwind Loose / Upon the wheels the stormy seas howl at his dread command" (9:809–10, E 406).

Los/Urthona: Spiritual Poetic Persona

As might be understood from the interaction and co-operation of Tharmas and Los/Urthona, if the zoas are to be divided into two couples in line with the emanations these two zoas constitute one of them. Adhering to the binary paradigm of *The Four Zoas*, it is therefore relevant to continue our discussion with the character Los/Urthona. In Blake criticism Los is traditionally considered to be something of the contrary of Urizen, and in Blake's later poetry it is difficult not to see much of Blake himself and his main aesthetic ideas in Los. Significantly, Damrosch devotes a whole chapter of his book, "Blake and Los," to analysing the relation between Blake and his alter ego, or rather poetic persona.

As we have already seen, the unfallen form of Los is called Urthona: "Los was the fourth immortal starry one ... Urthona was his name in Eden" (*FZ* 1:14; 16–17, E 301). But, again, since *The Four Zoas* is a story of human affliction in a fallen world the eternal form of the character, Urthona, does not appear until the last judgement in the final Night. To increase the symbolic complexity there is also a character called the Spectre of Urthona who co-operates and almost merges with Los in the fallen existence.

When we first encounter Los and Enitharmon in *The Four Zoas* they live a complacent life of pure innocence:

> But Los & Enitharmon delighted in the Moony spaces of Eno
> Nine Times they livd among the forests feeding on sweet fruits
> ....
> A male & female naked & ruddy as the pride of summer
> [1:232–33; 236, E 305]

Already in the following stanza they are described as fallen characters, and Los is endowed with the power to control time and Enitharmon to control space:

> He could control the times & seasons & the days & years
> She could control the spaces regions desart flood & forest
> But had no power to weave a Veil of covering for her sins
> She drave the Females all away from Los
> And Los drave all the Males from her away
> [1:240–44, E 305]

We notice the similar, negative, gender interaction here as with Tharmas and Enion. After the gender division both male and female react with jealousy. In the rest of the first Night Los acts in consequence of this. As we remember, he hits his emanation violently and threatens her: "Sickning lies the Fallen Man his head sick his heart faint / Mighty atchievement of your power! Beware the punishment!" (1:288–89, E 306). Enitharmon is quick to reply: "Threaten not me, O visionary thine the punishment / The Human Nature shall no more remain nor Human acts / Form the rebellious Spirits of Heaven, but War & Princedom & Victory & Blood" (1:309–11, E 306).

To manifest the afflictions of the world the great negation Urizen descends to proclaim his superior position: "Now I am God from Eternity to Eternity" (1:319, E 307). In the first of their many combats Los replies:

> ...Art thou one of those who when most complacent
> Mean mischief most? If you are such Lo! I am also such.
> One must be master. Try thy Arts. I will also try mine
> For I perceive thou hast Abundance which I claim as mine
> [1:331–34, E 307]

For most of the poem Urizen takes the upper hand, and, as Blake satirizes the negation of legal marriage through the wedding feast of Los and Enitharmon, his darkness overspreads the world:

> But Los & Enitharmon sat in discontent & scorn
> Craving the more the more enjoying drawing out sweet bliss
> From all the turning wheels of heaven & the chariots of the Slain
> [1:439–41, E 310]

In line with this, Enitharmon in the next Night accuses Los of infidelity:

> But if among the virgins
> Of summer I have seen thee sleep & turn thy cheek delighted
> Upon the rose or lilly pale or on a bank where sleep
> The beamy daughters of the light starting they rise they flee
> From thy fierce love for tho I am dissolvd in the bright god
> My spirit still pursues thy false love over rocks & valleys
> [2:312–17, E 323]

As we have seen so many times in Blake's long poems, infidelity is only one of several expressions of "false love" in a fallen existence. However, nowhere is the battle of the sexes as intense and omni-present as in *The Four Zoas*. In my view, this is a major cause of the overall chaotic structure of the poem. Here though, in spite of being deluded by female beauty, Los still relies on Enitharmon for final restoration:

> Cold & repining Los
> Still dies for Enitharmon nor a spirit springs from my dead corse
> Then I am dead till thou revivest me with thy sweet song
> Now taking on Ahanias form & now the form of Enion
> I know thee not as once I knew thee in those blessed fields
> Where memory wishes to repose among the flocks of Tharmas
> [2:321–26, E 323]

Inevitably, in the fallen world Los is at the mercy of the ultimate female negation, Enitharmon, who, after confessing she had assumed the shape of Ahania, again accuses Los of betrayal. "I decievd thee & will still deceive" (2:328, E 323), Enitharmon finally declares before leaving Los desolate and without hope.

In the fourth Night the interactivity, or conflict rather, between Los and Tharmas takes its beginning. Now Los realizes that instead of Urthona he is "all powerful Los" (4:43, E 332), and begins using his hammer and anvil in order to construct a better society:

> Then Los with terrible hands siezd on the Ruind Furnaces
> Of Urizen. Enormous work: he builded them anew
> Labour of Ages in the Darkness & the war of Tharmas
> And Los formd Anvils of Iron petrific. For his blows
> Petrify with incessant beating many a rock.
> [4:165–69, E 335]

Entreated as we know by Tharmas to perform this eternal duty, Los acquires his most well-known shape as the blacksmith labouring evermore in his forge for the sake of art, the shape that he is later to have in *Jerusalem*. His work is interrupted by sudden Godly intervention, and it is as if Los's ceaseless labour has brought him closer to his maker with existence suddenly on the verge of the apocalypse of the second coming:

> Then wondrously the Starry Wheels felt the divine hand. Limit
> Was put to Eternal Death Los felt the Limit & saw
> The Finger of God touch the Seventh furnace in terror
> And Los beheld the hand of God over his furnaces
> Beneath the Deeps in dismal Darkness beneath immensity
> In terrors Los shrunk from his task. His great hammer
> Fell from his hand his fires hid their strong limbs in smoke
> For with noises ruinous hurtlings & clashings & groans
> The immortal endur'd. Tho bound in a deadly sleep
> Pale terror seizd the Eyes of Los as he beat round
> The hurtling Demon. Terrified at the shapes
> Enslavd humanity put on he became what he beheld
> He became what he was doing he was himself transformd
> [4:275–87, E 338]

Transformed by having seen the divine and the seventh furnace, Los in Night Five continues the battle with his eternal archenemy Urizen with renewed strength. At this apex of mental struggle and activity the son of Los and Enitharmon, Orc, is born:

> The groans of Enitharmon shake the skies the labring Earth
> Till from her heart rending his way a terrible Child sprang forth
> In thunder smoke & sullen flames & howlings & fury & blood
> [5:36–8, E 339]

Orc, who roughly symbolizes revolutionary spirit and activity, has no real function in *The Four Zoas*. Blake uses Orc, however, to illustrate the conflict between parent and child. When Orc is said to be fourteen years old "Los beheld the ruddy boy / Embracing his bright mother & beheld malignant fires / In his young eyes discerning plain that Orc plotted his death" (5:80–82, E 340). This is indeed a remarkable passage in Blake, since he clearly shows here that the designs of jealousy work not only between male and female but also between child and parent. It gives rise to the most frightening emotions, what Blake calls "the chain of Jealousy":

> He went each morning to his labours with the spectre dark
> Calld it the chain of Jealousy. Now Los began to speak
> His woes aloud to Enitharmon. Since he could not hide
> His uncouth plague. He siezd the boy in his immortal hands
> While Enitharmon followd him weeping in dismal woe
> Up to the iron mountains top & there the Jealous chain
> Fell from his bosom on the mouintain. The Spectre dark
> Held the fierce boy Los naild him down binding around his limbs
> The accursed chain O how bright Enitharmon howld & cried
> Over her son. Obdurate Los bound down her loved Joy
> [5:94–103, E 341]

It is not too difficult to visualize this vivid picture of a father's despair over the natural, unbreakable and reciprocal chain of love between mother and child, around puberty creating a chain of jealousy in the father similar to jealousy felt towards another man. We should here also remember the two poems from *Songs of Innocence and of Experience*, "A Little Boy Lost" and "A Little Girl Lost," where Blake works with a similar context of parental despair.

This rift is not to be mended, Blake suggests, as the passage continues. Los goes on working in even greater fury: "The hammer of Urthona smote the rivets in terror. Of brass / Tenfold. The Demons rage flamd tenfold forth rending / Roaring redounding. Loud Loud Louder & Louder" (5:104–06, E 341). The work is of no avail though, not even the sincere remorse of Los:

> Los & Enitharmon
> Felt all the sorrow Parents feel. They wept toward one another
> And Los repented that he had chaind Orc upon the mountain
> And Enitharmons tears prevaild parental love returnd
> Tho terrible his dread of that infernal chain They rose
> At midnight hasting to their much beloved care
> ....
> He thought to give to Enitharmon
> Her son in tenfold joy & to compensate for her tears
> Even if his own death resulted so much pity him paind
> [5:143–54, E 342]

In this difficult situation too, then, Los's repentance and the tears of Enitharmon make parental love return. Not even male-female cooperation, however, or Los's extreme unselfish compassion, are of any help since the chain of jealousy has already bound them: "In vain they strove now to unchain. In vain with bitter tears / To melt the chain of Jealousy. Not Enitharmon's death / Nor the Consummation of Los could ever melt the chain" (5:160–62, E 342). The two parents finally have to concede the impossibility of finding a solution:

> Despair & Terror & Woe & Rage
> Inwrap the Parents in cold clouds as they bend howling over
> The terrible boy till fainting by his side the Parents fell
> [5:170–72, E 342–43]

This is a most intriguing section that demonstrates two things. First, the inclusion of parental love suggests the extraordinarily far-reaching scope of Blake's poem, underlining the omnipresent workings of jealousy on all emotional levels. Second, and most importantly, in this incident the interactivity of the two sexes does not lead to anything positive and there is no solution to the problem. This is of course even more remarkable since male-female interactivity leads to the positive conclusion of the entire poem, as we shall shortly see, when Los as the last zoa reunites with his emanation Enitharmon. Here, what has started with glorious delight and the utmost activity in the birth of Orc finishes in utter despair with the victory of the great negation Urizen.

URIZEN: GOD-FIGURE AND COMPLEX NEGATION

One of the most established and well-known facts of the Blakean mythos is that Urizen is the great negation and that he is supposed to be a devilish creature and associated with Satan. He is also the arch-enemy of Los. Urizen represents the negative reasoning power in man that, at its worst, works to curb creative imagination. In *The Four Zoas*, however, the symbol of Urizen is not only used for negative purposes. Compared with the Urizen of *Milton* he is more of one character among many, forming part of the action just like his three fellow zoas. In line with Blake's idea of the interrelated zoas, he rather acts within that intricate scheme as one of four equally important components.

As Blake moves along to the subsequent epic *Milton*, and leaves the fourfold structure behind, Urizen seems to become increasingly identified with the Hebrew Yahweh/Elohim God-figure that Blake abhors as manifesting and sustaining the ancient patriarchal moral law of the Commandments, although Blake's concept of God becomes even more complex as he realizes that he has to develop the somewhat simplified dualistic divine concept of his earlier prophecies. This transformation has already taken place in *The Four Zoas,* where the role of the Judaeo-Christian God is basically taken by Urizen.

There is a fierce battle for Godlike power throughout *The Four Zoas* between Tharmas, Los and Urizen. Already in Night the First the latter, in a most self-assured and arrogant manner, proclaims: "Now I am God from Eternity to Eternity" (1:319, E 307). A further example of this attitude appears in the third Night: "Am I not God said Urizen. Who is Equal to me" (3:106, E 328). His position and Godlike status seem to be undisputed, as Los also verifies: "Our God is Urizen the King. King of the Heavenly hosts / We have no other King but he" (4:38–39, E 332). Then suddenly Tharmas usurps the God-position: "Now all comes into the power of Tharmas. Urizen is falln" (4:129, E 334). Urizen from then on disappears into the afflictions of the fallen world. Thus he assumes the same proportion as any of the other zoas. In the post-lapsarian world of Generation, Urizen returns to executing what Frye has characterized as the passive forms of jealousy.

Like the other three zoas Urizen is dependent, or interdependent rather, on the four female emanations of the poem. It is Enitharmon, the most negative emanation, who introduces him in the poem as a kind of protection against her zoa, Los: "Descend O Urizen descend with horse & chariots" (1:308, E 306). Since Enitharmon is the kind of woman who has "power over Man from Cradle to corruptible Grave" *(Jerusalem* 30:26, E 175), Urizen must obey:

> The Wandering Man bow'd his faint head and Urizen descended
> And the one must have murderd the other if he had not descended
> Indignant muttering low thunders; Urizen descended
> Gloomy sounding, Now I am God from Eternity to Eternity
> [1:316–19, E 306–7]

From the very onset we get a well-fitting description of Urizen's character: "Indignant muttering low thunders," "Gloomy sounding"—a warmonger who proclaims himself to be God for all time. His epithet in *The Four Zoas,* "Prince of Light," is also established from the start. The arrogant assertion of the light of reason ironically makes him a Satan-figure, the Prince of Darkness.

As a God-like authority Urizen finds himself in a position to exercise his power over the female, proclaiming that "Vala shall become a

Worm in Enitharmon's Womb" (3:20, E 326), without mentioning the expulsion of his own emanation, Ahania. Here he seems to take advantage of the evil Vala, who is already in a fallen state, in order to infiltrate the other emanations, above all the consort of his foremost enemy Los/Urthona, Enitharmon. Ahania, in spite of her humble attitude towards Urizen, cannot avoid his wrath. He cannot stand the risk of her becoming another Vala, which of course, cast out into a fallen state, is just what she becomes. Urizen's wrath in the fallen world inevitably becomes futile.

This is obvious in the passage in Night Six where Urizen, like all the other characters in *The Four Zoas*, is trapped in a fallen existence where woman is the usurper of power through her sexual strategies. A desperate Urizen is met only with female reticence:

> Answerest thou not said Urizen. then thou maist answer me
> Thou terrible woman clad in blue, whose strong attractive power
> Draws all into a fountain at the rock of thy attraction
> With frowning brow thou sittest mistress of these mighty waters
> She answered not but stretchd her arms & threw her limbs
>   abroad
>   [6:12–16, E 345]

The powerless Urizen can only continue to condemn woman, planning a, probably futile, scheme of revenge:

> O horrible O dreadful state! those whom I loved best
> On whom I pourd the beauties of my light adorning them
> With jewels & precious ornament labourd with art divine
> ....
> Now I will pour my fury on them & I will reverse
> The precious benediction. for their colours of loveliness
> I will give blackness for jewels hoary frost for ornament
>   deformity
> For crowns wreathd Serpents for sweet odors stinking
>   corruptibility
> For voices of delight hoarse croakings inarticulate thro frost
> For labourd fatherly care & sweet instruction. I will give
> Chains of dark ignorance & cords of twisted self conceit
>   [6:25–27; 35–41, E 345]

By using a language of remarkable poetic precision, immersed in biblical imagery, Blake manages to convey a forceful picture of the powerful work of love in its negative state in a fallen existence.

In the remaining three Nights of *The Four Zoas* Urizen never fully recovers from this central, and to him unexpected, negative experience. Like the other zoas, he can only look forward to the redemptive powers of the apocalypse. Urizen, in his spectral form, speaks:

> The Spectre said. Thou lovely Vision this delightful Tree
> Is given us for a Shelter from the tempests of Void & Solid
> Till once again the morn of ages shall renew upon us
> To reunite in those mild fields of happy Eternity
> Where thou & I in undivided Essence walkd about
> [7:267–71, E 359]

The only option for Urizen, then, is to repent and confess his sins in order to gain access to Eden. After suffering and repentance, Urizen reunites in joy with his emanation Ahania and they ascend into the apocalypse of the final Night.

Luvah/Orc: Apocalyptic Initiator and Agent

To follow the poem full circle it is logical to conclude with Luvah, the zoa corresponding to Vala, the emanation with whom we began our investigation of the main characters. For most of *The Four Zoas* Luvah collaborates with two of the characters, Vala and Urizen. Just introduced into the poem, Luvah seems to be another competitor for the dominating position: "Luvah & Urizen contend in war around the holy tent" (1:480, E 311). Above all, it looks as though Luvah wants to challenge the Prince of Light, Urizen: "Luvah replied Dictate to thy Equals. Am not I / The Prince of all the hosts of Men nor Equal know in Heaven" (1:504–05, E 311). The cunning and power-mad Urizen, however, has already laid the scheme for their activities by suggesting to Luvah that they should let fallen man remain in that state:

> Thou Luvah said the Prince of Light behold our sons & daughters
> Reposd on beds. Let them sleep on. Do thou alone depart
> Into thy wished Kingdom where in Majesty & Power
> We may erect a throne. Deep in the North I place my lot
> Thou in the South
> [1:488–92, E 311]

Luvah does not find the proposal acceptable since he understands that Urizen is a false and calculating figure:

> If I arise into the Zenith leaving thee to watch
> The Emanation & her Sons the Satan & the Anak
> Sihon & Og. wilt thou not rebel to my laws remain
> In darkness building thy strong throne & in my ancient night
> Daring my power wilt arm my sons against me in the Atlantic
> My deep My night which thou assuming hast assumd my Crown
> I will remain as well as thou & here with hands of blood
> Smite this dark sleeper in his tent then try my strength with thee
> [1:506–13, E 311]

This is a very important section of the poem since it provides us with much of the background to what will follow in the remaining eight Nights. Here Blake is obviously influenced by *Paradise Lost* with its war in heaven and the banishment of Satan and his archangels. This opening struggle between Luvah and Urizen is the symbolic beginning of the chaotic fallen existence in Blake's world of Generation with the war between the sexes related in *The Four Zoas:*

> While thus he spoke his fires reddend oer the holy tent
> Urizen cast deep darkness round him silent brooding death
> Eternal death to Luvah. Raging Luvah pourd
> The Lances of Urizen from chariots. Round the holy tent
> Discord began & yells & cries shook the wide firmament
> [1:514–18, E 312]

Furthermore, and very interestingly bearing in mind some comments on the poem, it is evident which are the positive and the negative characters in it. Both Los / Urthona, "Beside his anvil stood Urthona dark. A mass of iron / Glowd furious on the anvil" (1:519–20, E 312), and Tharmas, "And Tharmas took her in pitying" (1:525, E 312), are mustered into the first of these categories together with Luvah, as we have already seen. Luvah is the most controversial of these, and many commentators read Luvah negatively. Frye, for instance, links this character with the fallen world of Generation as a representation of the sexual aspect of existence (235). Quite as expected Urizen sides with evil: "But Urizen with darkness overspreading all the armies / Sent round his heralds secretely commanding to depart / Into the north" (1:535–37, E 312).

There is some justification, though, for placing Luvah on the side of the negative characters, especially since the bonds between him and Urizen are so close:

> Albion calld Urizen & said. Behold these sickning Spheres
> ....
> For I am weary, & must sleep in the dark sleep of Death
> Thy brother Luvah hath smitten me but pity thou his youth
> [2:3–7, E 313]

But, as we see here, Luvah's young age is a mitigating circumstance, and the stern Urizen seizes this unique opportunity through the commands of Albion to settle the dispute and assumes dominion over Luvah and his emanation Vala. The couple react with fear: "Luvah & Vala trembling & shrinking, beheld the great Work master / And heard his Word! Divide ye bands influence by influence" (2:22–23, E 314). In Urizen's fallen world Luvah and Vala inevitably lose their original innocence:

> Luvah was cast into the Furnaces of affliction & sealed
> And Vala fed in cruel delight, the furnaces with fire
> ....
> In joy she heard his howlings, & forgot he was her Luvah
> With whom she walkd in bliss, in times of innocence & youth
> [2:72–79, E 317]

In *Jerusalem*, as we shall see, Luvah, little as he participates in the poem, is definitely negative.

At this point the two disappear "physically" from the poem for quite some time. Vala, as we recall, is an absent character for most of the poem, and so is Luvah. In his lamentations Luvah recalls the memory of Vala a few times. Just as Los, and, especially, Tharmas miss their respective emanations, he mourns her absence for some Nights. In the second Night, for instance, he complains to Urizen:

> O first born Son of Light
> O Urizen my enemy I weep for thy stern ambition
> But weep in vain O when will you return Vala the Wanderer
> These were the words of Luvah patient in afflictions
> Reasoning in the loins in the unreal forms of Ulros night
> And when Luvah age after age was quite melted with woe
> The fires of Vala faded like a shadow cold & pale
> [2:108–13, E 318]

First and foremost the activity of Luvah, or rather his and Vala's interaction, is crucial in the final Night. The gender interactivity of these two characters is decisive for the progress of the apocalypse, and they are the main actors in the second part of the final Night. Together with Vala, Luvah descends in the final Night to initiate the apocalypse: "Luvah & Vala descended & enterd the Gates of Dark Urthona" (9:375, E 395). They are the second of the four couples to be reconciled and serve as an example for the others in the continued apocalypse of the remainder of the poem. With their descent we are led step by step towards Urizen's announcement nearly two hundred lines later that time as we know it has ended. Thus, as together they enter "Vala's Garden":

> They saw no more the terrible confusion of the wracking universe
> They heard not saw not felt not all the terrible confusion
> For in their orbed senses within closd up they wanderd at will
> [9:380–82, E 395]

They can now walk freely in a renewed state of innocent bliss:

> Invisible Luvah in bright clouds hoverd over Valas head
> And thus their ancient golden age renewd for Luvah spoke
> With voice mild from his golden Cloud upon the breath of morning
> Come forth O Vala from the grass & from the silent Dew
> Rise from the dews of death for the Eternal Man is Risen
> [9:385–89, E 395]

In this perhaps most decisive and central passage of the whole poem, we can notice that, significantly, "their ancient golden age" is not recovered but *"renewd,"* which is in line with Blake's notion of apocalypse as a continuation of the sublunary world.

Luvah's observation that the eternal Man Albion is awoken again and the entreatment of his emanation make Vala rejoice and run eagerly forward, realizing her origin as well as what is just happening: "To yonder brightness there I haste for sure I came from thence / Or I must have slept eternally nor have felt the dew of morning" (9:402–03, E 396). Through a remarkably interactive dialogue between her and Luvah she is finally led into her garden of innocence where, significantly, she encounters Tharmas and Enion as children. Mankind is on the very verge of apocalypse.

The Apocalypse of The Four Zoas

Inspired by the Book of Revelation Blake gave Night Nine the subtitle "The Last Judgment." There are already intimations of apocalypse in the preceding Nights, but it is only in the final ninth Night that apocalypse in *The Four Zoas* really begins. In Blake's later work, it is Los, mostly with the spiritual aid of his emanation Enitharmon, who is the primary apocalyptic labourer in Blake's major epics. This is particularly the case in *The Four Zoas* in which the mental strife of these two characters is a prerequisite for the advent of the apocalypse. As we have seen, after the fall at the beginning of the poem the basic urge of their activity is to finally reunite with each other and thereby initiate the apocalypse. Consequently, it is only when Los and Enitharmon, as precursors of the other characters, are finally reunited at the end of the poem that there are positive repercussions.

The apocalypse sets in quite early in the final Night, and it seems that Blake wants to underscore the metaphorical status of his particular form of apocalypse. It is Los alone, in great strength, who launches the apocalypse:

> Los his vegetable hands
> Outstretchd his right hand branching out in fibrous Strength
> Siezd the Sun. His left hand like dark roots coverd the Moon
> And tore them down cracking the heavens across from immense
>   to immense
> Then fell the fires of Eternity with loud & shrill
> Sound of Loud Trumpet thundering along from heaven to
>   heaven
> A mighty sound articulate Awake ye dead & come
> To judgment from the four winds Awake & Come away
>   [9:6–13, E 386]

By taking down the illuminating sources of sun and moon Los eclipses the light of the world, inflicting darkness on mankind, something which is described in the biblical apocalypses of Ezekiel, Isaiah, and particularly Revelation. This passage is very close to the apocalypse of Isaiah: "For the stars of heaven and the constellations thereof shall not give their light: the sun shall be darkened in his going forth, and the moon shall not cause her light to shine.... Therefore I will shake the heavens, and the earth shall remove out of her place" (13:10, 13; 704). We can also make a comparison with the apocalypse of Revelation: "And I beheld when he had opened the sixth seal, and, lo, there was a great earthquake; and the sun became black as sackcloth of hair, and the moon became as blood; And the stars of heaven fell unto the earth, even as a fig tree casteth her untimely figs, when she is shaken of a mighty wind. And the heaven departed as a scroll when it is rolled together; and every mountain and island were moved out of their places" (6:12–14, 1222). Existence as we know it has come to an end, but with the sound of the apocalyptic trumpet humanity is awoken to new, eternal, life. In Revelation a peaceful millennium is announced, in which Christ is to reign for a thousand years with all his disciples: "This is the first resurrection. Blessed and holy is he that hath part in the first resurrection: on such the second death hath no power, but they shall be priests of God and of Christ, and shall reign with him a thousand years" (20:5–6, 1233). In *The Four Zoas*, and in Blake's two other epics, it is not quite clear whether a millennium is proclaimed or not. Nevertheless, in these three poems we find ample evidence of a peaceful and harmonious existence to come, so in Blake, as Paley has pointed out, millennium and utopia are interchangeable.

The first sign that *The Four Zoas* is drawing near to its resolution in the apocalypse is the creation of a universal female character, Jerusalem, as the counterpart of the universal male character, Albion, and also, symbolically, of Christ, the Lamb of God:

> Thus forming a Vast family wondrous in beauty & love
> And they appeard a Universal female form created
> From those who were dead in Ulro from the spectres of the dead
> And Enitharmon namd the Female Jerusalem the holy
> Wondring she saw the Lamb of God within Jerusalem's Veil
> The Divine Vision seen within the inmost deep recess
> Of fair Jerusalem's bosom in a gently beaming fire.
> [8:187–193, E 376]

Jerusalem through her late appearance in the poem becomes a portent of the apocalypse. "Now we behold redemption" (8:197, E 376), some of the characters sing in praise as they become more reassured of what is actually taking place. Jerusalem is of course to become the eponymous key character in Blake's final epic, but already in *The Four Zoas* she has a vital function in discovering the dead body of Christ. Together with Los she takes the body down from the cross and buries it in a sepulchre:

> Los took the Body from the Cross Jerusalem weeping over
> They bore it to the Sepulcher which Los had hewn in the rock
> Of Eternity for himself he hewd it despairing of Life Eternal
> [8:338–40, E 379]

Towards the end of Night Eight there is no doubt that the apocalypse is on its way, as is testified by several textual instances. To begin with, Enion announces that "the time of love / Appears upon the rocks & hills" (8:538–39, E 384). The negative aspects of man and of every individual are annihilated: "For I am now surrounded by a shadowy vortex drawing / The Spectre quite away from Enion that I die a death / Of bitter hope" (8:545–47, E 384). When the negations are extinguished an enhanced and improved existence emerges as "the time approaches fast…. When the man gently fades away in his immortality / When the mortal disappears in improved knowledge cast away / The former things" (8:549–53, E 384–85).

However, it is Christ, the Lamb of God, who symbolically initiates the apocalypse through the Second Coming: "The Lamb of God has rent the Veil of Mystery soon to return / In Clouds & Fires around the rock & the Mysterious tree" (8:556–57, E 385). The work is not wholly done, though, and Christ who "regulates the forms / Of all beneath & all above … weeps / That Man should Labour & sorrow & learn & forget & return / To the dark valley whence he came to begin his labours anew" (8:568–75, E 385). To escape the labour and conflicts of the fallen world mankind must return to the innocence of the original Paradise:

> And in the cries of birth & in the groans of death his voice
> Is heard throughout the Universe whereever a grass grows
> Or a leaf buds The Eternal Man is seen is heard is felt
> And all his Sorrows till he reassumes his ancient bliss
> [8:580–83, E 385]

Since this state can only be realized through the Second Coming, Los and Enitharmon now take down the body of Christ from the cross:

> And Los & Enitharmon took the Body of the Lamb
> Down from the Cross & placd it in a Sepulcher which Los had hewn
> For himself in the Rock of Eternity trembling & in despair
> Jerusalem wept over the Sepulcher two thousand years
> [8:593–96, E 385]

The female counterpart of Christ, Jerusalem, mourns his death for two thousand years of Christian religion. It is also significant of the gender politics of the whole poem that this symbolic action must be carried out by male and female together.

Los and Enitharmon then start building the heavenly city of Jerusalem, "weeping / Over the Sepulcher & over the Crucified body" (9:1–2, E 386). Still crucial, however, is the presence of Christ: "But Jesus stood beside them in the Spirit Separating / Their Spirit from their body" (9:4–5, E 386). Through the spiritual inspiration of Christ, Los gains strength to once and for all begin the final process of the apocalypse as he seizes the sun, in the passage quoted above. This passage differs from most of the other apocalyptic passages in Blake's work in blending traditional biblical images like "fires" and "Trumpet" with the original typical posture of Los seizing the sun and covering the moon to tear up the whole expanse of the universe. In the next few lines Blake again relies on the Bible, and to begin with we hear echoes from Daniel in which the narrator states: "Daniel spake and said, I saw in my vision by night, and, behold, the four winds of the heaven strove upon the great sea" (7:2, 887):

> A mighty sound articulate Awake ye dead & come
> To judgment from the four winds Awake & Come away
> Folding like scrolls of the Enormous volume of Heaven & Earth
> With thunderous noise & dreadful shakings rocking to & fro
> The Heavens are shaken & the Earth removed from its place
> The foundations of the Eternal hills discoverd
> [9:12–17, E 386–87]

The last four lines here remind us of the apocalypses in Isaiah and Revelation. The lengthy Isaiah apocalypse stretches from 24:1 to 27:13, and the following lines are most strikingly similar to the above passage: "[F]or the windows from on high are open, and the foundations of the earth do shake. The earth is utterly broken down, the earth is clean dissolved, the earth is moved exceedingly. The earth shall reel to and fro like a drunkard, and shall be removed like a cottage; and the transgression thereof shall be heavy upon it; and it shall fall, and not rise again" (24:18–20, 713). The episode in Revelation is shorter and perhaps less significant here: "And the temple of God was opened in heaven, and there was seen in his temple the ark of his testament: and there were lightnings, and voices, and thunderings, and an earthquake, and great hail" (11:19, 1226).

If we continue reading the apocalypse in Isaiah we can compare it with the final few lines of this first apocalyptic section in *The Four Zoas*:

> The thrones of Kings are shaken they have lost their robes & crowns
> The poor smite their oppressors they awake up to the harvest
> The naked warriors rush down to the sea shore
> Trembling before the multitudes of slaves now set at liberty
> They are become like wintry flocks like forests stripd of leaves
> The oppressed pursue like the wind there is no room for escape
> [9:18–23, E 387]

In Isaiah we notice a similar royal reference: "And it shall come to pass in that day, that the LORD shall punish the host of the high ones that are on high, and the kings of the earth upon the earth" (24:21, 713). We can also observe that Blake has maintained his political stance, advocating the revolutionary upheaval displayed in for instance *America* and *The French Revolution* by the use of more concrete vocabulary: "oppressors," "warriors," and "slaves now set at liberty." To Blake, then, the apocalypse entails both a substantial socio-political transformation and a metaphorical mental transcendence.

As a whole, one can certainly argue that *The Four Zoas*, and possibly also *Jerusalem* with its shorter and more condensed apocalypse, have given us the most detailed existing literary account(s) of the apocalypse. In general Blake provides us with a more comprehensive description than does the Bible through his wide range of vocabulary and images. At the same time as he adheres to the biblical apocalyptic tradition, he also manages to create new signifiers; sometimes he even combines these two strategies. A good example of such an image is the frequent use of the sun as a symbol in the ninth Night, indicating both the immersion in the biblical tradition and the relation to the character Los, so crucial for the apocalypse. Hence, one connotation of Los's name is sun, mainly through the anagram "sol." Blake gives the light of the sun credit for finally waking up the Eternal Man from his long repose in Beulah, almost one epic poem in duration:

> Eternally thou must have slept nor have felt the morning dew
> But for yon nourishing sun tis by which thou art arisen
> The birds adore the sun the beasts rise up & play in his beams
> And every flower & every leaf rejoices in his light
> [9:404–07, E 396]

In *The Four Zoas* the sun is several times addressed directly as the source of life: "Rise up O sun most glorious minister & light of day (9:434, E 397).

Another significant example occurs in Night Nine where Blake even succeeds in illustrating the harmonious sound of the apocalypse in a convincing image:

> Look how the opening dawn advances with vocal harmony
> Look how the beams foreshew the rising of some glorious power
> The sun is thine he goeth forth in his majestic brightness
> [9:397–99, E 396]

As the apocalypse approaches, the characters wake up from their eternal sleep. Arising, filled with strength and activity after a long absence in the poem, the eponymous character Vala now returns to search for her counterpart zoa: "Where dost thou dwell for it is thee I seek & but for thee / I must have slept Eternally" (9:395–96, E 396). From this we understand that the reunion of the two sexes is crucial also for bringing about the anticipated utopian existence. It is not, however, until the very end of *The Four Zoas* that this ultimate reconciliation is finally achieved. The trope "vocal harmony" which occurs in several places in the poem is then reiterated at the advent of the apocalypse: "The Elements subside the heavens rolld on with vocal harmony" (9:800, E 405).

Somewhat surprising perhaps is Blake's use of traditional biblical imagery to describe existence in Eden, and also in Beulah. For instance, flocks of woolly lambs occur in the final Night after Luvah and Vala have descended to earth. The lambs with their bleating manifest the innocence of Blake's utopia, and not only the association with Christ: "I walk among his flocks & hear the bleating of his lambs" (9:425, E 396). Vala intends to erect a house in the peaceful Beulah to return to for rest: "So spoke the sinless soul & laid her head on the downy fleece / Of a curld Ram who stretchd himself in sleep beside his mistress" (9:455–56, E 397). This is only a dream, however, and Vala awakes to find her lambs gone: "And then from her white door she lookd up to see her bleating lambs / But her flocks were gone up from beneath the trees into the hills" (9:472–73, E 397).

In the episode, commonly known as "Vala's Garden," the images of an innocent state continue as Vala sees a vision of Tharmas and Enion as small children in front of her newly-built house:

> And now her feet step on the grassy bosom of the ground
> Among her flocks & she turnd her eyes toward her pleasant house
> And saw in the doorway beneath the trees two little children playing
> She drew near to her house & her flocks followd her footsteps
> The Children clung around her knees she embracd them & wept over them
> Thou little Boy art Tharmas & thou bright Girl Enion
> How are ye thus renewd & brought into the Gardens of Vala?
> [9:505–11, E 398]

In innocent playfulness the two children represent the positive counterparts of the negations of the fallen world, here labelled "Valas world." As a key figure, Vala is a fallen character throughout *The Four Zoas*, from the very beginning of the poem to the final redemption in the apocalypse:

> Thus in Eternal Childhood straying among Valas flocks
> In infant sorrow & joy alternate Enion & Tharmas playd
> Round Vala in the Gardens of Vala & by her rivers margin
> They are the shadows of Tharmas & of Enion in Vala's world
> [9:553–56, E 400]

The section "Vala's Garden" is a notorious source of difficulty and disagreement in Blake criticism. As I see it, Blake portrays Tharmas and Enion as innocent children since they are already consumed by the apocalypse at this point in the poem. As a whole, "Vala's Garden" is perhaps the most pastoral utopian passage in Blake's epic poems. We find a number of traditional utopian images: the Garden of Eden, fruits, flowers and, again, lambs—all seen in Vala's vision. But, typical of Blake's dialectical mythology, Tharmas also recalls the deceptive temptation in Paradise:

> O Vala I am sick & all this garden of Pleasure
> Swims like a dream before my eyes but the sweet smelling fruit
> Revives me to new deaths
> [9: 538–40, E 399]

"Vala's Garden" is the final initiation of apocalypse in *The Four Zoas*. Shortly after these visions of innocence seen from the pastoral idyll of Beulah have faded, the ultimate negation Urizen with great joy announces that "Times are Ended" (9:568, E 400). This is the beginning of the Golden Feast that concludes *The Four Zoas*:

> This sickle Urizen took the scythe his sons embracd
> And went forth & began to reap & all his joyful sons
> Reapd the wide Universe & bound in Sheaves a wondrous harvest
> They took them into the wide barns with loud rejoicings & triumph
> Of flute & harp & drum & trumpet horn & clarion
> The feast was spread in the bright South & the Regenerate Man
> Sat at the feast rejoicing & the wine of Eternity
> Was servd round by the flames of Luvah all Day & all the Night
> [9:582–89, E 400]

Beside the more familiar utopian references such as "flute," "harp," "drum," "trumpet," "horn," "clarion," and "wine" we can also observe more striking images related to harvest: "sickle," "scythe," "reap," "Sheaves," "wondrous harvest," and "wide barns." By the introduction of this new kind of imagery Blake indicates that the poem is drawing towards its close with the human harvest of the ensuing consummation of the apocalypse.

The apocalyptic Golden feast continues and as another sign of an imminent improved existence the Eternal Man, Albion, rises to new life:

> The Eternal Man arose he welcomed them to the Feast
> The feast was spread in the bright South & the Eternal Man
> Sat at the feast rejoicing
> [9:617–19, E 401]

But the utopian existence of Eden cannot be fully realized before man and woman are finally reconciled, and at this point the two sexes are still divided:

> And Many Eternal Men sat at the golden feast to see
> The female form now separate They shudderd at the horrible thing
> Not born for the sport and amusement of Man but born to drink up all his powers
> They wept to see their shadows they said to one another this is Sin
> This is the Generative world they remembered the days of old
> [9: 621–25, E 401]

It is obvious here that the apocalyptic work is not completed and that it is still a fallen world, Blake's Generation, from which the Eternal Men cast glances of reminiscence at "the days of old" when man and woman walked in undivided essence before the split at the fall. In this fallen world, however, everything becomes abstractions and negations. Instead of experiencing the enjoyment of true love, "the sport and amusement," woman is, symbolically, placed in the role of drinking up all the powers of Man.

Hence, the human harvest must continue so Urizen seized "in his hand the Flail" (9: 650, E 402), and "Tharmas took the Winnowing fan" (9: 654, E 402). Shortly the human harvest is complete and it is time to gather the rich store of the vintage:

> Luvah the vintage is ripe arise
> The sons of Urizen shall gather the vintage with sharp hooks
> And all thy sons O Luvah bear away the families of Earth
> I hear the flail of Urizen his barns are full no room
> Remains & in the Vineyards stand the abounding sheaves
>   beneath
> The falling Grapes that odorous burst upon the winds.
>   [9:693–98, E 403]

As the "prince of Love," Luvah is significant for the apocalypse and accordingly he has to reappear in the poem before the apocalypse can be fully consummated:

> The shepherds shout for Luvah prince of Love
> Let the Bulls of Luvah tread the Corn & draw the loaded
>   waggon
> Into the Barn while children glean the Ears around the door
>   [9:700–02, E 403]

Thus Luvah assumes God-like status, showing that in Blake's mythological scheme any of the four zoas can assume the function of God. Blake raises his symbolic language here to an even more advanced level, emphasizing the innocent state of the approaching utopia still more, exemplified by the word "children." This becomes even clearer as Blake manifests innocence through the use of a number of tropes that remind us of nursery rhyme symbols in the *Songs of Innocence*, particularly "The Lamb":

> Then shall they lift their innocent hands & stroke his furious nose
> And he shall lick the little girls white neck & on her head
> Scatter the perfume of his breath while from his mountains high
> The lion of terror shall come down & bending his bright mane
> And couching at their side shall eat from the curld boys white lap
> His golden food and in the evening sleep before the Door
> [9:703–08, E 403][15]

These passages show Blake's great intratextual, as well as intertextual, awareness, and we can find this idea originally expressed in Isaiah: "The wolf and the lamb shall feed together, and the lion shall eat straw like the bullock" (65: 25, 748).

As the apocalypse is now fully set in motion, the agency of Luvah is emphasized. Particularly effective is the metonymical use of the symbol of Luvah's "wine presses" denoting the consummation of the apocalypse:

> Then fell the Legions of Mystery in maddning confusion
> Down Down thro the immense with outcry fury & despair
> Into the wine presses of Luvah howling fell the Clusters
> Of human families thro the deep. The wine presses were filld
> The blood of life flowd plentiful
> [9: 722–26, E 404]

The whole of humanity, or in Blake's pertinent term "the Human Grapes" (9: 748, E 404), is consumed in great suffering and with loud screaming, all according to what the Bible has told us about revelatory

---

[15] *Two more of the poems from* Songs of Innocence *reflect this passage. First, the innocent lamb also appears in the final stanza of "Spring." As in the passage above from* The Four Zoas *Blake juxtaposes the two symbols of innocence, the "Little Lamb" (Plate 27, E 15) and the child. In the poem "Night" also the taming of the wild "lion of terror" is implied as it lies down in innocence beside the meek lamb:*

> And now beside thee bleating lamb,
> I can lie down and sleep;
> Or think on him who bore thy name,
> Graze after thee and weep.
> For wash'd in lifes river,
> My bright mane for ever,
> Shall shine like the gold,
> As I guard o'er the fold
> (Plate 31, E 14)

damnation and resurrection. Luckily, however, all living organisms gather for the rescue of humanity: "The little Seed / The Sportive root the Earthworm the small beetle the wise Emmet / Dance round the Wine Presses of Luvah" (9:755–57, E 404). As Blake has formerly told us in "Auguries of Innocence," everything is contained in a grain of sand. These other forms of life "Dance around the Dying & they Drink the howl & groan / They catch the Shrieks in cups of gold they hand them to one another / These are the sports of love & these the sweet delights of amorous play" (9:767–69, E 405). The agony and torment of mankind in the wine presses of Luvah is a reminder that the biblical apocalypse also prescribes damnation for those who cannot be redeemed from sin, but through all their collective positive activity of love mankind manages to prevent this, thus finally revoking the negations of the fallen world. Again Blake emphasizes the need for unified action and shared responsibility in order to reach the final goal of male-female togetherness. Therefore the next step is for the remaining three zoas to come together:

> Then Tharmas & Urthona rose from the Golden feast satiated
> With Mirth & Joy Urthona limping from his fall on Tharmas
>   leand
> In his right hand his hammer Tharmas held his Shepherds crook
> Beset with gold were the ornaments formd by sons of Urizen
>   [9:774–77, E 405]

The activity of the zoas in turn inspires their emanations to come forth and ascend in joy:

> Then Enion & Ahania & Vala & the wife of Dark Urthona
> Rose from the feast in joy ascending to their Golden Looms
> There the wingd shuttle Sang the spindle & the distaff & the
>   Reel
> Rang sweet the praise of industry. Thro all the golden rooms
> Heaven rang with sweet Exultation
>   [9:778–82, E 405]

Blake's use of traditional female symbols, "Golden Looms," "the wingd shuttle," "the spindle," "the distaff," and "the Reel," to denote female activity through their metonymical function is significant. Consequently, to complete the process of the apocalypse Blake makes these female symbols of weaving harmonize with the male symbol of Luvah's "wine presses."

From the point of view of gender roles, this proves that Blake's utopia is not a "perfect" society, and the women still perform typically female tasks. On the other hand, Blake again uses exceptionally active images here: "wingd," "Sang," "Rang." Woman hereby becomes a character participating in the labour of the apocalypse. We get a picture of her as being just as active, and toiling as hard and with correspondingly ceaseless ardour, as the freedom-fighting Los, struggling to find poetic inspiration in order to create with his hammer at the anvil in his forge.

The last symbol with a metonymic function that Blake effectively uses in *The Four Zoas* is the Corn "Mills of Urthona" (9:808, E 406). In these mills the stored human harvest is finally ground, and

> Thunders Earthquakes Fires Water floods
> Rejoice to one another loud their voices shake the Abyss
> Their dread forms tending the dire mills
> [9:812–14, E 406]

"Such are the works of Dark Urthona" (9:821, E 406), and the apocalypse is finally completed:

> The Sun has left his blackness & has found a fresher morning
> And the mild moon rejoices in the clear & cloudless night
> And Man walks forth from midst of the fires the evil is all
>   consumd
> His eyes behold the Angelic spheres arising night & day
> The stars consumd like a lamp blown out & in their stead behold
> The Expanding Eyes of Man behold the depths of wondrous
>   worlds
> One Earth one sea beneath nor Erring Globes wander but Stars
> Of fire rise up nightly from the Ocean & one Sun
> Each morning like a New born Man issues with songs & Joy
> [9:825–33, E 406]

To manifest the all-encompassing scope of the apocalypse, domesticated wild animals, represented here by Urthona's lions, are "conversing with the Man" (9:843, E 406). The trope of conversation, symbolizing eternal intellectual activity, is repeated in *Jerusalem* where the characters "conversed together in Visionary forms dramatic" (98:28, E 257). A final echo from the Bible is heard as *The Four Zoas* draws towards its close:

> And the fresh Earth beams forth ten thousand thousand springs
>   of life
> Urthona is arisen in his strength no longer now
> Divided from Enitharmon no longer the spectre Los
> Where is the Spectre of Prophecy where the delusive Phantom
> Departed & Urthona rises from the ruinous walls
> In all his ancient strength to form the golden armour of science
> For intellectual War The war of swords departed now
> The dark Religions are departed & sweet Science reigns
>   [9:848–55, E 407]

Since the dream of the poem *The Four Zoas* is near its end, all things are now indeed changed. A new life is growing on the "fresh Earth." The fallen aspect of Urthona, Los, is departed. Urthona with all his regained strength is from now on to concentrate on intellectual instead of sexual warfare. Blake is still working here with a dualistic method; the impulse of war is turned into its opposite, love, and there is final harmony in the world of *The Four Zoas*. Blake has eventually achieved a preliminary visionary conclusion in *The Four Zoas*. It is only preliminary, however, as Blake is to carry on his visionary prophetic labour in his two concluding epics *Milton* and *Jerusalem*.

Finally, then, the regenerated unfallen Urthona has regained his pre-lapsarian strength and the spectral negations of the fallen world are eventually annihilated. But the conclusive step into Blake's utopian world is accomplished through the reunion of the male zoa, Urthona, with his female emanation, Enitharmon. The two of them can now enter Eden in togetherness, and the omniscient narrator Blake can announce that this is indeed the "End of the Dream" (9:856, E 407).

The Gender Reunion and Male-Female Togetherness of The Four Zoas

Male-female togetherness, then, is the conclusion of *The Four Zoas*, and it is only in relation to the very final phases of the poem that this term can be used. Togetherness is the state of harmony between male and female in Blake's higher radical innocence, to combine two terms coined by commentators of Blake. It is a prerequisite of this state that man and woman have by then gone through a fallen existence and through the metaphorical transcendence of the apocalypse been elevated to a higher level.

Ahania is the first female will/emanation to return from the life-in-death of Generation in order to rejoice with her zoa, Urizen. As we noticed earlier, she actually "died" only some lines earlier in Night Nine, somewhat to our surprise, since she now exults with joy:

> Ahania rose in joy
> Excess of joy is worse than grief—her heart beat high her blood
> Burst its bright Vessels She fell down dead at the feet of Urizen
> [9:196–98, E 391]

This passage is one of many which remind us of *The Marriage of Heaven and Hell*, where Blake declares that "Excess of sorrow laughs. Excess of joy weeps" (8:6, E 36), thus emphasizing the need for equilibrium of opposites. As the turbulence and chaos of the first eight Nights of *The Four Zoas*, with the zoas and emanations in a constant state of sexual warfare, suggest, the need for balance and stability is particularly important for the relation between man and woman in this poem. Therefore, in spite of the fact that Ahania "bursts" with joy, in the positive connotation of the word, she cannot be reconciled with her male counterpart Urizen, who at this stage has not been quite redeemed. We have to wait before the two can be reconciled. This is an important passage in the poem since Ahania and Urizen are the first couple to reunite:

> And Lo like the harvest Moon Ahania cast off her death clothes
> She folded them up in care in silence & her brightning limbs
> Bathd in the clear spring of the rock then from her darksom cave
> Issud in majesty divine Urizen rose up from his couch
> On wings of tenfold joy clapping his hands his feet his radiant
>   wings
> In the immense as when the Sun dances upon the mountains
> A shout of jubilee in lovely notes responding from daughter to
>   daughter
> From son to Son as if the Stars beaming innumerable
> Thro night should sing soft warbling filling Earth & heaven
> And bright Ahania took her seat by Urizen in songs & joy
> [9: 344–53, E 394–95]

Blake's use of a strong and positive imagery, denoting great activity, is striking here. This is a poetic strategy of Blake when he tries to express male-female reunion at a few crucial instances in the poem. Here, as in other similar passages, both male and female activity are important. To begin with, Urizen together with his sons "drink," "sing" and "view the flames of Orc." Next Urizen rises "up from his couch / On wings of tenfold joy clapping his hands his feet his radiant wings." This trope is particularly striking since, as we shall notice, some of these words are used in crucial positions. Furthermore, the beams from Urizen's "radiant wings" point ahead to the next line "when the Sun dances upon the mountains," the sun being, as we recall, a significant symbol in Night Nine. Also Ahania shows activity; she "[c]ast off her death clothes," and "[i]ssud in majesty divine." The decisive step is when, on her own initiative, "bright Ahania took her seat by Urizen in songs & joy." Significantly, she is not the female passive bystander here who exults with and for her male counterpart in a supportive but submissive way, only to be invited by the powerful male to take the seat beside him to share his power. In an emancipatory way she instead seizes joint power.

Even more forceful language is used to denote female activity when Vala as the second emanation in turn reunites with her zoa Luvah, as ordered by the Eternal Man: "Luvah & Vala henceforth you are Servants obey & live / You shall forget your former state return O Love in peace (9:363–64, E 395). Like Ahania, who "cast off her death clothes," Vala and Luvah leave the death-in-life state of the fallen existence of Blake's Eden: "Luvah & Vala descended & enterd the Gates of Dark Urthona / And walkd from the hands of Urizen in the shadows of Valas Garden" (9:375–76, E 395). It is apparent that it is the world of Eden they enter since they have "their ancient golden age renewd" (9:386, E 395). Luvah successfully inspires his counterpart to greater activity:

> She rises among flowers & looks toward the Eastern clearness
> She walks yea runs her feet are wingd on the tops of the bending grass
> Her garments rejoice in the vocal wind & her hair glistens with dew
> [9:390–92, E 395]

The images evoked here are among the most powerful in the poem. For one thing they indicate great velocity: Vala "runs" with "wingd" feet. The latter image is used several times in *The Four Zoas* and harks back to Urizen's "radiant wings" referred to some lines before. "Vocal wind" points ahead a few lines to the expression "vocal harmony" (9:397, E 396), which is also reiterated later in the poem. Furthermore, we can visualize the image of a woman whose "hair glistens with dew," which, in spite of its traditional gender political position with female beauty, also conveys a sense of newfound freshness. By evoking these metaphors of movement in order to picture a female character, actively participating, Blake offers an alternative to the traditional image of woman as passive.

Vala's great and positive activity continues in the following section, "Vala's Garden," where Blake again emphatically uses the word "run" as Vala leads her flocks of lambs forward in a rejoicing mood: "For from my pleasant hills behold the living living springs / Running among my green pastures delighting among my trees" (9:441–42, E 397). It seems, though, that "running" here refers to the "living living springs." However, it is not Vala's speed as such that is the positive activity, rather her significant function at this juncture of the poem. The repetition of the word "living" also emphasizes a dynamic joyful activity.

In the next passage which is important for the issue of female activity, Vala is again displayed, or unveiled, as it were, in beauty as she undresses and wades naked into the river. By taking off her clothes, both in a material substantial sense and in a philosophical symbolical sense, Vala attains true spiritual existence. As Damrosch has clarified: "[W]hereas visible clothes are generally negative symbols (especially Vala's veil), the body itself is a form of clothing, so that although in visual terms nakedness is good, in philosophical terms the true spiritual existence is attained by taking off the garment of the body" (192). In this naked, pure and innocent state she sees a vision of a lonely and miserable Tharmas:

> And on the rivers margin she ungirded her golden girdle
> She stood in the river & viewd herself within the watry glass
> And her bright hair was wet with the waters She rose up from
>   the river
> And as she rose her Eyes were opend to the world of waters
> She saw Tharmas sitting upon the rocks beside the wavy sea
> He strokd the water from his beard & mournd faint through the
>   summer vales
>   [9:480–85, E 398]

In his loneliness Tharmas mourns the absence of his emanation Enion and he calls out to wake her up from eternal sleep:

> Arise O Enion Arise & smile upon my head
> As thou dost smile upon the barren mountains and they rejoice
> When wilt thou smile on Tharmas O thou bringer of golden day
> Arise O Enion arise for Lo I have calmd my seas
>   [9: 491–94, E 398]

As a sign that he is ready to reunite with Enion and await the apocalypse together with her, Tharmas has "calmd [his] seas," the element of which he is the ruler. Vala, who is also prepared for this decisive step, recognizes her own conquered despair in Tharmas and in an empathetic way aids him by invoking Enion: "Then Vala lifted up her hands to heaven to call on Enion" (9:498, E 398).

As Vala's vision continues, the interlude from Tharmas and Enion's childhood follows. This difficult passage has already been discussed, but one line needs to be focused on here. When Vala has managed to wake up the two children, "They rose they went out wandring sometimes together sometimes alone" (9:529, E 399). This is probably the most enigmatic line in what is generally a notoriously difficult section, and it raises two pertinent queries. First, we must question the time-perspective of this line both in relation to the section and to the poem as a whole. The section "Vala's Garden" is a vision within a vision, a dream within the dream of the poem *The Four Zoas*; that two of its main characters suddenly revert back to childhood seems odd only on a superficial level. It is not so odd when we realize that the innocence of the children is evoked here in order to give a tangible intimation of the higher innocence to come in Blake's regained Paradise of Eden at the end of the poem. Odder, I believe, is the relation of this single line to the dialogue it is inserted into. We must at least question the time-perspective that is indicated by the word "sometimes." This word seems to be indicative of a time-span of a longer duration, which is quite a sudden and abrupt intrusion here.

Secondly, the line also questions the stability of gender relations through the two words "together" and "alone," and in this position in the poem signals that Tharmas and Enion as a couple are yet not quite ready for reunion. As we understand later they are still negations in a fallen world, or, as Blake puts it: "They are the shadows of Tharmas & of Enion in Valas world" (9:556, E 400). But, significantly, the great negation Urizen is soon to proclaim the end of time, and the golden feast of human harvest can begin. Finally, then, Enion is ready to rise and cast off her death clothes as she says:

> O Dreams of Death the human form dissolving companied
> By beasts & worms & creeping things & darkness & despair
> The clouds fall off from my wet brow the dust from my cold limbs
> Into the Sea of Tharmas Soon renewd a Golden Moth
> I shall cast off my death clothes & Embrace Tharmas again
> [9: 595–99, E 401]

As the third of the couples in *The Four Zoas* Tharmas and Enion are reunited, which is manifested by Tharmas as "Joy thrilld thro all the furious form of Tharmas humanizing" (9:613, E 401).

Three out of four couples are thus reunited at this point of the poem. However, it is only at the very end of *The Four Zoas* that the final couple, Los and Enitharmon, are reconciled. Even though "The Eternal Man arose" (9:617, E 401) and all are welcomed to the golden feast to drink "the wine of Eternity" (9:619, E 401), man and woman are still separated. Luvah humbly makes the confession that "Attempting to be more than Man We become less" (9:709, E 403), and mankind is thrown into the afflictions of apocalypse in Luvah's wine presses.

It is after humanity has been crushed as human grapes in the wine presses that Enitharmon eventually reappears in the poem. Together, Enitharmon and Los joyfully ascend with her three fellow emanations from the feast to their looms to reweave human bodies, bodies ready to enter the utopia of Eden as the apocalyptic work is now nearly done. At this moment it is only for the regenerated form of Los, Urthona, to complete the apocalyptic work in his corn mills where he grinds all "the distress / Of all the Nations of Earth" (9:807–08, E 406). Henceforth all is rejoicing, and Urthona takes "his repose in Winter in the night of Time" (9:824, E 406), "no longer now / Divided from Enitharmon" (9:849–50, E 407), the last emanation to reunite with her zoa.

Conclusion: The Utopia of The Four Zoas

The reconciliation of the final couple in *The Four Zoas* is not only a reunion—it is a reunion in male-female togetherness. As such it is different from the reconciliation of the other three couples of *The Four Zoas*, and it provides the conclusion to the whole poem. Urthona and Enitharmon enter Eden together in harmony at the closure of the poem, while Urizen/Ahania, Luvah/Vala, and Tharmas/Enion are still in progress towards complete togetherness after their respective reunions. At the end of the poem we can assume, but not be certain, that also the remaining three couples enter Blake's utopia in harmonious togetherness, since all opposites in the poem are by now reconciled. Consequently, the concluding male-female reconciliation of Urthona and Enitharmon may be taken as a metonymic symbolic representation of the reunion of all four zoas with their respective emanations, and at the same time of the communal male-female reunion of all mankind.

Since there is no explicit textual evidence, however, that more than one couple of four reaches the final level of male-female togetherness and enters the utopia of Eden, *The Four Zoas* is not a conclusion to Blake's vision of gender equality, and the open ending of the poem implies a continuation of the task in the two following epics, *Milton* and *Jerusalem*. As three of the couples do not find harmony and togetherness at the end of *The Four Zoas*, the vision is incomplete and the characters are still in progress.

4
The Gender Utopia of *Milton*

At some point, probably around the time of his return to London after the three years at Felpham, Blake abandoned *The Four Zoas* to concentrate on either *Milton* or *Jerusalem*, or both. There are textual indications in *Milton* that this poem was already begun at Felpham where Blake lived between 1800–1803:

> Milton of the land of Albion.
> Should up ascend forward from Felphams Vale & break the
>   Chain
> Of Jealousy from all its roots
>   [22:36–38, E 119]

Further on in the poem Blake even illustrates his rural intermission with a portrait of the cottage where he and his wife lived, and an imaginative description of how Los conducted him there:

> For when Los joind with me he took me in his firy whirlwind
> My Vegetated portion was hurried from Lambeths shades
> He set me down in Felphams Vale & prepard a beautiful
> Cottage for me that in three years I might write all these Visions
>   [36: 23–24, E 137]

This is the most concrete textual evidence of Blake's residence on the south coast, and as a whole, plate 36 is substantially autobiographical. If we consider the designs, we discover that it is into Blake's garden that Milton's emanation Ololon descends. This is even indicated on the plate, where at the bottom in the left-hand corner we can read the engraved inscription "Blakes cottage at Felpham." Anyhow, it is verified by Morton Paley (*Continuing* 3) and other commentators that Blake had produced a substantial amount of material at Felpham which he took back to London when moving home. It is therefore likely that for some time he worked on all three epics before deciding to put most of his effort into finalizing *Milton*.

Milton is something of an amendment to *The Four Zoas*, with its relative limitation as a gender utopian poem. In *The Four Zoas* Blake finds no effective single symbol to represent either the preparatory step towards male-female reunion, or the elevated utopian state of male-female togetherness. In *Milton* Blake finds a superior image to represent the male-female reunion through the male character Milton and his emanation Ololon. Convincingly, Blake allows Ololon, as a six-part character, to represent the three wives and three daughters of the poet John Milton, whose difficulties in relations with women is a sub-theme of *Milton*. The main theme of *Milton* is the journey and descent of the immortal Milton from heaven, Blake's level of Eden, down to earth, Blake's Generation, in search of his female counterpart, the emanation Ololon. This is the superficial story of the first book. Since Milton cannot find her at this lower level, Ololon too has to descend down to earth, which forms the story of the second book. In the finale of *Milton* the two are reunited the moment immediately before apocalypse.

Like *The Four Zoas*, both *Milton* and *Jerusalem* are prophetic utopian poems. At the beginning of *Milton* Blake emphasizes the urgency of his prophecy by numerous repetitions of one crucial phrase: "Mark well my words! They are of your eternal salvation" (1:25; 2: 5, passim). To underline the prophetic aspect of his poem even further Blake introduces a new character, the Bard, to give voice to his ideas in this section at the beginning of *Milton,* popularly called the "Bard's Song." The two later poems relate to *The Four Zoas* in different ways. Inevitably, this circumstance implies that also the relation between *Milton* and *Jerusalem* is quite vital. For one thing, this is corroborated by the likelihood that Blake for some time worked simultaneously on the two manuscripts.

While *Jerusalem* adheres in a more conspicuous way to the apocalyptic structure of *The Four Zoas, Milton* is a pre-apocalyptic poem. Even though it breaks the pattern of fully apocalyptic poems, it remains a development of Blake's gender utopia. This development is mainly manifested in the improved representation of more forcefully active female characters, which more effectively counterbalance the traditional activity of the male characters. Ololon is a new, dynamic female character, whose activity has clear positive ramifications for the outcome of the poem, which has no equal in *The Four Zoas*. It is particularly in this respect that *Milton* is a development of the gender politics from *The Four Zoas*, where we find no single female character as dynamic in activity and portrayed in such a successful way as Ololon. This more vital portrayal of female characters Blake continues in *Jerusalem* where the eponymous heroine of the poem is also a strong female character.

In *Milton*, then, female activity works on a more consistent level than in *The Four Zoas*. It is obvious that this activity is meant to be positive in the long run, bearing in mind the outcome of the poem in the final vision of gender reunion between Milton and Ololon. This is one of the most important aspects of William Blake's poetry—that we have to consider each poem in a holistic mode, viewing the *whole* poem from its final point. It goes without saying that we have to assess his oeuvre as a whole, viewing it from the poetic conclusion in *Jerusalem*.

Another important aspect is that *Milton* is Blake's most personal poem. This is notable on two separate levels. First, as nowhere else in his poetry Blake makes personal references to his own life here, in this case rural Felpham. Secondly, a sub-theme of the poem is the life of the poet John Milton. Blake's general idea is, somewhat ambitiously, to provide a revision of the fateful gender-political errors committed by John Milton in the relations with his three wives and three daughters through the poem bearing the earlier poet's name. It is Blake's view that Milton's unsuccessful gender relations had a negative impact on his poetry. Blake's poem *Milton* is therefore also an attempt to correct the flaws of John Milton's poetry.

It is maybe significant then that *Milton* is a more well-structured poem than *The Four Zoas*, organized into more or less strict units in a synthesis of instant and temporal duration. In *Milton* Blake made no tentative alterations as he did in *The Four Zoas*, but more confidently divided the poem into two books and roughly 50 plates. Of the four known copies of the poem, the last copy completed by Blake consists of 50 plates. Although in these four copies Blake changed the order of some of the plates as well as incorporating new ones, *Milton* seems rather well-planned compared with its predecessor, with its neat division into two books. *Jerusalem* is of course also well-planned and well-structured in this respect, containing 100 plates divided into four chapters.

In *Milton* the apocalypse is not fully achieved and the poem ends, and indeed takes place, at the moment before apocalypse, the eternal moment, "a Pulsation of the Artery" (28:3, E 127). This moment in fact comprises the whole poem, thus again manifesting the metaphorical status of Blake's poetry. Nevertheless, *Milton* is also a gender-utopian poem. From the beginning of *Milton*, Blake continues his gender-utopian theme from *The Four Zoas*. After the epic invocation of the muses Milton's spiritual journey is indicated, and as in *The Four Zoas* the narrative is located in a world of fallen sexuality:

> Record the journey of immortal Milton thro' your Realms
> Of terror & mild moony lustre, in soft sexual delusions
> Of varied beauty, to delight the wanderer and repose
> His burning thirst & freezing hunger!
> [2:2–5, E 96]

The language in this passage is reminiscent of similar images from *The Four Zoas*, and as in the previous poem it indicates the impact of the female characters on the male characters in the poem. At this early point of the poem the images have clearly negative implications, related to the strong sexual power of the female over the male: "mild moony lustre," "soft sexual delusions," "varied beauty," "burning thirst," "freezing hunger." It is one of the aims of the poem to abolish metaphorically these negative expressions of a twisted sexual politics and recover the lost unity and equality of the two sexes. Taking the life of John Milton as a poetic vehicle, Blake, as we shall notice, goes so far as to succeed in reuniting his two main characters, Milton and Ololon, as a result of their demanding spiritual quest.

Even though *Milton* continues the gender-utopian theme from *The Four Zoas*, the expression of gender utopia in *Milton* is quite different. It seems that in *Milton* Blake more and more realizes the urgent need of gender interactivity, and particularly positive female activity, to accomplish his utopian ideas. In contrast to *The Four Zoas* there is constant and productive positive activity, both male and female, throughout the whole poem. The major manifestation of this is the relationship and interactivity between Milton and Ololon in their search for each other in a fallen world.

Accordingly, as in its predecessor, the respective roles and actions of the male and female characters are an important component of Blake's gender utopia. Susan Fox points to the great importance of the dimension of activity and passivity, but strangely enough sees only negative implications for the female sex:

> Throughout the poem females are either passive or pernicious. Females presented positively are passive. Emanations cannot long endure the strife of Eden, Enitharmon is uncomplainingly cut off from full vision by Los, Ololon mourns by her river in Eden and only descends to Generation when she sees Milton there, Catherine is ill in her house. Active females are pernicious: Leutha, Tirzah, the Shadowy Female all create disaster by their actions, which are only imitations of the actions of males anyway, and which need the further actions of males to complete them [214].

As with so many other Blake commentators, Fox is too hasty to classify all female and male characters in one homogeneous way. But Blake's sexual politics is much more complex than that and goes beyond narrow classification. The activity of Leutha, Tirzah and the Shadowy Female is certainly mainly negative, but this is not the case with Ololon. She is in fact one of Blake's most positive female characters and her activity in the poem unquestionably has positive results.

In accordance with Blake's scheme of gender interactivity, the male character counterbalancing Ololon's positive female activity is Milton. It is Milton who initiates the interaction with its positive outcome through his appearance in the poem, when he descends into the left foot of the character Blake. Through this extraordinary idea, poetic inspiration is channelled into one body, or one character. Their fusion is only one in a number of unions in *Milton*. At this stage the character Blake has already merged with the Bard, who is the narrator of the "Bard's Song" between plate 2:25 and plate 13:44, and his poetic persona, the character Los. The most important union, though, is the reunion of Milton and Ololon at the end of the poem.

The Characters of Milton

To develop and improve the structure of his gender utopia from *The Four Zoas* Blake had to launch new symbolic ideas. The structure comprising four zoas and four emanations apparently did not offer that possibility. As an essential complement Blake therefore introduces a number of important new characters. This is one of two major new components in *Milton*; the other is the downright dualistic or parallel structure, based on the two opposed characters Milton and Ololon. While *The Four Zoas* and *Jerusalem* both offer dialectic conclusions by the elevation into a utopian level, *Milton* stops and hovers at the point before apocalyptic transcendence.

Thus the range of characters is different in *Milton* compared with *The Four Zoas*. However, even if Blake does not keep the structure with four male zoas and four corresponding emanations, some of the characters from *The Four Zoas* reappear in *Milton*: Albion, Urizen, Los, Enitharmon, Orc. Neither Tharmas nor Luvah take any active part in the poem. These two zoas are mentioned only a few times, and through Blake's intricate strategy Luvah is generated into Orc who assumes his function. The female characters Enion and Ahania are mentioned only one time each, while there is no reference to Vala at all, although sometimes the rather similar Shadowy Female appears instead. The hasty and complete disappearance of Vala is of course most remarkable, bearing in mind the original title of *The Four Zoas*.

A few significant new characters crucial to the overall paradigm of gender interactivity are introduced in *Milton*: Leutha, Ololon, and Elynittria are all female while Milton, Palamabron, and Rintrah are male. Here we can notice a development in Blake's gender utopia, since we have as many new female as male characters in *Milton*. This may be one of the reasons that the balance of *Milton* is better than *The Four Zoas* from a gender perspective, and that it in fact adheres to the parallel, dualistic structure throughout. The main reason, I believe, for the improved gender politics in *Milton* is the focus on two representative metonymic characters, Milton and Ololon, who are equally strong and active.

ENITHARMON: IMPROVED POSITIVE ACTIVITY

In *The Four Zoas* the activity of the female characters is conspicuous and crucial mainly in the apocalyptic vision of the finale. In *Milton*, on the other hand, female activity is of great importance throughout the poem. This is for instance obvious in the constant activity of Enitharmon, who works diligently at her looms on the occasions she appears in the poem.

Enitharmon is the only one of the four emanations from *The Four Zoas* to take an active part in *Milton*. As in the earlier poem she is the counterpart and emanation of Los and the gender interactivity of the two characters is still important. While the hammer, tongs and anvil are the conventionally male tools of Los, the loom is the traditionally female tool of Enitharmon: "Three Classes are Created by the Hammer of Los, & Woven / By Enitharmons Looms when Albion was slain upon his Mountains" (2–3:26, 1, E 96). Enitharmon's task is similar to the task of Los. Creating the three classes of humanity is obviously one aspect of that task. Often Enitharmon and Los are seen working together:

> Loud sounds the Hammer of Los, loud turn the Wheels of
>   Enitharmon:
> Her Looms vibrate with soft affections, weaving the Web of Life
> Out from the ashes of the Dead; Los lifts his iron Ladles
> With molten ore: he heaves the iron cliffs in his rattling chains
>   [6:27–30, E 100]

As Los hammers out the human forms of the three classes, so Enitharmon weaves their bodies on her looms. What is as obvious here as in *The Four Zoas* is that a masculinist signifying economy, to use Judith Butler's term, very much dominated the discourse of that age, and governed the distribution and representation of the original gender-political ideas even of such a radical thinker as Blake. In his poetry this influence, in varying degrees, can be traced in his way of representing the two sexes through a language that invokes traditional images of the male and the female. In the passage above, for instance, "soft affections" are linked to a female character, Enitharmon, thus cementing the politics of gender.

Compared with *The Four Zoas* the paradigms of gender interactivity and male-female togetherness work at a consistent level throughout *Milton*. Enitharmon and Los keep their unity through the poem, and their degrees of activity do not vary greatly. The activity of Enitharmon and Los in the poem is more carefully planned than in the haphazard structure of *The Four Zoas* and the atmosphere is more harmonious, since in *Milton* we are in "the Universe of Los and Enitharmon" (19:25, E 113). *Milton* has a parallel structure, as Susan Fox has explained, and, accordingly, as Los "physically" departs from the poem at the end of Book I, so does Enitharmon.

Furthermore, while in *The Four Zoas* male-female reunion and togetherness is a significant feature at the time of apocalypse in the final Night, in *Milton* Los and Enitharmon seem to find some kind of togetherness early on in their joint efforts at anvil and loom, respectively. They also manage to maintain this intense co-operative spirit throughout the whole of book one. At the end of the first book, however, they both disappear, only to reappear as two apocalyptic co-workers in the final plate.

That Enitharmon disappears from the poem only to return at the moment before apocalypse in the final plates is reminiscent of *The Four Zoas* where, as we may recall, Enitharmon and Los were one of the four couples to reappear and reunite at the time of the apocalypse. In *Milton* it is to Los and Enitharmon in Eden that the main female representation in the poem, Ololon, descends: "In this Moment Ololon descended to Los & Enitharmon / Unseen beyond the Mundane Shell Southward in Miltons track" (35:46–47, E 136). Overall, Enitharmon is a more positive character in *Milton* than in *The Four Zoas*. Since she is closely linked with the act of creation, and hence to regeneration, her activity clearly has positive connotations, artistic creativity being a major focus in *Milton*. Although without participating as much in *Milton* as in the former poem, Enitharmon, together with Los, is an important character for the progress of gender interactivity in *Milton*. Since Enitharmon is the most negative female character in *The Four Zoas*, her positive impact here is of great significance for the overall development of Blake's gender utopia.

Leutha: Scapegoat Surprised by Sin

It seems that in *Milton* it is Leutha who assumes Enitharmon's symbolic function from *The Four Zoas* as a negative female character. Leutha is an important character since she roughly represents Blake's notion of original sin: "I am the author of this Sin! by my suggestion / My Parent power Satan has committed this transgression" (11:35–36, E 105). This, of course, is reminiscent of Book II of *Paradise Lost* and the very sudden conception within Satan of Sin, as a darting flash which surprisingly issues forth from his head:

> All on a sudden miserable pain
> Surpris'd thee, dim thine eyes, and dizzy swum
> In darkness, while thy head flames thick and fast
> Threw forth, till on the left side op'ning wide,
> Likest to thee in shape and count'nance bright,
> Then shining heav'nly fair, a Goddess arm'd
> Out of thy head I sprung: amazement seiz'd
> All th'Host of Heaven; back they recoil'd afraid
> At first, and call'd me Sin, and for a Sign
> Portentous held me
> [II:752–61]

Concomitantly, Leutha is the most straightforward representation of fallen female sexuality in Blake's poetry. Here she can be compared with Enitharmon in *The Four Zoas* who, as we know, symbolizes the delusive female will as Alicia Ostriker, among others, has pointed out. In contrast, the negative activity of Leutha is directly linked with a male object, the character Palamabron, who is one of several poetic personas of Blake in the poem, and to a female character, Palamabron's emanation Elynittria. Hence, Leutha appropriates the role of a negative female agent. Leutha immediately confesses herself to be the author of Sin and quite blatantly states her reason: "I loved Palamabron & I sought to approach his Tent, / But beautiful Elynittria with her silver arrows repelld me" (11:37–38, E 105). Seemingly a case of classical *crime passionel*, where Palamabron's emanation Elynittria is furious with jealousy, it provokes Leutha into even more intrigues further on in the poem.

In Blake's adaptation of the episode from *Paradise Lost* Leutha takes possession in Satan's brain, transferring her love for Palamabron to Satan:

> This to prevent, entering the doors of Satans brain night after night
> Like sweet perfumes I stupified the masculine perceptions
> And kept only the feminine awake. hence rose his soft
> Delusory love to Palamabron: admiration join'd with envy
> [12:4–7, E 105]

Possibly the most complex of the many male-female relations in Blake's poetry, the pair Satan and Leutha provide an important example of the negative results of a relationship where one side dominates the other, thereby draining the counterpart of all energy. In plate 12 Leutha as Sin gains complete control over her symbiotic companion Satan through delusive sexual strategies. This plate is quite complicated to follow since Leutha as Sin has taken her place within Satan, and Satan somehow becomes Leutha and by force performs her dirty tricks. Satan cannot handle the situation: "Satan astonishd, and with power above his own controll" (12:16, E 106). Leutha, however, continues her confessional and immediately takes the blame:

> I form'd the Serpent
> ....
> To do unkind things in kindness! with power armd, to say

> The most irritating things in the midst of tears and love
> These are the stings of the Serpent!
> [12:29; 32–34, E 106]

Through her act of betrayal she leads Satan on to his deluded love for Palamabron. His emanation Elynittria naturally turns against Satan, in a representative example of the result of negative female activity in a fallen existence:

> Soon
> Day sunk and Palamabron return'd, trembling I hid myself
> In Satans inmost Palace of his nervous fine wrought Brain:
> For Elynittria met Satan with all her singing women.
> Terrific in their joy & pouring wine of wildest power
> They gave Satan their wine: indignant at their burning wrath.
> Wild with prophetic fury his former life became like a dream
> Cloth'd in the Serpent's folds, in selfish holiness demanding
>   purity
> Being most impure, self-condemn'd to eternal tears, he drove
> Me from his inmost Brain & the doors clos'd with thunders
>   sound
> O Divine Vision who didst create the Female: to repose
> The Sleepers of Beulah: pity the repentant Leutha.
> [12:39–50, E 106]

Again, lack of balance and domination in a male-female relation proves disastrous, leading to separation of the two counterparts. As in similar passages in *The Four Zoas*, Blake uses the female here as a kind of catalyst for faults committed by male and female alike. Therefore Leutha is one of Blake's most important female characters, a fact sometimes neglected by critics.

Elynitttria: Passive and Forgiving Emanation

Since the gender utopia of *Milton* is more elaborate than that of *The Four Zoas*, Blake contrasts the negative female activity of Leutha with the positive female activity of Elynittria. As Blake is to emphasize to a greater extent in *Jerusalem*, the forgiveness of sins is one of the foremost means of accomplishing the gender equality of the utopia of Eden. Accordingly, Elynittria actively approaches Leutha in order to forgive her:

> But Elynittria met Leutha in the place where she was hidden.
> And threw aside her arrows, and laid down her sounding Bow;
> She sooth'd her with soft words & brought her to Palamabrons bed
> In moment new created for delusion, interwoven round about
> [13:36–39, E 107]

With this act of compassion, the "Bard's Song" ends. Blake lets the inspired Bard conclude his song with an evocation of the positive alternative force—the unselfish forgiveness of sins, with Elynittria soothing the sinner Leutha, in the humanist path of Jesus. Through this, mankind takes one step further towards the utopia of Eden. It even suggests a gender utopia with shared sexual pleasures, indicated by the sudden appearance of Oothoon, the female advocate of a liberal view of sexuality from *Visions of the Daughters of Albion*: "Leutha lived / In Palamabron's Tent and Oothoon was her charming guard" (13:44, E 107). This is all the more remarkable bearing in mind that commentators, notably Leopold Damrosch, have claimed that Blake's Eden lacks sexual expression.

The Bard's Song is the only part of *Milton* where Elynittria is active. Or, rather, passive, since Elynittria is in fact one of the few female characters in the three long poems that fits into the scheme proposed by so many commentators that a female character in Blake's poetry is passive and good. For example, there is one scene in *Milton* where Elynittria most tolerantly puts aside her natural jealousy and goodheartedly forgives her counterpart Palamabron's infidelity, bringing his mistress Leutha to his bed.

Many critics have believed that this scene and the whole Bard's song reflect Blake's private life. And knowing that *Milton* is his most personal poem, there might be some foundation in this idea. Since *Milton* was partly composed in the Felpham years, where then the character Palamabron is a representation of Blake who has a hard time fighting the urizenic directives of his patron William Hayley in the form of the character Satan. This would make Elynittria into Blake's wife Catherine. Due to our lack of knowledge of Blake's biography, this will all inevitably remain speculation with more or less qualified guesses. However, if we are to continue to be somewhat speculative, I would like to suggest that some of the components in the Bard's song were actually fetched from earlier years in Blake's life. Adhering to poetic licence, I believe that Blake went back in time some ten years and that we are to find some clues to the Bard's song in the context of the Joseph Johnson circle. It is at that time we find Blake uncertain about his emotional life and he seems to be sexually, and intellectually, tempted by some other woman, or even women, for instance the two Marys, Hays and Wollstonecraft. It is then that Catherine has good reason to suffer from jealousy, and eventually has to take a tolerant stance towards her husband, something which has obviously been put into Elynittria.

OLOLON: ACTIVE AND POSITIVE SYMBOLIC INVENTION

While the first of Blake's new female characters in *Milton*, Leutha, already departs from the poem in plate 13, the second, Ololon, only enters in book two. Ololon is the emanation of Milton and, adhering to the dualistic structure of the poem, Book I belongs to Milton and Book II to Ololon. As we already know, the first book describes Milton's descent from heaven to the generative world and, accordingly, the second book describes the descent of Ololon.

Ololon is the most important character addition to *Milton* compared to *The Four Zoas*. Together with the character Jerusalem in the poem of that name and Oothoon in *Visions of the Daughters of Albion*, she is the most positive female character in Blake's poetry. At the same time as these three are positive characters, they are active, in stark contradistinction to the traditional view of Blake criticism that a positive female character is passive.

Even though she does not appear at this stage of the poem, already in Book I Ololon realizes the problems of her counterpart Milton in the fallen world. At this early point she therefore decides to descend:

> Milton goes to Eternal Death!
> ....
> And Ololon said, Let us descend also, and let us give
> Ourselves to death in Ulro among the Transgressors.
> [21:43–46, E 116]

But for quite a few plates Ololon is a passive character. She laments for Milton during the rest of the book, and it is only in Book II that she becomes active and descends materially. In contrast to Milton's descent, Ololon's descent is made in two steps. At first to Blake's third level; and thus "into this pleasant Shadow Beulah, all Ololon descended" (31:8, E 130). Ololon's descent at this moment is a portent of the utopia of Eden:

> O how the Starry Eight rejoic'd to see Ololon descended!
> And now that a wide road was open to Eternity,
> By Ololons descent thro Beulah to Los & Enitharmon.
> [35:34–36, E 135]

The moment of Ololon's descent is an important event in Blake's gender utopia. Its great importance is emphasized by the unconventional use of time. In one single moment the poet's work, the poem *Milton*, is done and it is in this prophetic instant that Ololon descends:

> There is a Moment in each Day that Satan cannot find
> Nor can his Watch Fiends find it, but the Industrious find
> This Moment & it multiply. & when it once is found
> It renovates every Moment of the Day if rightly placed[.]
> In this Moment Ololon descended to Los & Enitharmon
> Unseen beyond the Mundane Shell Southward in Miltons track
> [35:42–47, E 136]

Accordingly, Ololon's search for Milton occurs at the same moment as his search for her.

Milton is Blake's most personal poem and Ololon now, almost literally, as a tangible portent descends into his garden in his residence at rural Felpham:

> Walking in my Cottage Garden, sudden I beheld
> The Virgin Ololon & address'd her as a Daughter of Beulah[:]
> Virgin of Providence fear not to enter into my Cottage
> What is thy message to thy friend: What am I now to do
> Is it again to plunge into deeper affliction? behold me
> Ready to obey, but pity thou my Shadow of Delight
> Enter my Cottage, comfort her, for she is sick with fatigue
> [36:26–32, E 137]

Probably nowhere else in Blake's poetry can we find such a direct personal reference. It seems that Blake had domestic problems related to the issue of gender interactivity. Worried about his own female Shadow of Delight, his wife Catherine Blake, he introduces the character Ololon as a vehicle in his poem to seek to solve his dilemma. We know that Catherine frequently, and sometimes Blake himself, lay ill in bed during the last year of their residence at Felpham. This is one of the most important passages in the poem since Blake, through this peculiar mixture of fiction and autobiography, makes *Milton* a much more "ordinary" and matter-of-fact, or rather down-to-earth, poem than *The Four Zoas*, and *Jerusalem*, particularly. These lines are important also since from this moment Ololon finds herself on the same level of existence as her counterpart Milton, and from then on she can substantially start her factual search for him. It is at the advent of the apocalypse in the final plates of *Milton* that Ololon is most significant as a utopian character. There she reunites with her counterpart Milton to await the apocalypse.

Furthermore, and importantly so, the character Ololon is probably Blake's greatest symbolic invention. Although Ololon is a female character, Blake refers to this character with plural pronouns: "our," "us," "we," "they."[16] In fact, Ololon is a six-part character, Milton's six-fold emanation Ololon, consisting of John Milton's three wives and three daughters. Through the symbol Ololon Blake covers and explores the problematic levels of all six women in John Milton's life inclusively in one single character, in "the multitudes of Ololon" (35:37, E 135). By the use of Ololon and John Milton's female relations as poetic vehicles Blake also incorporates his own personal problems into the material.

Los: Inspiration Retained

Los is the most important of the characters from *The Four Zoas* also to participate in *Milton*. As Los roughly represents poetic inspiration, the character symbolizes one of the main themes of the poem very well, the creative process itself. Already in plate 3 Los has begun his mission of poetic creation, with the same artistic tools as in *The Four Zoas*: "Los siezd his Hammer & Tongs; he labourd at his resolute Anvil" (3:7, E 96).

In *Milton* Blake defines the difference between the threefold Beulah and the fourfold Eden, outlining the sexual/human distinction: "The Sexual is Threefold: the Human is Fourfold" (3: 5).[17] To enter the

---

[16] *Feminine desire has often been referred to as polymorphous and even polyphonic, and in line with this Rita Felski claims that "[t]he celebration of 'feminine' desire as plural, spontaneous, chaotic, and mysteriously 'other' itself reiterates and is easily assimilated into a long-standing cultural symbolization of woman in Western society" (37). Here Blake can be said to be a forerunner and two centuries ahead of some contemporary feminist critics with their insistence on the use of neutral pronouns. Anne K. Mellor points to the feminist writer Marge Piercy as an outstanding example with her use of the pronoun "per," in* A Woman on the Edge of Time, *referring to both male and female persons. ("Blake's Portrayal of Women" 154) It is Mellor's argument that Blake fails to transform his use of language, but compared with Blake's Ololon Piercy's device seems rather insignificant.*

[17] *This plate is not included in E. Plates 2(b) and 3(a) only appear in copies C and D of* Milton.

fourfold level of Blake's gender utopia Eden one of the obstacles, the three classes of men, must be abolished, and this is part of Los's inspired task. To accomplish this task Los labours on in his London forge: "Loud sounds the Hammer of Los, & loud his Bellows is heard / Before London to Hampsteads breadths & Highgates heights" (6:8–9, E 99). Los continues his inspired labour all through the first book of *Milton*, much resembling the Los of *The Four Zoas*, working to redeem mankind from the fall. As always, increased activity is the hallmark of Los's labour:

> So Los said, Henceforth Palamabron, let each his own station
> Keep: nor in pity false, nor in officious brotherhood, where
> None needs, be active. Mean time Palamabrons horses.
> Rag'd with thick flames redundant, & the Harrow maddend with
>   fury.
> Trembling Palamabron stood, the strongest of Demons trembled:
> Curbing his living creatures; many of the strongest Gnomes,
> They bit in their wild fury, who also madden'd like wildest
>   beasts
> Mark well my words; they are of your eternal salvation
>   [5:41–48, E 101]

Condemning the negative passive "officious brotherhood" of organized state-religion, Los visualizes the individual activity of Palamabron's raging horses, the fury of the harrow and the wild fury of "the strongest Gnomes" as the means to redemption. To underline the importance of his message Blake repeats the last line no less than seven times in the first eleven plates of *Milton*. It is also of significance that the number in this context is the symbolically important number seven.

In spite of this, the Los of *Milton* is not the Los of *The Four Zoas*. The best illustration of the alteration is Los's descent into the soul of the first-person narrator, the character Blake, in plate 22. His descent forebodes the advent of Blake's utopian version of the biblical millennium of peace. Humanity's struggle through six thousand years is ended with the inauguration of the millennium:

> I am that Shadowy Prophet who Six Thousand Years ago
> Fell from my station in the Eternal bosom. Six Thousand Years
> Are finishd. I return! both Time & Space obey my will.
>   [22:15–17, E 117]

Los's union with Blake, and consequently also with the character Milton, who at this instant is already united with the character Blake, is one of many examples of the great importance of unity not only in *Milton* but in Blake's gender utopia as a whole. Through these unions, either spiritual unions as in this passage or gender reunions, humanity takes a symbolic step towards a utopian existence through Blake's poetry.

As in *The Four Zoas,* Los in *Milton* is one of the most notable apocalyptic agents. As we have already seen, he exits from the poem at the end of the first book and does not reappear until the last few pre-apocalyptic plates. In the final plate he is one of several harbingers of the apocalypse:

> And Los & Enitharmon rose over the Hills of Surrey:
> Their clouds roll over London with a south wind, soft Oothoon
> Pants in the Vales of Lambeth weeping oer her Human Harvest
> Los listens to the Cry of the Poor Man: his Cloud
> Over London in volume terrific, low bended in anger.
> [42:31–35, E 144]

At this point the poem is on the very verge of the apocalypse which, in contrast to *The Four Zoas* and *Jerusalem,* never occurs in *Milton,* as we shall shortly see.

As a paradoxical character in terms of presence/absence the Los of *Milton* resembles three of the emanations from *The Four Zoas*: Ahania, Enion and Enitharmon. These three female characters depart early from the poem, cast out from the garden of innocence, as it were. From then on although absent as positive emanations, they are however present and act as negated female wills for almost the entire poem. Like Los in *Milton* they only resurface as emanations in the final Night just in time for the apocalypse, to reunite with their male counterparts. In *Milton,* by contrast, Los is never reconciled with his emanation, Enitharmon, and the apocalypse is never completed in this poem.

Urizen/Satan: Inspiration Negated

Of the remaining characters from Blake's first epic, Los's adversary Urizen is the most active. Significantly, he enters *Milton* bound up in the "forg'd manacles" of his reasoning mind: "Urizen lay in darkness & solitude, in chains of the mind lock'd up" (3:6, E 96). Compared with *The Four Zoas* Urizen is a more evil and negative character in *Milton.* To emphasize his negated status Blake equates him with Satan: "Then Los & Enitharmon knew that Satan is Urizen / Drawn down by Orc & the Shadowy Female into Generation" (10:1–2, E 104). In doing so

Blake also lets Satan descend into the fallen world to become a vehement antagonist of his character Blake and, as the characters merge, also of Milton and Los. The battle between man/Milton and demon/Urizen thus takes its beginning:

> Urizen emerged from his Rocky Form & from his Snows,
> And he also darkend his brows: freezing dark rocks between
> The footsteps. and infixing deep the feet in marble beds:
> That Milton labourd with his journey, & his feet bled sore
> Upon the clay now chang'd to marble; also Urizen rose,
> And met him on the shores of Arnon; & by the streams of the
>   brooks
>
>   [18–19:51, 1–5, E 112]

The struggle between Milton and Urizen, or Satan, continues throughout the whole poem. In *Milton* Satan is the more important aspect of this negative dual character, and he is in fact a manifestation of the fallen Urizen, as Damrosch correctly has stated (294).

Towards the end of the poem Milton realizes the urgent need to eliminate his antagonist in order to be able to reach the state in which he can unite with his lost emanation:

> In the Eastern porch of Satan's Universe Milton stood & said:
> Satan! my Spectre! I know my power thee to annihilate
> And be a greater in thy place & be thy Tabernacle
> A covering for thee to do thy will, till one greater comes
> And smites me as I smote thee & becomes my covering
>   [38:28–32, E 139]

At this point in the poem, just before the apocalypse, the positive force Milton overcomes the negative force Satan to prepare for the second coming of "one greater." The negation of spectres must be replaced, in the terminology of *The Four Zoas*, by zoas and emanations in time for the gender reunion.

In spite of showing some characteristics reminiscent of the Satan of *Paradise Lost*, Satan in *Milton* is a representation of the morally censorious and law-proclaiming God whom Blake equates with Urizen. Urizen/Satan in *Milton* is surely a development, and while Urizen in *The Four Zoas* enquires, "Am I not God ... Who is equal to me" (3:106, E 328), Satan in *Milton* self-assuredly certifies: "[I] am God alone / There is no other! let all obey my principles of moral individuality" (9:25–26, E 103).

This may of course also be compared to Satan in *Paradise Lost*, as he plans his vengeance on God:

> To bow and sue for grace
> With suppliant knee, and deify his power
> Who from the terror of this arm so late
> Doubted his empire—that were low indeed;
> That were an ignominy and shame beneath
> This downfall
> [I:111–16]

However, after roughly half the poem it is not difficult to realize that John Milton has no intention of making Satan a good character. Blake's Satan in *Milton*, on the other hand, is a fallen and negative character from his very first entrance in the poem, in accordance with Blake's allegorical scheme of the fall as original sin.

Paradoxically enough, in *Milton* the activity of Satan ceases at an early stage and he more or less withdraws from the poem: "He sunk down a dreadful Death, unlike the slumbers of Beulah" (9:48, E 103). His fall is further confirmed: "Satan is fall'n from his station & never can be redeem'd" (11:19, E 105). He is, in a manner of speaking, redeemed by his emanation Leutha, who unselfishly takes his blame upon herself, and even enters his brain. Urizen/Satan's only further function in *Milton* is as the spectre or negation of Milton, and as such he is annihilated in the finale of the poem when all negations have to be destroyed before the apocalypse.

Orc: Revolutionary Inspiration

In *The Four Zoas* Orc is only a minor character, but in *Milton* he assumes larger proportions. As a representation of the revolutionary artistic spirit Orc, together with Los, becomes the natural enemy of Urizen/Satan. Already at the inception of the three characters there is an indication of how the relations between them will develop: "First Orc was Born then the Shadowy Female: then All Los's Family / At last Enitharmon brought forth Satan" (3:40–41, E 97).

Both in *The Four Zoas* and *Milton* Orc is the son of Los and Enitharmon as, according to this passage, is also Satan. Further on in the poem Blake writes that "[S]atan is the Spectre of Orc & Orc is the generate Luvah" (29:34, E 127). This might be logical since a spectre is the negative fallen aspect of a male character. More difficult to grasp at once is that Orc is the generate, lower aspect of Luvah. As in *The Four Zoas,* Orc is the representation of this character in the fallen world, while Luvah is the eternal aspect belonging to Blake's utopia of Eden. More obvious throughout *Milton,* though, is that the Shadowy Female is the emanation of Orc. Her eternal aspect is Vala, the emanation of Luvah. "Orc's consort," Damon explains, "is the Shadowy Female, who is this material world—a lower form of Luvah's Emanation, Vala" (309).

In the fallen world of *Milton* Luvah of *The Four Zoas* becomes Orc. Luvah is only briefly mentioned in *Milton,* then only manifesting his close relation to "Orc, who is Luvah" (18:1, E 111). His sole importance, in a recapitulation of the events from *The Four Zoas,* is as the usurper of Urizen:

> But when Luvah assum'd the World of Urizen to the South:
> And Albion was slain upon his mountains, & in his tent;
> All fell towards the Center in dire ruin, sinking down.
> [19:19–21, E 112]

These lines might be an indication of the negative role Orc will have in *Jerusalem,* where he assumes some of the functions of Urizen, who has no part in that poem.

Also reminding us of the utopian eternal existence which we get some retrospective glimpses of in *The Four Zoas,* is the moment when Orc tries to prevent his emanation from entering the fallen world of Generation:

> Orc answerd. Take not the Human Form O loveliest. Take not
> Terror upon thee! Behold how I am & tremble lest thou also
> Consume in my Consummation; but thou maist take a Form
> Female & lovely
>
> ....
> When thou attemptest to put on the Human Form, my wrath
> Burns to the top of heaven against thee in Jealousy & Fear.
> Then I rend thee asunder, then I howl over thy clay & ashes
> When wilt thou put on the Female Form as in times of old
> With a Garment of Pity & Compassion like the Garment of God
> [18:26–29, 31–35, E 111–12]

Blake juxtaposes the sexual connotations of two levels here, the fallen existence in Generation in which Vala becomes the Shadowy Female, and the utopian existence in Eden where "Pity & Compassion" are the hallmarks of the female. In Eden Orc sees woman as "Female & lovely," while in a fallen human world his love turns into wrath because of "Jealousy & Fear."

Palamabron: Compassionate and Redeemed Character

In *Milton* Blake launches the concept of the three classes. Like so much in Blake this has a religious foundation: "In Calvinist theology, the three classes of the elect, redeemed, and reprobate are those who are predestined to receive grace from God and go to heaven, those who have received (or are capable of obtaining) grace, and those who are damned" (*Milton,* Essick and Viscomi, ed. 122). *Milton* is the only Blake poem where this idea is exhaustively used. Here Blake figures this concept to be a development of his dualism from the earlier poetry, and he states: "Hence the three Classes of Men take their fix'd destinations. / They are the Two Contraries & the Reasoning Negative" (5:13–14, E 98). He was later to refine this development in *Jerusalem* by positing his definite representation of the four levels of existence: Ulro, Generation, Beulah, Eden.

The concept of the three classes is mainly used in the first book of *Milton,* particularly in the Bard's song. It is also this section which has been considered as the most autobiographical in the poem, in which some of the characters correspond to Blake's own contemporary social environment. This is true for the two companion characters Palamabron and Rintrah, who reflect two sides of the personality of William Blake. Palamabron is the most Blake-like, representing the poet and more specifically his compassion and pity, which is reflected in his tolerant and forgiving emanation Elynittria. Of the three classes this character is among the redeemed.

To Palamabron belongs his raging horses, with wild activity:

> So Los said: Henceforth, Palamabron, let each his own station
> Keep: nor in Pity false, nor in officious brotherhood, where
> None needs, be active. Mean time Palamabron's horses
> Rag'd with thick flames redundant, & the Harrow madden'd
>   with fury
> Trembling Palamabron stood; the strongest of Demons trembled,
> Curbing his living creatures; many of the strongest Gnomes
> They bit in their wild fury, who also madden'd like wildest
>   beasts.
>
>   [7:43–50, E 101]

That Palamabron is "the strongest of demons" is opposed to his piteous and mild side. In *The Four Zoas* he is said to be "good naturd" (8:391, E 381). Seemingly incompatible, this again demonstrates the great complexity of Blake's characters in the long epic poems. The passage also emphatically shows the urgency of activity.

If we are to follow the biographical interpretation of *Milton*, then Blake in the representation of Palamabron has serious arguments of disagreement with Hayley/Satan. Palamabron pins down Satan's deceitfulness: "You know Satan's mildness and his self-imposition / Seeming a brother, being a tyrant, even thinking himself a brother / While he is murdering the just" (7:23–5, E 100). But the hypocritical Satan returns the accusation: "Satan wept / And mildly cursing Palamabron, him accus'd of crimes / Himself had wrought" (7:35–7, E 101). The dispute is linked to certain women with key-functions in this context. That it is of a serious nature is obvious since the end of the Bard's song presents the first apex of the poem when Blake, the narrator, lets his character Milton leave heaven in order to find his six-fold emanation Ololon, and symbolically correct the serious mistakes he committed to his three wives and three daughters.

Rintrah: Energetic and Reprobate Character

Also the relations between the characters are complex. If Palamabron is of a compassionate nature, Rintrah represents energy in the form of wrath. We immediately understand this as Rintrah is the first character to be introduced in *The Marriage of Heaven and Hell:* "Rintrah roars & shakes his fires in the burden'd air" (2:1, E 33) Palamabron and Rintrah are among the great number of contrasting characters of the same sex, working well together by complementing each other, by providing different personality-traits. In line with the Rintrah-Palamabron character division, Rintrah unlike his twin-brother belongs to the reprobate class. In *Milton* we early notice the particulars of Rintrah and his propensity for instant wrath: "Till Satan had assum'd Rintrahs wrath in the day of mourning / In a feminine delusion of false pride self-deciev'd" (11:25–6, E 105). Since Rintrah is also associated with fire, his connection with Satan is not all that surprising.

Just like the two female characters Vala and Jerusalem collaborate and complement each other in *Jerusalem,* Rintrah and Palamabron work together in *Milton.* They rise to activity when the Bard has ceased his song and when, significantly, the inspired positive characters of the poem are symbolically united. Since Palamabron and Rintrah are two of Los's four sons, they also work in unison with their father. Los is at this point of the poem already merged with the Bard and now finally descends into the character, and even the poet/narrator, Blake (22:4–14, E 116–17). To rectify the errors committed by fallen sexuality and thus redeem mankind from corrupt sexual expressions, the character Milton is sent down to Generation to find his emanation Ololon to symbolically reconcile with her. Los directs him thus: "Milton of the land of Albion / Should up ascend forward from Felpham's Vale & break the Chain / Of Jealousy from all its roots" (23:36–8, E 119). Los then takes command and spurs his two sons on:

> [B]e patient therefore, O my Sons!
> These lovely Females form sweet night and silence and secret
> Obscurities to hide from Satan's Watch-Fiends Human loves
> And graces
>   [23:38–41, E 119]

 The rest of Book One of *Milton* abounds with sexual symbolism, hitherto not recognized and commented on at any length to my knowledge. One reason for this critical negligence, I believe, is the predominant focus on the Bard's song in the analytical comments of the poem. Read carefully, however, the last six plates open up a rich source of refences to the beauty of male and female bodies, and particularly the genitals. Thanks to Keri Davies's recent ground-breaking archival discoveries this can now easily be referred to Blake's Moravian family background, a religious orientation that venerated the sexual reproductive organs like no other. A "Moravian" interpretation of the text in these plates can also, in my view, be strengthened by analysing some of the illustrations. For instance, in plate 23 we see five human figures. To be a work by Blake, it is here uncommonly easy to notice that three of them are female characters, for one thing indicated by the marked declivities between their legs and distinctly drawn female breasts on at least one of them, and that two are unusually muscular male characters. This corresponds well with the text of the plate.

 Most of these symbols have their origin in Blake's, or rather Los's, city of "Art & Manufacture" (24:50, E 120), Golgonooza. This city is most elaborately described in *Jerusalem*, where plates 12 and 13 give a detailed account of this place, which is of course close to Blake's edenic city Jerusalem. Since Blake in *Milton* writes about "Jerusalem's Inner

Court, Lambeth" (25:48, E 122), we may rather safely draw some parallels between Jerusalem and Golgonooza, amply described in much of the text in these plates, and Jerusalem and Blake's own home in Lambeth, the residence which saw him more productive than any other.

As so frequently elsewhere in the three epics, Blake in the final plates of the first Book proposes sexuality as the salvation of mankind. Like so many times in world art, the body of woman is represented as the vehicle to the liberation through the sexual act. Cathedron, the female body, is situated at Los's palace at the centre of Golgonooza. If one enters into Cathedron, delightful and magnificent bodies are reproduced:

> And Every Generated Body in its inward form
> Is a garden of delight & a building of magnificence
> ....
> Continually woven in the Looms of Enitharmon's Daughters
> In bright Cathedron's golden Dome with care & love & tears
> [26:31–2; 35–6, E 123]

The entrance to the pleasures of Cathedron is Luban, the vagina/the cunt. If one accepts these definitions, a reading of the glorious sexual intercourse between man and woman unfolds in the following lines. To begin with, Antamon signifies the semen: "Antamon takes them into his beautiful flexible hands: / As the Sower takes the seed or as the Artist his clay" (28:13–14, E 126). The penis is then ready to penetrate the vagina: "But Theotormon & Sotha stand in the Gate of Luban anxious ... they create the crested Cock" (28:21; 24, E 126). In spite of the hesitation, the intercourse is accomplished, with the cock-cunt symbolism continued:

> [H]ardening it into a bone
> Opake and like the black pebble on the enraged beach
> While the poor indigent is like the diamond which, tho' cloth'd
> In rugged covering in the mine is open all within
> And in his hallow'd center holds the heavens of bright eternity.
> [28:34–38, E 126]

"The diamond"/cunt is concealed by the "rugged covering"/pubic hair, but the hardened "bone"/cock still manages to find the hole of "the mine"/cunt to experience the bliss of "the heavens of bright eternity" in the "hallow'd center" of the depth of the vagina.

Sexual intercourse, then, leads to "the heavens of bright eternity" at the spur of the Moment, the well-known Pulsation of the Artery (28:47; 29: 3, E 126; 127):

> And between every two Moments stands a Daughter of Beulah
> To feed the Sleepers on their Couches with maternal care.
> And every Minute has an azure Tent with silken Veils:
> And every Hour has a bright golden Gate carved with skill:
> And every Day & Night has Walls of brass & Gates of adamant
> Shining like precious Stones & ornamented with appropriate
>   signs
>
> [28:48–53, E 126]

Again, the genital metaphors are abundant: "Tent" and "golden Gate" for the vagina and "silken Veils" for the surrounding pubic hair. Further on it seems that Blake has retained some of Wollstonecraft's, or his own, ideas of "free love":

> The Starry heavens reach no further, but here bend and set
> On all sides, & the two Poles turn on their valves of gold
> And if he move his dwelling-place, his heavens also move
> Where'er he goes, & all his neighbourhood bewail his loss.
> Such are the Spaces called Earth & such its dimension.
>
> [29:10–14, E 127]

Mankind has scented the redemption of the apocalypse and its subsequent edenic existence, even "in the Nerves of the Nostrils" (29:35, E 128), denoting love and emotions. But it is still a fallen world, where fallen sexuality is dominant:

> But Enitharmon and her Daughters take the pleasant charge
> To give them to their lovely heavens till the Great Judgment Day
> Such is their lovely charge. But Rahab & Tirzah pervert
> Their mild influences
>
> [29: 51–54, E 128]

Thus, the narrator Blake must find the means to set things right. That is why he lets Ololon descend to Milton's level in the second Book of the poem.

Significantly, Palamabron and Rintrah end *Milton* together, as all living forms stand prepared for apocalypse: "Rintrah & Palamabron view the Human Harvest beneath" (42:36, E 144). Like all other positive symbols they reappear as harbingers before the apocalypse.

MILTON: REDEEMING BARD

In order to correct what the author Blake saw as errors committed by John Milton during his lifetime, he lets the character Milton descend into the character Blake's left foot. Having made fatal errors in the emotional field during his lifetime, thereby destroying the relations with his three wives and three daughters, Milton, through his union with the character Blake, assumes earthly form in order to correct his errors. In his poetry he had not been visionary enough, but rather gave in too easily to the destructive principles of reason. In family matters he had had great problems in his relations with his three wives and his three daughters.

Milton's task is defined at the beginning of the first book:

> Say first! what mov'd Milton, who walkd about in Eternity
> One hundred years, pondring the intricate mazes of Providence
> Unhappy tho in heav'n, he obey'd, he murmur'd not. he was
>   silent
> Viewing his Sixfold Emanation scatter'd thro the deep
> In torment! To go into the deep her to redeem & himself perish?
>   [2:16–20, E 96]

Accordingly, the first part of Milton's task is to restore, and improve, his relations with the female sex. The Sixfold Emanation Ololon is the central female character in this scheme, since she incorporates all six Milton's women.

The central character of the second part of Milton's task is the Bard. Most noteworthy the Bard is in "the Bard's Song":

> What cause at length mov'd Milton to this unexampled deed[?]
> A Bards prophetic Song! for sitting at eternal tables,
> Terrific among the Sons of Albion in chorus solemn & loud
> A Bard broke forth! all sat attentive to the awful man.
>   [2:21–24, E 96]

Through the Bard, Milton is to correct his poetic errors under Blake's guidance. This task of correction becomes Milton's own through the union Bard/Blake/Milton and, later in the poem, also Los. The Bard ceases his song in plate 13 and "the loud voic'd Bard terrify'd took refuge in Miltons bosom" (14:9, E 108).

It is obvious at once to Milton that the apocalypse must be imminent: "When will the Resurrection come; to deliver the sleeping body / From corruptibility" (14:17–18, E 108). The situation appears so desperate to Milton that he poses perhaps the most central question of the entire poem:

> What do I here before the Judgment? without my Emanation?
> With the daughters of memory, & not with the daughters of inspiration[?]
> [14:28–29, E 108]

The main reason for his despair is that he has been separated from his emanation Ololon, something not obvious to Milton this early in the poem. In the fallen existence that he has now become part of, "the daughters of inspiration" have been changed to the negation "the daughters of memory." For the rest of the poem Milton tries to amend his existence, starting with his search for Ololon in book one. Possibly this is also a biographical reference to John Milton's problematic relations with his three daughters. In Milton's view, his own daughters would certainly be "daughters of memory" rather than "daughters of inspiration."

Significantly, the first conflict the character Milton deals with is the gender issue. Confronting his six women, Milton draws them down to his own present human level:

> In those three females whom his Wives, & those three whom his Daughters
> Had represented and containd, that they might be resum'd
> By giving up of Selfhood: & they distant view'd his journey
> In their eternal spheres, now Human, tho' their Bodies remain clos'd
> In the dark Ulro till the Judgment: also Milton knew: they and
> Himself was Human, tho' now wandering thro Death's Vale
> In conflict with those Female forms, which in blood & jealousy
> Surrounded him, dividing & uniting without end or number.
> [17:1–8, E 110]

This is of course on a superficial level a biographical comment on the life of John Milton. Through the device of making the long dead Milton return to human life, the level of the author William Blake, to sort out his unsettled affairs, Blake finds an unorthodox way of commenting on and analysing his own mundane difficulties. Therefore Milton

> [s]aw the Cruelties of Ulro, and he wrote them down
> In iron tablets: and his Wives & Daughters names were these
> Rahab and Tirzah, & Milcah & Malah & Noah & Hoglah.
> [17:9–11, E 110]

In this parody of God's promulgation of the Decalogue in Exodus Blake uses the biblical names of Zelophehad's daughters to represent Milton's six women. Blake thereby manifests the divine and basic character of his/Milton's/humanity's difficulty in gender relations. In an earthly existence the God-given law is impossible to transgress.

The daughters of Zelophehad are important symbols in this context, not only because they represent Milton's wives and daughters. Since they are six in number, the connection with Milton's Sixfold Emanation Ololon is evident. However, they are isolated negated female wills, and as such, representations of Blake's view of what happens to the female, and the male, when separated from their counterparts. One of Zelophehad's daughters, Tirzah, together with the additional character Rahab, symbolizes the ultimate female negation in Blake's poetry.

Blake lets Milton take an active part in the poem to perform the task of awakening mankind in time for the approaching apocalypse:

> And they lamented that they had in wrath & fury & fire
> Driven Milton into the Ulro; for now they know too late
> That it was Milton the awakener: they had not heard the Bard
> [21:31–33, E 116]

As we have seen before, male and female activity is a crucial step in the movement towards the male-female reunion proclaiming apocalypse and utopia. In the fallen world, though, the inhabitants "had not heard the Bard."

However, it is only in the first book that Milton is really active. In the second it is Milton's emanation Ololon who descends to take an active part in the poem, thus illustrating the parallel and equal gender structure of *Milton*. Milton is not able to find his emanation in his wanderings in the first book, and the best solution is for Blake to make also Ololon descend in book two to search for her male counterpart. In the first book male activity is crucial; in the second, female activity. With this structure Blake again stresses that both male and female activity working reciprocally, equally forceful, are needed to bring about the apocalypse. To achieve this male-female reconciliation, crucial for the apocalypse and eternal utopia, Blake must also let Ololon descend to the generative world:

> Knowest thou of Milton who descended
> Driven from Eternity; Him I seek! terrified at my Act
> In Great Eternity which thou knowest! I come him to seek
> [37:1–3, E 137]

As Ololon's quest indicates, the essential moment in *Milton* is the reunion between the two characters Ololon and Milton.

THE HERMAPHRODITE

The reconciliation of Milton and Ololon is the positive outcome of Blake's gender utopia in *Milton*. In this unified double character male and female are portrayed as equally strong. This is the ultimate ideal in Blake's gender utopia, which he expresses even more successfully in *Jerusalem* through the androgynous character Albion, who, as the universal man, unites all mankind. In *Milton*, however, the negation of gender unity and the opposite of the androgynous man, the hermaphrodite, or the female hidden within the male, is still a significant character. In *Milton* this character is more elaborate than in *The Four Zoas* where the very few references are linked to the character Satan. In *Jerusalem* the hermaphrodite is of even less significance.

As we have seen, through fateful mistakes in the relations with his women Milton has been divided from his emanation. Now he stands before God's judgement on the final day alone without his counterpart, and as he is about to confront eternal death, "his own Shadow" in the shape of a negated hermaphrodite appears as a warning:

> And Milton said. I go to Eternal Death!
> ....
> Then on the verge of Beulah he beheld his own Shadow;
> A mournful form double; hermaphroditic: male & female
> In one wonderful body. and he enterd into it
> In direful pain
>   [14:33; 36–39, E 108]

As he stands face to face with this negative, incomplete form of being, Milton realizes that if he leaves his gender troubles unresolved he will not be allowed to enter the utopia of Eden after the apocalypse. At the biographical level Blake is pointing out the steps John Milton should have taken to solve his family dilemma. At a broader level this symbolizes the urgency of gender reconciliation in society as a whole. Milton must therefore return to the fallen world to find his feminine counterpart Ololon and reunite with her to be able to enter the utopian level, just as society as a whole needs to aim at equal balance between the two sexes.

The hermaphrodite represents all female negations in one unified symbol. Milton encounters all of them on his return to the fallen world. In line with the negated sexual politics of a post-lapsarian existence the females entice Milton with beauty and sexual temptations:

> The Twofold form Hermaphroditic: and the Double-sexed;
> The Female-male & the Male-female, self-dividing stood
> Before him in their beauty, & in cruelties of holiness!
> Shining in darkness, glorious upon the deeps of Entuthon.
> [19:32–35, E 113]

At this crucial point in the poem, Milton withstands these female temptations, and is thus able to continue his journey in pursuit of gender reunion with his own emanation Ololon. Disregarding the negative influence of other females, represented by Rahab, Tirzah and Vala, Milton moves forward towards apocalypse:

> At last when desperation almost tore his heart in twain
> He recollected an old Prophecy in Eden recorded,
> And often sung to the loud harp at the immortal feasts
> That Milton of the land of Albion should up ascend
> Forwards from Ulro from the Vale of Felpham; and set free
> Orc from his Chain of Jealousy, he started at the thought
> [20:56–61, E 115]

The hermaphrodite is Blake's ultimate single representation of the result of negative gender interactivity. It is strongly opposed by its antithesis through different symbols throughout Blake's poetry, of which the most successful representation is the androgynous man Albion in *Jerusalem*. Damrosch has explained the relation between the two opposing representations of the different degrees of gender interactivity: "The hermaphrodite is the appalling union of Satan and Rahab, a hideous parody of the Edenic androgyny, doubling its sexual organs instead of casting them away" (289). Thus, while the hermaphrodite moves towards the lowest level Ulro, the androgynous man moves towards the other extreme of the utopia of Eden.

In *The Four Zoas* there is no single character who represents the positive, reconciled state of male and female. In *Milton* we find the gender reunion of Milton and Ololon as an improved representation of positive gender interactivity. Finally, in *Jerusalem* Blake, in a more complex mythological structure, makes his androgynous character Albion represent this ultimate union. As a result, there is an atmosphere of harmony throughout *Jerusalem*, not only at the concluding apocalyptic moment.

The Pre-Apocalypse of Milton

The character Albion represents unified mankind in all Blake's three epics. As in the other two poems, Albion in *Milton* slumbers in the fallen world as a symbol of the great need for mankind to awaken and correct the errors of this existence. When Milton descends to the fallen world this sleeping character, associated with a number of negative symbols, is what he first encounters:

> First Milton saw Albion upon the Rock of Ages,
> Deadly pale outstretchd and snowy cold, storm coverd;
> A Giant form of perfect beauty outstretchd on the rock
> In solemn death
> [15:36–39, E 109–110]

The confrontation of images like "Deadly pale," "snowy cold," "storm coverd" and "solemn death" makes it obvious to the character Milton that he must move on to accomplish his task of awakening mankind.

The reawakening of Albion is the main symbolic indicator that the apocalypse is imminent in *Milton*, just as it is in *The Four Zoas* and *Jerusalem*. Near the end of the first book of *Milton* there are signs of a not too distant arousal in Albion: "Now Albions sleeping Humanity began to turn upon his Couch; / Feeling the electric flame of Miltons awful precipitate descent" (20:25–26, E 114). This moment occurs just after Milton has resisted the temptations of the alluring hermaphroditic females in the previous plate. Having refused the female negations, the strong and positive force of Milton's "electric flame" is now obvious.

Milton is on the right path but it still remains for him to find and reunite with his emanation, Ololon, for Albion, mankind, to fully wake up.

The first signs of an imminent apocalypse are to be found already in plate 18 where a number of apocalyptic images are introduced in a passage foreboding the pre-apocalyptic ending of *Milton*:

> Thus darkend the Shadowy Female tenfold & Orc tenfold
> Glowd on his rocky Couch against the darkness: loud thunders
> Told of the enormous conflict[.] Earthquake beneath: around;
> Rent the Immortal Females, limb from limb & joint from joint
> And moved the fast foundations of the Earth to wake the Dead
> [18:46–50, E 112]

In this early passage we recognize the symbols from *The Four Zoas* as well as from the apocalyptic books in the Bible: "darkness," "loud thunders," "earthquake." However, since the apocalyptic instances in *Milton* are far fewer than in *The Four Zoas* with its lengthy apocalypse, the biblical symbols are not so dominant in the later poem.

In *Milton* there are other portents of gender reunion and, ultimately, of apocalypse, expressed through symbols Blake did not use in *The Four Zoas*. In plate 31 the lark, a traditional symbol of the advent of apocalypse, mounts to the sky:

> The lark sitting upon his earthy bed: just as the morn
> Appears; listens silent; then springing from the waving Corn-
>   field! loud
> He leads the Choir of Day! trill, trill, trill, trill,
> Mounting upon the wings of light into the Great Expanse:
> Reechoing against the lovely blue & shining heavenly Shell:
> His little throat labours with inspiration; every feather
> On throat & breast & wings vibrates with the effluence Divine
> [31:29–35, E 130]

At this point the lark concentrates all the creative energy in the poem, from the inspired union of Bard/Blake/Milton/Los, into one refined image as the morning of the final day dawns. Although this is not the only apocalyptic moment of the poem, the significance of the passage becomes even clearer as we also notice another traditional apocalyptic harbinger, "the Wild Thyme" (31:51, E 131), further on in the same plate.

More than in *The Four Zoas*, Blake in *Milton* points to the need for co-operation in general: "Such are the Laws of Eternity that each shall mutually / Annihilate himself for others good, as I for thee" (38:35–36, E 139). In *Jerusalem* Blake emphasizes this idea even more through his concept of "the Brotherhood of Man." Here Milton, through his fierce opposition to the negative principle finally manages to arouse the sleeping Albion: "Then Albion rose up in the Night of Beulah on his Couch / Of dread repose seen by the visionary eye" (39:32–33, E 140). As mankind regains consciousness through Albion the last obstacle to the apocalypse is removed. It takes the "visionary eye" of a Bard, of a Los, of a Milton, or of a Blake through almost a whole epic poem to awaken him.

As the final augury of the approaching apocalypse, like utopian envoys from the previous poem, all the four zoas appear at the very end of *Milton* blowing the "Four Trumpets" (42:23, E 143) that announce the apocalypse. The four zoas, as we know, are aspects of Albion, and when they appear we understand that it is the final moment just before the apocalypse when mankind has regained consciousness. However, in this frozen instant the author Blake also awakes as the narrative "I," the vision ends, and he returns to his mortal body in the fallen world:

> Terror struck in the Vale I stood at that immortal sound.
> My bones trembled. I fell outstretchd upon the path
> A moment, & my Soul returnd into its mortal state
> To Resurrection & Judgment in the Vegetable Body
> [42:24–7, E 143]

Thus the apocalypse has to be postponed, and the poem finishes on the very threshold of Eden. As an indication of this all the apocalyptic harbingers depart from the poem:

> Immediately the Lark mounted with a loud trill from Felphams Vale
> And the Wild Thyme from Wimbletons green & impurpled Hills
> And Los & Enitharmon rose over the Hills of Surrey
> Their clouds roll over London with a south wind, soft Oothoon
> Pants in the Vales of Lambeth weeping oer her Human Harvest
> Los listens to the Cry of the Poor Man: his Cloud
> Over London in volume terrific, low bended in anger.
> [42:29–35, E 143–44]

But still there is a potential of apocalypse and utopia at the end of the poem:

> Rintrah & Palamabron view the Human Harvest beneath
> Their Wine-presses & Barns stand open; the Ovens are prepar'd
> The Waggons ready: terrific Lions & Tygers sport & play
> All Animals upon the Earth, are prepard in all their strength
> To go forth to the Great Harvest & Vintage of the Nations
> [42–43:36–39, 1, E 143–44]

Notable here are the new apocalyptic images from *The Four Zoas* where Blake compares the apocalypse to the time of harvest. In this "human harvest" significant symbols like "wine-presses," "barns," "ovens" and "waggons" denote the preparation of both human beings and animals for "the Great Harvest" of Eden, again to be found in the fully apocalyptic poem *Jerusalem*. The pre-apocalyptic conclusion of *Milton*, then, is that mankind is prepared for the advent of apocalypse. However, to be ready to take the subliminal leap to the gender-utopian level of Eden more is needed in male as well as female activity—and most of all, in gender interactivity.

The Gender Reunion of Milton and Ololon

It is the reunion of male and female that is still the foremost symbol of the advent of apocalypse and utopia in Blake's poetry. In the relatively incomplete gender vision of *The Four Zoas* there is no successful single representation for the improvement of gender relations, in spite of the reunited couples at the end. As I have argued, in *Milton* this is symbolized through the characters Milton and Ololon in their quest for each other and their ultimate reunion. Towards the end of the poem Blake announces the proximity of the gender utopia of Eden the moment Ololon descends to find her counterpart: "[A] wide road was open to Eternity / By Ololon's descent thro' Beulah to Los and Enitharmon!" (35:35–6, E 135). In a spiritually charged moment which, as it were, contains the whole poem, Ololon descends to the fallen level in plate 35. To be fully redeemed, however, all negations must be destroyed. This is only achieved the moment Ololon and Milton are reunited:

> There is a Negation, & there is a Contrary
> The Negation must be destroyd to redeem the Contraries
> The Negation is the Spectre; the Reasoning Power in Man
> This is a false Body: an Incrustation over my Immortal
> Spirit; a Selfhood, which must be put off & annihilated alway

> To cleanse the Face of my Spirit by Self-examination.
> To bathe in the Waters of Life; to wash off the Not Human
> [40–41:32–37, 1, E 142]

In this instant Ololon realizes the need for the negations to be annihilated:

> Altho' our Human Power can sustain the severe contentions
> Of Friendship, our Sexual cannot, but flies into the Ulro
> Hence arose all our terrors in Eternity! & now remembrance
> Returns upon us! are we Contraries O Milton, Thou & I
> [41:32–35, E 143]

Thus, it is Blake's view that in the fallen world sexuality has become reduced to a mere negation and is therefore referred to here as belonging to Blake's lowest level, Ulro. However, as Ololon and Milton stand on the threshold of apocalypse there is hope of recovery on a higher transcendent level where they can return to the remembered state of original unity in which they were contraries, not negations. Although it is obvious that Ololon's negation "a Double Six-fold Wonder" is annihilated, "away from Ololon she divided & fled into the depths" (42:4–5, E 143), the actual reunion with her counterpart Milton is never completed in *Milton*.

One reason why the gender vision of *Milton* is more complete than that of *The Four Zoas* is that its symbolism has been improved and the interaction of its characters is more balanced. Also, through the insertion of some more successful new characters and images, Blake manages to represent the crucial gender interactivity of male and female. Blake develops his language and symbols in his three main epics, as Essick and Viscomi indicate: "Blake does not—indeed, could not, if he wanted any audience at all—completely dispense with the grammar and syntax of his inherited language, but he goes a long way in forcing English to its outer boundaries" (12). *Milton* is indeed a valid example of this, and an indication that Blake has already managed to force the English language a long way towards its outer boundaries. In this poem Blake comes close to a representation of his ideal through the pre-apocalyptic reunion of Milton and Ololon. *Milton* therefore offers an improved representation of gender utopia compared with *The Four Zoas*, so at one level this poem must be read as a development of an idea that was to be finally expressed in Blake's last epic, *Jerusalem*.[18]

---

[18]*Interestingly, Judith Butler has described the signification of the relation between the genuinely male/masculine and female/feminine as almost impossible. In* Gender Trouble *she writes:*

Conclusion: The Utopia of Milton

In *The Four Zoas*, as we remember, the apocalypse eventually takes place at the end and the four couples are therefore reunited. One couple, Los and Enitharmon, even reach the state of male-female togetherness that is required to step over the threshold into Blake's gender utopia. In *Milton*, despite numerous apocalyptic indications, no apocalypse occurs. One reason that *Milton* is only pre-apocalyptic may be that it is not as irrevocably a fallen poem as *The Four Zoas* and *Jerusalem*. Unlike these two poems, *Milton* is not entirely fictional; to a great extent it is personal and at times even autobiographical. Consequently, the reunited couple Milton and Ololon never reach the state of male-female togetherness and the poem concludes at the very moment before apocalypse.

Milton is a much more well-organized poem, and in this respect it points ahead to the final prophetic poem *Jerusalem*. The outcome of my examination of *Milton* is that, even though it shares both characters and the main apocalyptic and utopian theme with *The Four Zoas*, the connections and structural affinities are closer to *Jerusalem*. This is after all rather natural, since we can assume with some certainty that Blake worked for quite a few years on both *Milton* and *Jerusalem* simultaneously. The superficial similarity in the designs of the plates of the two poems also supports this hypothesis.

In *Milton* Blake finished the poem with the characters still waiting for the apocalypse. Even though the male character Milton is reunited with his emanation Ololon, the two main characters of the poem never reach the utopian state of male-female togetherness since the apocalypse is never realized in *Milton*. *The Four Zoas*, on the other hand, includes a completed apocalypse and, as I have demonstrated, at least two of the characters in this poem achieve the utmost utopian state of male-female togetherness.

The final verdict on *Milton* as one of the three gender utopias of Blake's major epics is that it is both an improvement and a step backwards. Through the activity of the two characters Milton and Ololon, it is an improvement as an account of the need for gender interactivity

(continued) "The relation between masculine and feminine cannot be represented in a signifying economy in which the masculine constitutes the closed circle of the signifier and signified" (11). In Milton, *Blake provides evidence to contest Butler's view of the impossibility of this kind of signification.*

for the advent of apocalypse, and eventually, utopia. But since the gender utopian state of male-female togetherness is never in fact realized it must, paradoxically, also be regarded as a retreat from the effort to visualize this state, which was partly achieved in *The Four Zoas*. In *Milton*, then, Blake leaves the two main characters standing at the threshold, just about to enter the gender utopia of Eden. He therefore continues the story in the fully apocalyptic poem *Jerusalem*.

5
The Gender Utopia of *Jerusalem*

Symbolically speaking, one might claim that *Jerusalem* continues at the very point where *Milton* finishes. It begins at the moment on the verge of apocalypse where the earlier poem ends. The impending apocalypse transferred from *Milton* eventually materializes in the final plates of *Jerusalem*, and in contrast to its predecessor this epic is therefore a genuine apocalyptic poem. On the other hand, compared with the quite lengthy apocalypse in *The Four Zoas*, *Jerusalem* offers a rather compressed version of the final judgement.

The full depiction of apocalypse is one major common denominator between these two poems, and *Jerusalem* is, in many respects, more similar to *The Four Zoas* than to *Milton*. This is particularly the case on a deeper level, although at a casual glance the similarity between *Jerusalem* and *Milton* may be more conspicuous. Both are well-organized poems with their respective fifty and one hundred plates and both are wonderfully illustrated works of art, probably the two most successful products of Blake's illuminated writing. If we move beyond these immediately striking features, however, *Jerusalem* has more in common with *The Four Zoas*. Instead of developing the ideas in the earlier abortive poem it seems that Blake transferred them to *Jerusalem*. Succinctly put, *Jerusalem* is the utopian poem that *The Four Zoas* could have been, if Blake had gone on to finish it.

The resemblance between the two poems is most obvious on a thematic level. To begin with, *Jerusalem* is also a poem mainly taking place in a fallen existence. Like in *The Four Zoas* we are in the first two lines immediately introduced to the fallen world of the poem: "Of the Sleep of Ulro! and of the passage through / Eternal Death! and of the awaking to Eternal Life" (4:1–2, E 146). Thus concisely introducing the main theme of the poem, Blake goes on to present the two protagonists, Jerusalem and Albion. The first speaker of the poem is Christ, who tries in vain to reassure the fallen Albion that God and man are one in an eternal unity of brotherhood. He cannot understand why Albion has hidden the vision of eternity from his emanation:

> Where hast thou hidden thy Emanation lovely Jerusalem
> From the vision and fruition of the Holy-one?
> I am not a God afar off, I am a brother and friend;
> Within your bosoms I reside, and you reside in me
> [4:16–19, E 146]

This of course reminds us of how Enitharmon in jealousy hides the other emanations from Tharmas at the beginning of *The Four Zoas*. The jealous Albion is not to be saved at this juncture of the poem, however, and remonstrates against love, faith and friendship as the guiding principle. It is his view that love is only capable of creating the symbolic enchainment of "forg'd manacles":

> Seeking to keep my soul a victim to thy Love! which binds
> Man the enemy of man into deceitful friendships:
> Jerusalem is not! her daughters are indefinite:
> By demonstration, man alone can live, and not by faith.
> [4:25–28, E 146–47]

Instead of the love of Albion's faithful emanation Jerusalem, love in a fallen existence only produces the negated replicas, the daughters of Albion, with their deceitful jealousy. This is to be compared with the negation of the emanations in the fallen world of *The Four Zoas*, the female will. In line with the standards of a fallen world, Albion keeps his emanation hidden until the apocalypse at the end of the poem. He states: "Humanity shall be no more: but war & princedom & victory" (4:32, E 147).

However, there are also similarities between *Jerusalem* and *Milton*. Like its predecessor, *Jerusalem* emphasizes the creative moment. While in *Milton* "a Moment is a Pulsation of the Artery," Blake, in *Jerusalem*, prophecies "I see the Past, Present & Future, existing all at once" (15:8, E 159). There are a number of passages in the poem where Blake's use of time is quite unconventional. Blake's original use of time is a compelling indication of the need for a basic symbolic interpretation of *Jerusalem*, and the other two major epics.

As in *Milton* there are two main protagonists in the poem. While *Milton* is the story of the male character Milton and the female Ololon, *Jerusalem* is the story of Albion and his emanation in eternity, Jerusalem. The progress of the respective poems hinges on the gender interactivity of the two main characters. Thus, Blake has kept the basic dual structure of characters from *Milton* in his final epic.

The strong female character in the poem is Jerusalem, who in this respect resembles Ololon from *Milton*. Many commentators have compared Jerusalem with Ololon and Oothoon in *Visions of the Daughters of Albion*, and most of them believe these three to be the only strong female characters in the Blake canon. However, the issue is more complicated than that. In *The Four Zoas* we saw that Enion is an important female character with positive connotations as a utopian harbinger, and even the activity of Vala had some positive ramifications in the poem. In *Milton* the negative female agent from the *Zoas*, Enitharmon, has turned into a positive character. In *Jerusalem* Enitharmon is still often positive, particularly near the end, while Vala, who is absent in *Milton*, is more negative here than in *The Four Zoas*. The altering positions of the female characters in the major epics underline the great complexity of Blake's mythological system, and that the meaning and connotations of Blake's symbols change from poem to poem.

Jerusalem was probably finished and definitely first printed in illuminated writing as late as 1820, according to the title page of the poem: "Written and etched 1804–1820." Hence we can be sure that Blake started working properly on *Jerusalem* after having returned from Felpham in 1803, even though it is likely that he had sketched the rough outlines of the poem before then. Of a total of six known finished copies of *Jerusalem* only one is coloured. A proof of Blake's relative confidence in the structure of *Jerusalem* and in its greater overall harmony compared with the other two epics is the fact that he did not alter the order of the plates, as he so frequently did in the other illustrated poems. Of the six copies only one has a different order of plates. It is also significant, bearing in mind the theme of the poem, that Blake finished the only coloured copy just shortly before his death.

Also in *Jerusalem* gender interactivity is stressed, and as in *The Four Zoas* "mutual" is a key word. Los continues his labour to achieve complete gender equality in his vision of a future gender utopia where intellectual interactivity is the cornerstone:

> I care not! The swing of my Hammer shall reassure the starry round
> When in Eternity Man converses with Man they enter
> Into each others Bosom [which are Universes of delight]
> In mutual interchange.
>
> [88:2–5, E 246]

Certainly, this is a more effective trope to describe the humanitarian gender utopia encompassing all mankind, "Man," advocated by Blake throughout his three major prophetic poems, than he ever accomplished in *The Four Zoas*. This is only one of several striking images of male-female togetherness and gender equality in *Jerusalem*, which makes it an outstanding poem in the Blake canon. As Peter Ackroyd puts it, in his eulogy of the poem: "*Jerusalem* is an epic of extraordinary power and beauty, which suggests no less than a sea-change in our understanding of human history and human personality; it is clear that the message is unique because, after two hundred years, it has still to be properly understood. It establishes the truth of all that Blake had written, and painted, before" (322). Notably, however, even though *Jerusalem* is a more accessible poem than *The Four Zoas* in most respects, to some degree it shares the interpretative difficulty of Blake's first major epic.

Overall, in *Jerusalem* Blake conveys an atmosphere of harmony not achieved in *The Four Zoas*, and this is one reason why *Jerusalem* as a gender-utopian poem surpasses the first epic. *Jerusalem* appears to be a much more confident poem, both at the micro-level and at the superficial structural macro-level, organized in four equally long books consisting of twenty-five plates each, making a total of the even figure of one hundred. This harmony is in fact what mainly distinguishes *Jerusalem* from the two earlier epics, especially *The Four Zoas*. In contrast with the turbulent narration in this poem, in *Jerusalem* we encounter for example the almost serene voice of Enitharmon. We can sense a certain harmony in the characteristic flashback narrations describing the lost innocence of the original Eden: "In Eden our loves were the same here they are opposite" (87:17, E 246). Even though she is still part of a fallen world, she merely states this as a fact, calmly, as she remembers the innocent existence of bygone days.

The Characters of Jerusalem

As we know, the prerequisite of Blake's gender utopia is a creative activity of both sexes. This is compellingly emphasized in *The Four*

Zoas where the gender interactivity of the male and female characters paves the way for the reunion of the zoas and emanations in the final Night. The structure of *The Four Zoas*, with four opposed and complementary male and female characters, may suggest that interactivity is a more important component in this poem, since in *Jerusalem* we do not find a similar binary dialectical structure.

Even though the structure of *Jerusalem* is not conspicuously binary, the zoas and their emanations all, in various degrees, take part in the poem. As Paley explains, "[t]here are Zoas in *Jerusalem*, but their effective role is much reduced. The myth of division is transferred to paternity and to geography" (*Continuing* 197). The partial transfer to geography is obvious in the following passage, where the four zoas are related to British place names:

> For Four Universes round the Mundane Egg remain Chaotic
> One to the North; Urthona: One to the South; Urizen;
> One to the East: Luvah: One to the West, Tharmas;
> They are the Four Zoas that stood around the Throne Divine
> Verulam: London: York & Edinburgh: their English names
> [59:10–14, E 208]

As the increased use of geography indicates, the mythological structure of *Jerusalem* has a quite different foundation, with two unifying main characters. Albion, England, is the basic core for the male characters of the poem. Although all the four zoas are still important individual characters, they are subordinated to Albion, who assumes all of their basic functions, with Los as the sole exception. Already in *The Four Zoas* the various characters were aspects of Albion, but in *Jerusalem* this model is more potently exploited. Albion thus becomes the most important male character of *Jerusalem*.

The corresponding female character is Jerusalem, who is the basic female symbol in the poem. By altering the minor character Jerusalem who only appeared quite late, just in time for the apocalypse, in *The Four Zoas* to the all-embracing character in *Jerusalem*, Blake succeeds in representing an improved and balanced vision of gender relations in his final poem. It is beyond doubt that Jerusalem in all her strength is the counterpart of the male power of Albion. Jerusalem being equally strong, the two characters at the end of the poem are thus reunited in togetherness, making them the most successful representation of gender equality in the whole Blake canon.

We recognize a few of the major characters from the two earlier epic poems in *Jerusalem*. Los is still a central character, but strangely enough his constant antagonist Urizen has no part at all in the poem. This may be another reason that, in its definite expression, *Jerusalem* is a more harmonious poem. Most of the evil traits of this character are assumed by Albion, who thus becomes a complex composite character of both good and evil.

VALA: ACTIVE NEGATIVE CHARACTER

After her absence in *Milton*, Vala substantially reappears in *Jerusalem*. In this poem she is an even more negative, but also more fully drawn, character than in *The Four Zoas*. Vala's function and relation with the other main characters of *Jerusalem*, particularly Jerusalem and Albion, is different and more complex than in *The Four Zoas*. In the earlier poem, as we may recall, Vala is the emanation of Luvah. In *Jerusalem*, on the other hand, Albion as the eternal and androgynous man assumes the functions of the split zoas in the former poem. Through this construction, Albion is the counterpart to both Vala and Jerusalem.

As in *The Four Zoas*, Vala is a fallen character throughout *Jerusalem*. In this poem she is even more markedly *the* negative character, even though she shares some evil traits with other female characters like Gwendolen, Cambel, Rahab and Tirzah. Moreover, in *Jerusalem* the positive Jerusalem and the negative Vala stand in clear opposition. In the fallen world of *Jerusalem* Vala dominates Jerusalem through negative sexual strategies. To begin with, Jerusalem in a mood of great loss explains to Vala how the sexes were undivided in original innocence before the fall occurred:

> Albion lov'd thee! he rent thy Veil! he embrac'd thee! he lov'd thee!
> Astonish'd at his beauty & perfection, thou forgavest his furious love:
> I redounded from Albions bosom in my virgin loveliness.
> The Lamb of God reciev'd me in his arms he smil'd upon us:
> He made me his Bride & Wife: he gave thee to Albion.
> Then was a time of love: O why is it passed away!
> [20:36–41, E 165–66]

It seems that we can take this passage as an account of how some form of sexual love in fact existed before the fall in Blake's view. Albion in "his furious love" disrobes Vala, by rending her veil. Accordingly, we can assume that Blake envisions some expression of sexuality to exist both before the fall and after the apocalypse.

Another similarity with *The Four Zoas* is that there are several accounts of the fall and its results. In plate 79 Jerusalem blames Vala for the gender division in the fall:

> Tell me O Vala thy purposes; tell me wherefore thy shuttles
> Drop with the gore of the slain; why Euphrates is red with blood
> Wherefore in dreadful majesty & beauty outside appears
> Thy Masculine from thy Feminine hardening against the heavens
> To devour the Human! Why dost thou weep upon the wind among
> These cruel Druid Temples: O Vala! Humanity is far above
> Sexual organization; & the Visions of the Night of Beulah
> Where Sexes wander in dreams of bliss among the Emanations
> Where the Masculine & Feminine are nurs'd into Youth & Maiden
> By the tears & smiles of Beulah's Daughters till the time of Sleep is past.
> [79:68–77, E 236]

Although Beulah is a sublevel of Eden we notice here that male and female are still divided. In this world sexuality is organized, which is not the case on the Human fourfold level of Eden, not necessarily implying that sexuality does not exist there. Vala, however, believes there is no redemption from the fall:

> [t]hey scent the odor of War in the Valley of Vision.
> All Love is Lost! terror succeeds & Hatred instead of Love
> ....
> I have looked into the secret Soul of him I loved
> And in the dark recesses found Sin & can never return.
> [22:9–10, 14–15, E 167]

In contrast, Vala's positive sister-emanation Jerusalem still believes in redemption through the forgiveness of sins: "Why should Punishment Weave the Veil with Iron Wheels of War / When Forgiveness might it Weave with Wings of Cherubim" (22:34–35, E 168). By questioning the negations in these effective alliterative lines, Blake asserts the positive outcome of forgiveness. The brotherhood of man, with the forgiveness of sins as the guiding light and Christ as the central figure, becomes the most essential concept in *Jerusalem*. In contrast with *Milton* and *The Four Zoas*, Blake in *Jerusalem* emphasizes the need for a humble and humanistic view of life to achieve the harmony required for the highest utopian level of his mythology.

To be consistent with the main mythological structure of the poem, Jerusalem should be the emanation of Albion. But through the all-embracing capacity of Albion, also Vala becomes his counterpart. Considering the overall frame of *Jerusalem*, with the two basic characters Jerusalem and Albion, it is more logical to accept the former construction. In this complex scheme Blake also uses the words Bride and Wife. Therefore, as rivals for Albion, Vala and Jerusalem are in dispute. Jerusalem says:

> Albion I cannot be thy Wife.
> ....
> wherefore is Vala
> Clothd in black mourning upon my rivers currents, Vala awake!
> [45:44, 46–47, E 195]

In *The Four Zoas* Blake does not use "wife" and "bride," and in *Jerusalem* it is in fact not always easy to determine the signified of these two words. The relation between the characters is no clear guidance as Vala anwers Jerusalem: "[A]lbion is mine! Luvah gave me to Albion / And now recieves reproach & hate" (45:50–51, 195). The most logical interpretation would be that in a fallen world Vala is Albion's emanation. This is what at first seems to be the case:

> Albions Emanation which he had hidden in Jealousy
> Appeard now in the frowning Chaos prolifing upon the Chaos
> Reflecting back to Albion in Sexual Reasoning Hermaphroditic
> [29:26–28, E 175]

Typically, Vala belongs to the chaotic and jealous world of Hermaphroditic Sexual Reasoning. Again, Blake's sexual politics proves to be more complex than commonly believed. Looking ahead to a future gender utopia in Eden, Vala assumes positive characteristics:

> Vala was Albions Bride & Wife in great Eternity
> ....
> For the Divine appearance is Brotherhood, but I am Love
> Elevate into the Region of Brotherhood with my red fires
> [29:39, 52; 30: 1, E 175–76]

Further on, Blake in an intriguing passage, questions traditional gender identities. Vala accuses Los of being both male and female:

> She cries: The Human is but a Worm, & thou, O Male: Thou art
> Thyself Female, a Male: a breeder of Seed: a Son & Husband: & Lo.
> The Human Divine is Womans Shadow, a Vapor in the summers heat.
> Go assume Papal dignity thou Spectre, thou Male Harlot! Arthur,
> Divide into the Kings of Europe in times remote O Woman-born
> And Woman-nourishd & Woman-educated & Woman-scorn'd!
> [64:12–17, E 215]

Most interesting here is the epithet "Male Harlot," assigned to the Spectre of Los/Urthona. Clearly, Blake posits here the sexual status of male and female as already equal in a fallen existence. Just as the male scorns the female harlot, the "Woman-born," "-nourished" and "-educated" male harlot is naturally "scorn'd" by the female. To underline the fallen environment the Daughters of Albion appear as the ultimate negative amalgamated symbol of male-female, the hermaphrodite: "A dark Hermaphrodite they stood frowning upon Londons River" (64:31, E 215). We have already encountered this effective symbol in *The Four Zoas* and in a stronger and conscious development of the concept in *Milton*. It is only in *Jerusalem*, however, that the idea is fully developed where Blake, through the opposing force of the positive symbol Albion, provides a persuasive corrective to even out the twisted gender balance.

In *The Four Zoas*, we remember, Vala is the emanation of Luvah. Both Vala and Luvah are active characters in that poem, sometimes with positive repercussions for the gender balance of the *Zoas*. Vala's activity at the apocalypse is of clear importance for the resolution in gender reunion at the end of the poem, and Luvah is the instigator of the apocalypse. In *Jerusalem* Vala, along with her consort Luvah, is a markedly negative character:

> When the Four Zoas of Albion, the Four Living Creatures, the Cherubim
> Of Albion tremble before the Spectre, in the starry Harness of the Plow
> Of Nations. And their Names are Urizen & Luvah & Tharmas & Urthona

> Luvah slew Tharmas the Angel of the Tongue & Albion brought him
> To Justice in his own City of Paris, denying the Resurrection
> Then Vala the Wife of Albion, who is the Daughter of Luvah
> Took vengeance Twelve-fold among the Chaotic Rocks of the Druids
>
> [63:2–8, E 213–14]

We can notice here that the four zoas and Albion are still the basic characters in Blake's mythological system, and we can also grasp something of the interrelations between these characters. That the four zoas are components of the composite character Albion is comprehensible here, while the relations between Albion, Vala and Luvah are considerably more complex. Vala is now the daughter of Luvah, and that is why Luvah could earlier on give Vala to Albion.

The character most substantially changed in *Jerusalem* is in fact Luvah. In *The Four Zoas* he is more of a good than a bad character, with passionate love as his foremost feature. In *Jerusalem* Luvah is almost exclusively a negative character, and one gets the impression that Blake lets him assume some of the evil functions of Urizen. Urizen is mentioned a number of times, but has no real function in the poem and his role is shared by Luvah and Albion. The omission of the most negative character in Blake's mythological system is a clear indication that *Jerusalem* as a whole is a more positive poem than *The Four Zoas*.

Vala's last speech in the poem occurs in plate 80, and in the remaining plates her function is more or less transferred to other characters like Gwendolen and Cambel. Here, though, Vala explains how she was commanded to kill Albion:

> My Father gave to me command to murder Albion
> In unreviving Death; my Love, my Luvah orderd me in night
> To murder Albion the King of Men
>
> [80:16–18, E 236]

When this plot fails Albion conquers Luvah instead, and in an avenging scheme Vala changes from being protective to becoming deceitful: "But I Vala, Luvahs daughter, keep his body embalmd in moral laws" (80:27, E 236). Thus corrupting Albion, England, by enchaining his people with moral laws, Vala perpetuates the patriarchal system of the poem.

Enitharmon: Altering Complex Character

In contrast with *The Four Zoas*, Enitharmon in *Jerusalem* is a more complex character, in spite of the fact that she participates considerably less. In the earlier poem Enitharmon is an almost exclusively negative and evil character. The activity of Enitharmon in *Jerusalem* is negative for most of the poem, but towards the end she has a more positive function, and she is finally assimilated into the all-encompassing harmonious spirit of plate 100; one final time manifesting the integral nature of Blake's art and poetry. This sea-change from evil to positive is well in accordance with the final aim of *Jerusalem*—to achieve total harmony for all living material.

To begin with, Enitharmon is again the symbolic incarnation of the negative and evil Female Will:

> Enitharmon answerd: This is Womans World, nor need she any
> Spectre to defend her from Man
> ....
> A triple Female Tabernacle for Moral Law I weave
> That he who loves Jesus may loathe terrified Female love
> Till God himself become a Male subservient to the Female.
> [88:16–17, 19–21, E 247]

Enitharmon's activity increases as the poem draws to its close, and plates 86 to 88 are perhaps the most evident examples of gender interactivity in *Jerusalem*, with Los defending the position of male desire. First, Blake recapitulates the gender division in the fall: "She separated stood before him a lovely Female weeping / Even Enitharmon separated outside, & his Loins closed" (86:57–58, E 245). As we saw in *The Four Zoas*, after the gender division the negations of love, desire and jealousy, are immediately established. Accordingly, Los delights in the beauty of Enitharmon and his love for her:

> O lovely Enitharmon: I behold thy graceful forms
> Moving beside me till intoxicated with the woven labyrinth
> Of beauty & perfection my wild fibres shoot in veins
> Of blood through all my nervous limbs
> [87:3–6, E 246]

True to the principles of a fallen existence, Enitharmon answers Los with the negative activity of the female will. However, although the gist of the message is negative, in the enunciation "I never will be thy slave" there is also a strong assertion of female emancipation:

> Enitharmon answerd. No! I will sieze the Fibres & weave
> Them: not as thou wilt but as I will, for I will Create
> A round Womb beneath my bosom lest I also be overwoven
> With Love; be thou assured I never will be thy slave
> Let Mans delight be Love; but Womans delight be Pride
> In Eden our loves were the same here they are opposite
> [87:12–17, E 246]

The last line particularly is a crucial summing up of Blake's view of the issue. In the innocent state of original Eden male and female lived together in unity, but after the fall they have become divided opposites. Los, however, continues his labour to accomplish complete gender equality in his visions of a future gender utopia where interactivity is the key concept, here manifested by the words "mutual interchange":

> I care not! The swing of my Hammer shall reassure the starry
>   round
> When in Eternity Man converses with Man they enter
> Into each others Bosom [which are Universes of delight]
> In mutual interchange
> [88:2–5, E 246]

In the general utopian pursuit of the poem, Enitharmon in the final plates becomes mild, tender and loving:

> Enitharmon heard. She raisd her head like the mild Moon
> O Rintrah! O Palamabron! What are your dire & awful
>   purposes?
> Enitharmons name is nothing before you: you forget all my
>   Love!
> The Mothers love of obedience is forgotten & you seek a Love
> Of the pride of dominion
> [93:1–5, E 253]

At this crucial moment before apocalypse Enitharmon recalls the innocent love of original Eden and realizes that love has come to assume the negations of pride and dominion after the fall. Enitharmon's altered attitude at this late point in the poem is one of the auguries that apocalypse is imminent.

Rahab, Tirzah and the Daughters of Albion: Collaborating Female Negations

Yet another of the many co-operating same-sex couples in Blake's prophecies is Rahab and Tirzah. Rahab is the mother of Tirzah, and both are among the negative female characters in Blake's poetry. They both use sex as a means of dominating the male, but while Rahab is the whore Tirzah is the chaste, so they represent the two extreme poles of a twisted sexual expression. Their respective negative strategies thus are also different; Rahab freely displays her lust, while Tirzah withholds it.

Both these female characters take some part of *The Four Zoas* and *Milton*, but it is only in *Jerusalem* they become of importance. At the beginning of the poem they take command of the twelve Daughters of Albion, whom they divide between them:

> These are united into Tirzah and her Sisters on Mount Gilead,
> Cambel & Gwendolen & Conwenna & Cordella & Ignoge.
> And these united into Rahab in the Covering Cherub on
>   Euphrates,
> Gwiniverra & Gwinifrred & Gonoril & Sabrina beautiful,
> Estrild, Mehetabel & Ragan, lovely Daughters of Albion,
> They are the beautiful Emanations of the Twelve Sons of Albion
>   [5:40–45, E 148]

In line with Rahab and Tirzah, the Daughters of Albion are negative female characters who try to control their male counterparts. They are not significant in *The Four Zoas* and *Milton,* but in *Jerusalem,* with its different organization, they somehow assume the role of the four emanations when they occur in a fallen existence in the shape of female wills.

As Albion gradually disintegrates, Rahab, Tirzah and the Daughters of Albion disappear from the poem. They reenter in chapter 3 when Albion is fast asleep on his rock and the world is in its utmost fallen state, with male and female still divided. Significantly, at that point "The Human form began to be alter'd by the Daughters of Albion" (66:46, E 219). The Daughters separate and spread all over the world in order to delude the male: "[N]o one can consummate Female bliss in Los's World without / Becoming a Generated Mortal, a Vegetating Death" (69:30–31, E 223). At this point Rahab acquires a key function: "The Jealousies become Murderous, uniting together in Rahab / A Religion of Chastitiy, forming a Commerce to sell Loves" (69:33–34). Vala, who is a more evil character in *Jerusalem* than in the previous two poems, is substituted by Rahab: "Her name is Vala in Eternity: in Time her name is Rahab" (70:31, E 224). As now "Jerusalem lies in ruins" (84:6, E 243), which of course is a comment on the utterly degenerate state of Blake's contemporary residential city, "I see London, blind & age-bent, begging thro' the Streets" (84:11, E 243), human existence is at a bottom level and the complaining Daughters of Albion are usurped by Rahab: "Thus sang the Dauthers in lamentation, uniting into One / With Rahab as she turn'd the iron Spindle of destruction" (84:29–30, E 243). Even though the Daughters pray for Los to appear as an industrious labourer for the sake of mankind, "all is distress & woe" (84:16, E 243), "[i]n all the Cities of the Nations" (84:14, E 243).

Rahab the whore takes command and is joined by her daughter Tirzah. To complicate the relation of the characters in *Jerusalem*, Tirzah is also one of Zelophehad's daughters, who first appeared in *Milton*. She is the fifth of the daughters and is the representation of sex, more specifically in its corrupt and fallen expressions. By being a prude, or a pure woman, she leads the male characters into sin. She tempts them, and then by withholding her desire she succeeds in torturing them. Tirzah commands her depraved sisters, and in its turn she is dominated by her mother, Rahab. It is easy to understand how well the two characters collaborate: Rahab is the advocate and practitioner of free love and sex, while Tirzah puts restraint to all emotional outflow of sexuality. A classical scheme of dualistic co-operation among Blake's characters, of which we have a number of illustrative examples in the great prophecies. Rahab and Tirzah continuously work together, and as a final manifestation the extreme sexual negation the Hermaphrodite appears:

> In cruelties of Rahab & Tirzah, permanent endure
> A terrible indefinite Hermaphroditic form,
> A Wine-press of Love & Wrath, double, Hermaphroditic
> [J 89:2–4, E 248]

The divided Daughters of Albion finally are united "in Rahab and Tirzah / A Double Female" (67: 1–2, E 220). There is a point in the poem when Tirzah appears to be the dominant of the two. As Tirzah and Rahab have reunited the Daughters of Albion, she takes command:

> O thou poor Human Form! Said she. O thou poor child of woe!
> Why wilt thou wander away from Tirzah? Why me compel to
>   bind thee?

If thou dost go away from me I shall consume upon these Rocks
These fibres of thine eyes that used to beam in distant heavens
Away from me
                                                    [67:44–48, E 221]

What regards the relations between these characters we definitely can agree that Blake's own mythological system is indeed complex.

JERUSALEM: UNIVERSAL FEMALE CHARACTER

Just as Ololon is to *Milton*, the character Jerusalem is Blake's most successful symbolic addition to *Jerusalem*. There are many similarities between these two characters. Most importantly, both are strong and positive female characters. In fact, Jerusalem and Ololon are more positive than any of the four main female characters in *The Four Zoas*. Both are also composite characters representing several individuals. On the superficial level, the six-fold Ololon represents the three wives and three daughters of John Milton. However, the implication is that the level of representation goes beyond that since Blake uses Milton's life only as a poetic vehicle to cover both personal and universal issues. Regarding Jerusalem the case is clearer; she represents all four emanations as well as the female portion of mankind, as the eternal counterpart of the universal man, Albion. This construction implies a pronounced opposition and a dialectic interaction between the two leading protagonists, both in *Milton* and in *Jerusalem*. In *Milton*, Ololon and Milton overtly dominate the poem, while Jerusalem and Albion have an exclusive symbolic status in a more subtle and intricate way in *Jerusalem*.

The figure Jerusalem is, as we know, first described in the Bible. Both in Ezekiel and Revelation we find the idea of Jerusalem as a twofold or a split signifier. The narrator of Revelation tells us: "And I John saw the holy city, new Jerusalem, coming down from God out of heaven, prepared as a bride adorned for her husband" (21:2, 1234). The double signification of the symbol Jerusalem is obvious in the poem. As a woman, she is clearly the counterpart of Albion. As a city, the symbol is a representation of Blake's contemporary London as the utopian place that he envisions in his poetry, and sometimes labels Golgonooza. It is the utopian city which has St. Augustine's City of God as one of its models.

Jerusalem's status as both a woman and a utopian city is at the same time evident and confusing. With this in mind, one can understand

Robert Southey, when, in 1811, he had seen *Jerusalem* and condescendingly remarked to the diarist Crabb Robinson that it was "a perfectly mad poem" and that its author believed that "Oxford Street is in Jerusalem" (Bentley, *Blake Records* 229). As the most London-centered and urban writer in English literature, it was only natural for Blake to locate Oxford Street in Jerusalem. London is in fact the utopian vision of all Blake's poetry.

At the beginning of the poem, Jerusalem collaborates negatively with Vala:

> He [Albion] found Jerusalem upon the River of his City soft
>   repos'd
> In the arms of Vala, assimilating in one with Vala
> The Lilly of Havilah: and they sang soft thro' Lambeths vales,
> In a sweet moony night & silence that they had created
> With a blue sky spread over with wings and a mild moon,
> Dividing & uniting into many female forms
>   [19:40–45, E 164]

Characteristically, Blake uses traditional feminine associations here like "soft," "sweet" and "mild" to describe the female negations in a fallen world. Also worth of notice here is Blake's preference for lower case letters for negative words that elsewhere in his poetry would normally have been introduced with a capital letter to signify a positive status: "created," "wings," "female."

At this point in the poem, on the other hand, Jerusalem casts nostalgic glances back to pre-lapsarian innocence:

> I redounded from Albions bosom in my virgin loveliness.
> The Lamb of God reciev'd me in his arms he smil'd upon us:
> He made me his Bride & Wife: he gave thee to Albion.
> Then was a time of love. O why is it passed away!
>   [20:38–41, E 165–66]

Here, again, is the notable use of the word "Wife." It seems that Blake puts more weight on this word and uses it in a more positive sense than "Bride." The passage further suggests that in the innocence of original paradise love was mutual and for all to share.

Jerusalem is probably Blake's most successful female character. It seems that Blake came up with the idea already when he was writing *The Four Zoas,* and gradually developed this character in the three epics.

At the same time as she is a strong and powerful character, there is a clear aura of softness around her, and at the beginning of the poem Los calls her "the mild Emanation, Jerusalem" (14:31, E 158).

As the poem continues, the activity of Jerusalem increases. Shouldering the weight of responsibility, Jerusalem collectively represents the emanations, or all females, as it were:

> The Emanations of the grievously afflicted Friends of Albion
> Concenter in one Female form an Aged pensive Woman.
> Astonish'd ! lovely! Embracing the sublime shade: the
> Daughters of Beulah
> Beheld her with wonder!
> [48:27–30, E 197]

Jerusalem's activity induces Los "[t]o prepare Jerusalem a place" in his seventh furnace (48:46, E 197). In spite of Los's benevolence and Jerusalem's activity, it is too late to save fallen man. He is finally cast into the affliction of the furnaces and everything is consumed:

> Come & mourn over Albion the White Cliff of the Atlantic
> The Mountain of Giants: all the Giants of Albion are become
> Weak! witherd! darkend! & Jerusalem is cast forth from Albion
> [49:6–8, E 198]

Los's vision of Eternity is finally completely lost: "The Visions of Eternity, by reason of narrowed perceptions, / Are become weak Visions of Time & Space, fix'd into furrows of death" (49:21–22, E 198). Despite this, hope of a utopian existence is not wholly lost. As long as mankind has the strength to persevere in the ambition to build a better world, the aspiration can continue: "Striving to create a Heaven in which all shall be pure & holy" (49:27, E 199).

Towards the end of the poem, Jerusalem's collaboration with Vala becomes more positive. Since in *Jerusalem* Vala is the female negation per se, Jerusalem as the positive female character needs her as a complement to make up a complete female counterpart to the male, to be prepared for the advent of apocalypse. Through this structure the formation of these characters adhere well with Blake's dialectical method of writing.

Los: Indefatigable Poetic Inspiration

Los is at least as important in *Jerusalem* as in *The Four Zoas* and *Milton*, so it is a safe claim that he is the most central character throughout

Blake's major epics. To keep the balance of gender interactivity in the poem, Los, more clearly than in the other two poems, remains the zoa and counterpart of Enitharmon, who is here even characterized as his wife, a strongly positive word, as we have seen: "Enitharmon is a vegetated mortal Wife of Los: / His Emanation, yet his Wife till the sleep of death is past" (14:13–14, E 158). Enitharmon's particular status as a "mortal Wife" emphasizes that here she is not only a negative emanation as in *The Four Zoas*. Blake demonstrates this by introducing the word "Wife" in *Jerusalem*, which is not used elsewhere in his poetry.

Linked to this is Blake's use of the two concepts of "Negations" and "Contraries." Contraries is the positive dialectical term, so familiar to interpreters of Blake, derived from plates 3 and 4 of *The Marriage of Heaven and Hell*. But true to Blake's dualistic principle, also the negative opposition exists, negations. Blake makes this distinction clear:

> Negations are not Contraries: Contraries mutually Exist:
> But Negations Exist Not:
> ....
> but my Emanation, Alas! will become
> My Contrary
>
> [17:33–34, 38–39, E 162]

Significantly, the emanations are the female characters connected with the positive term contraries, while negations belong to the delusive strategy of the female will.

The negation of Los is the Spectre of Urthona. The name Urthona, denoting the eternal form of Los, is not used as frequently in *Jerusalem* as in *The Four Zoas*. Central to *Jerusalem* is the continuous struggle between Los and his Spectre. Early in the poem Los tries to subdue his Spectre:

> Los cries, Obey my voice & never deviate from my will
> And I will be merciful to thee: be thou invisible to all
> To whom I make thee invisible
>
> [10:29–31, E 153]

The battle with the Spectre is not easily won. In plate 17 Los continues to tame his negation, trying to protect Enitharmon from his negative influence:

> For Los said: Tho my Spectre is divided: as I am a Living Man

> I must compell him to obey me wholly: that Enitharmon may not
> Be lost: & lest he should devour Enitharmon
> [17:16–18, E 161]

In spite of Los's great effort it is too late to save Enitharmon, and he is definitely separated from his emanation in the fallen level of Generation:

> So Los in secret with himself communed & Enitharmon heard
> In her darkness & was comforted: yet still she divided away
> In gnawing pain from Los's bosom in the deadly Night
> [17:48–50, E 162]

It is notable in this version of the creation myth from Genesis that even though Enitharmon in fact "was comforted," in a fallen existence nothing can be rescued. At this point in *Jerusalem* the fall is definitive and everything is lost. Los finally underlines the fall, by turning love into hate: "[F]or I can hate also as well as they!" (17:63, E 162).

In contrast to the other two epics, in *Jerusalem* Los manages to resist sexual temptation, in the shape of the other three emanations:

> They wooe Los continually to subdue his strength: he continually
> Shews them his Spectre: sending him abroad over the four points of heaven
> In the fierce designs of beauty & in the tortures of repulse! He is
> The Spectre of the Living pursuing the Emanations of the Dead.
> Shuddring they flee: they hide in the Druid Temples in cold chastity:
> Subdued by the Spectre of the Living & terrified by undisguisd desire
> [17:10–15, E 161]

The fact that Los manages to withstand the seductive attempts of the emanations is probably the main reason that he has the ability and strength to toil on, for the rest of the poem, in his forge to build the utopian city Jerusalem. Through his ceaseless energetic activity the poem cumulatively moves towards its conclusion in apocalypse.

The urban poet Blake visualizes the fourfold city in his own earthly residence, and makes Los the foremost architect of the utopian city. Between 12:45 and 13:29 in *Jerusalem* Los describes his ideal city,

Golgonooza, in minute detail. Later in the poem we therefore find Los building Golgonooza in London:

> Here on the banks of the Thames, Los builded Golgonooza,
> Outside of the Gates of the Human Heart, beneath Beulah
> In the midst of the rocks of the Altars of Albion. In fears
> He built it, in rage & in fury. It is the Spiritual Fourfold
> London: continually building & continually decaying desolate
> [53:15–19, E 203]

At the end of the poem, Blake's vision of his own contemporary London can be identified both as Golgonooza and Jerusalem. Accordingly, Los's furnaces stand in London. In the fallen existence these are in ruins:

> Los was all astonishment & terror: he trembled sitting on the Stone
> Of London: but the interiors of Albions fibres & nerves were hidden
> From Los; astonishd he beheld only the petrified surfaces:
> And saw his Furnaces in ruins
> [46:3–6, E 195]

As effects of the fall, not only Los's furnaces are demolished, but also the whole city of Jerusalem: "But now Albion is darkened & Jerusalem lies in ruins: / Above the Mountains of Albion, above the head of Los" (71:54–57, E 226). Possibly this is seen as an ominous signal for the fallen characters, since in chapter four, from plate 76 onwards, the poem moves towards its conclusion in apocalypse.

As a further step towards apocalypse and utopia, Los commands the four zoas to act in order to save Albion, the falling Man, or themselves, as it were, since they are all aspects of the universal man, through the communal action of brotherhood:

> Then Los grew furious raging: Why stand we here trembling around
> Calling on God for help; and not ourselves in whom God dwells
> Stretching a hand to save the falling Man: are we not Four
> Beholding Albion upon the precipice ready to fall into Non-Entity
> [38:12–15, E 184]

This is one of the few instances in the epics where the symbolic merges with the real, and Blake's message touches on the political. Quite evidently Blake insists here on the need for the ordinary man, and woman, to spring into action. Eventually, we can only help ourselves.

The most important function of Los is to initiate the gender reunion before the apocalypse at the end of *Jerusalem:*

> Then Los again took up his speech as Enitharmon ceast
> Fear not my Sons this Waking Death. he is become One with me
> Behold him here! We shall not Die! we shall be united in Jesus
> [93:17–19, E 253]

Through Los's insistence on mutual male-female activity, mankind is prepared for the final clarion call, which sounds in the last line of the same plate.

Albion: Universal Male Character

Blake's great prophetic insight is more obvious in *Jerusalem* than anywhere else in his poetry. He sees the negative consequences of the industrial revolution already emerging, expressed through one of his favourite images, the "wheel." This is one of Blake's most pregnant and appropriate symbols, and can be used either in a negative sense, "wheel without wheel," or a positive, "Wheel within Wheel":

> [c]ruel Works
> Of many Wheels I view, wheel without wheel, with cogs
>   tyrannic
> Moving by compulsion each other: not as in Eden: which
> Wheel within Wheel in freedom revolve in harmony & peace
>   [15:17–20, E 159]

Quite fittingly, Blake, in this alliterative metonymic trope, as in most places in his poetry, lets a capital first letter denote a positive concept and a lower-case first letter signify a negative one. The obvious negative image conveyed by this passage implies severe times for mankind and, significantly, it is at this point in the poem that the representation of unified mankind, Albion, falls asleep as a reaction to the loss of innocence in the fall:

> But first Albion must sleep, divided from the Nations

5—*The Gender Utopia of* Jerusalem   179

> I see Albion sitting upon his Rock in the first Winter
> And thence I see the Chaos of Satan & the World of Adam
> [15:29–31, E 159]

First and foremost in this passage, Albion signifies the nation of England, "divided from the Nations," which becomes even more obvious in the next line where Blake gives a list of typical north London place names: "Hampstead Highgate Finchley Hendon Muswell hill: rage loud" (16:1, E 159). Noteworthy here is that we know that Blake personally did not particularly like the northern suburbs of London, a fact which underlines his views on the serious fallen condition of contemporary England. "On 31 January 1826, he wrote: 'When I was young Hampstead Highgate Hornsea Muswell Hill & even Islington & all places North of London always laid me up the day after & sometimes two or three days with precisely the same Complaint...'" (Beatley, *Stranger* 28).

It becomes more and more obvious at this stage of the poem that Blake has transferred the symbolic focus from particular characters, notably the zoas and their emanations, to geography, as the plate continues:

> Humber & Trent roll dreadful before the Seventh Furnace
> And Tweed & Tyne anxious give up their Souls for Albions sake.
> Lincolnshire Derbyshire Nottinghamshire Leicestershire
> From Oxfordshire to Norfolk on the Lake of Uddan Adan
> ....
> Scotland pours out his Sons to labour at the Furnaces
> Wales gives his Daughters to the Looms; England: nursing Mothers
> [16:16–19, 22–23, E 160]

Blake goes on to assign "Jerusalem's Gates" (16:30, E 160) to "the Fifty-two Counties of England & Wales / The Thirty-six of Scotland, & the Thirty-four of Ireland" (16:28–29, E 160).

Albion appears already on the title page of *The Four Zoas*, but is not a significant character in that poem. In *Milton* he is even less so; he is passive and asleep and takes no part in the action. Neither can one claim that he is particularly active in *Jerusalem*, since he is slumbering for most of the poem, being the foremost symbolic representation of fallen man. That Albion is a crucial character in this poem is beyond doubt, however, and much for the same reason: that he represents the whole of mankind. Through the increasing emphasis on Jerusalem as a contradictory and complementary female force, Blake makes Albion into a central character, to say the least.

In both the second and the fourth chapter Blake announces that Albion has spoken his last words. In chapter two Albion gives a long final speech, at first with a nostalgic remembrance of bygone days of utopian bliss: "Albion coverd the whole Earth, England encompassd the Nations, / Mutual each within others bosom in Visions of Regeneration" (24:44–45, E 170). In his final words in this chapter, Albion realizes the need for a corrective support for the fallen state of the world: "Descend O Lamb of God & take away the imputation of Sin / By the Creation of States & the deliverance of Individuals Evermore Amen" (25:12–13, E 170). As it turns out, these are not Albion's very last words. At 47:1 once again "Albion utterd his last words," (E 196) which is repeated at the end of the same plate:

> Therefore I write Albions last words, Hope is banish'd from me.
> These were his last words, and the merciful Saviour in his arms
> Reciev'd him, in the arms of tender mercy and repos'd
> The pale limbs of his Eternal Individuality
> Upon the Rock of Ages.
> [47:18, 48:1–4, E 196]

After this Albion falls asleep on his rock. He remains silent and sleeping for the whole of chapter three and until the apocalypse at the end of *Jerusalem*. Albion finally awakes in plate 95, and speaks again in the following plate. *Jerusalem* is a poem in a fallen state nearly all through, and Albion successively turns into the crucial character with the resolution in the end of the poem. In the last few plates he becomes the emblematic key-signifier for the onset of apocalypse. As Albion resumes consciousness the apocalypse is ready to commence.

The Apocalypse of Jerusalem

In plate 94 the apocalypse of *Jerusalem* suddenly begins. It is a much more abrupt onset than in *The Four Zoas*, where there are preparations and foretastes of an approaching apocalypse for more than a whole Night. At the end of the previous plate there is an indication that the sleeping eternal man Albion is soon to awaken: "Is it not that Signal of the Morning which was told us in the Beginning" (93:26, E 254).

5—The Gender Utopia of Jerusalem

Then, in rather an abrupt way, it is announced that traditional time is ended:

> Time was Finished! The Breath Divine Breathed over Albion
> Beneath the Furnaces & starry Wheels and in the Immortal
>   Tomb
> And England who is Brittannia awoke from Death on Albions
>   bosom
>   [94:18–20, E 254]

After this initiation of the introductory phases, the remaining six plates of *Jerusalem* deal with the apocalypse, in text and in illustrations.[19]

The apocalypse in *Jerusalem* is shorter and more concentrated than the apocalypse in *The Four Zoas*, mainly through the use of more effective imagery. We can certainly recognize the symbols from *The Four Zoas*, but in *Jerusalem* Blake manages to connect the purely utopian images with those of gender interactivity:

> [I]nto the Heavens he walked clothed in flames
> Loud thundring, with broad flashes of flaming lightning &
>   pillars
> Of fire, speaking the Words of Eternity in Human Forms, in
>   direful
> Revolutions of Action & Passion
>   [95:7–10, E 255]

The last line underlines the close relation between movement, "Revolutions," and activity as a guideline towards apocalypse. Both are needed in the aspiration towards utopia in the struggles of a fallen world.

It is even more crucial that Blake, at the end of *Jerusalem*, succeeds in emphasizing the great importance of a humanist dimension for the interactivity of the two genders, and consequently for everything else. The crucial moment in the poem is when Albion realizes that he is human: "[F]or Man is Love: / As God is Love" (96:26–7, E 256). With

---

[19] Partly, the illustrations tell their own, if not different, story. For one thing, the final illustration on the textless plate 100 offers another conclusion to Jerusalem, which is quite logical and plausible, as Morton Paley points out: "The design as a whole represents an alternative ending to Jerusalem, one in which all Human Forms are not awaking in the divine bosom but are, rather, participating in 'the Planetary lives of Years Months Days & Hours' (99:3) in the highest sense in which such activity is possible" (Jerusalem 297). In other words, Jerusalem is Blake's own London; when "we have built Jerusalem, / In England's green & pleasant Land" (Milton 1:15-16, E 96).

his discovery it naturally follows that through love man is equal to God, and thus Albion is both human and God:

> Albion saw his Form
> A Man. & they conversed as Man with Man, in Ages of Eternity
> And the Divine Appearance was the likeness & similitude of Los
> [96:5–7, E 255]

Blake takes this idea from the Christian principle of forgiveness of sins, a message that is reiterated throughout *Jerusalem* and this is the main reason for its prevailing atmosphere of harmony compared with Blake's other apocalyptic poem *The Four Zoas*: "[N]or can Man exist but by Brotherhood" (96:28, E 256). It is striking here also how well adapted to our own turbulent times Blake's message in fact is. For instance Jacques Derrida has in recent years emphasized the need for a global forgiving attitude, and in his talk "On Forgiveness" he discusses "unconditional forgiveness: beyond the exchange and even the horizon of a redemption or a reconciliation" (38). Thus, clearly pointing to a timeless eternal context similar to Blake's utopia, he claims in a characteristic Derridean manner that "forgiveness forgives only the unforgivable" (32).

Nevertheless, we can again notice that the key concepts for the Blakean apocalypse are unity and togetherness. As the workings of the apocalypse commence, we find traditional apocalyptic signifiers similar to the symbols in *The Four Zoas*, for instance, "Furnaces," "Fountains," "soft clouds" and "flaming fires," but in *Jerusalem* there is also a more intensive struggle towards unity as the four zoas reappear in search of their proper eternal positions in the fourfold vision:

> All was a Vision, all a Dream: the Furnaces became
> Fountains of Living Waters flowing from the Humanity Divine
> And all the Cities of Albion rose from their Slumbers, and All
> The Sons & Daughters of Albion on soft clouds Waking from
>   Sleep
> Soon all around remote the Heavens burnt with flaming fires
> And Urizen & Luvah & Tharmas & Urthona arose into
> Albions Bosom: Then Albion stood before Jesus in the Clouds
> Of Heaven Fourfold among the Visions of God in Eternity
> [96:36–43, E 256]

As in *The Four Zoas* the mental state of dreaming is linked with apocalypse and utopia, but the concept of vision is more compelling in

Jerusalem. But as we have also seen, to be absolutely fulfilled and to regain the lost paradise a reunion of male and female is required. Yet again, then, Blake emphasizes the need for man and woman to enter the utopian level in togetherness. Therefore Jerusalem, Albion's emanation in eternity, has to regain consciousness too: "For lo! the Night of Death is past and the Eternal Day / Appears upon our Hills: Awake Jerusalem, and come away" (97:3–4, E 256). With both male and female now having returned to consciousness, it only remains for the four zoas to resume their original and eternal positions for the lost harmony finally to be restored:

> And every Man stood Fourfold. each Four Faces had. One to the West
> One toward the East One to the South One to the North.
> [98:12–13, E 257]

Further on, in one of his most convincing and most well-known images Blake describes the ideal relation and communication between man and woman, or, rather, between Man and Man, the androgynous ideal, in the Fourfold state:

> [T]hese are the Four Rivers of Paradise
> And the Four Faces of Humanity fronting the Four Cardinal Points
> Of Heaven going forward forward irresistible from Eternity to Eternity
> And they conversed together in Visionary forms dramatic which bright
> Redounded from their Tongues in thunderous majesty, in Visions
> In new Expanses
> [98:25–30, E 257]

Significantly, this is one of the few instances of the word "Paradise" in the Blake canon.

Through forceful, animated and repetitive language Blake envisions the great activity and movement that are needed to achieve the togetherness of the "Visionary forms dramatic," "going forward forward irresistible from Eternity to Eternity," "in new Expanses." As male and female have now regained innocence through togetherness, the words of Blake's great epic seem to echo the concluding words of the great epic of John Milton: "[T]hey walked / To & fro in Eternity as One Man reflecting each in each" (98:38–9, E 258).

At the apocalyptic instant in *The Four Zoas* Blake relies rather heavily on the Bible for source material. The biblical references are considerably fewer in *Jerusalem*. This is evident in the very effective trope where the characters, at the moment of apocalypse, "conversed together in Visionary forms dramatic." Nothing in *The Four Zoas* can match this image, so it seems that *Jerusalem* is superior in apocalyptic images compared with the earlier poem. To emphasize that all sins are redeemed and that all negations are revoked, even the error itself, the tempter and cause of sin, the serpent, is finally human and fourfold: "And the all wondrous Serpent clothed in gems & rich array Humanize / In the Forgiveness of Sins according to the Covenant of Jehovah" (98:44–45, E 258). This ultimate representation of the abolishment of all negations is the final sign that the inhabitants of the world are now ready to step over the threshold into Blake's fourfold utopian existence.

The Male-Female Togetherness of Jerusalem

Gender interactivity in *Jerusalem* only becomes conspicuous late in the poem, from plate 86 onwards. In this aspect it is different from *The Four Zoas*, which depicts an eternal battle between the sexes throughout, and *Milton*, where gender interactivity is constant and parallel. In plate 86 Los addresses Jerusalem, who descends as a city from heaven, thus manifesting the symbol's two-fold image as city and woman:

> Thy Bosom white, translucent coverd with immortal gems
> A sublime ornament not obscuring the outlines of beauty
> Terrible to behold for thy extreme beauty & perfection
> ....
> I see the New Jerusalem descending out of Heaven
> Between thy Wings of gold & silver featherd immortal
> Clear as the rainbow, as the cloud of the Suns tabernacle.
> [86:14–16, 19–21, E 244–45]

That this is a passage with positive male-female interaction is indicated by images with positive connotations. For one thing, we find several symbols emphasizing innocence: "white," "beauty," "featherd." Even more symbols associated with the utopia of Eden can be detected:

"immortal gems," "sublime ornament," "Wings of gold & silver," "clear as the rainbow," "cloud of the Suns tabernacle."

Furthermore, Blake's unconventional use of the word "sometimes" in *The Four Zoas* reappears here:

> Thy Reins coverd with Wings translucent sometimes covering
> And sometimes spread abroad reveal the flames of holiness
> Which like a robe covers: & like a Veil of Seraphim
> In flaming fire unceasing burns from Eternity to Eternity
> [86:22–25, E 245]

As in Blake's first epic, this word gives a different sense of time, with an eternal perspective. Moreover, the last line is the start of a section denoting great activity and movement. Activity turns into interactivity further on:

> Thus Los sings upon his Watch walking from Furnace to Furnace.
> He siezes his Hammer every hour, flames surround him as
> He beats: seas roll beneath his feet, tempests muster
> Arou[n]d his head. the thick hail stones stand ready to obey
> His voice in the black cloud, his Sons labour in thunders
> At his Furnaces; his Daughters at their Looms sing woes
> His Emanation separates in milky fibres agonizing
> Among the golden Looms of Cathedron sending fibres of love
> From Golgonooza with sweet visions for Jerusalem, wanderer.
> [86:33–41, E 245]

Although Los performs traditionally male tasks with a male tool and his daughters and his emanation Enitharmon use a traditionally female instrument, this is nonetheless an important moment of gender interactivity, which leads the poem closer to apocalypse and utopia. That the passage is mainly positive is indicated by the many positive images in the last two lines: "golden Looms," "fibres of love," "Golgonooza," "sweet visions," "Jerusalem, wanderer." The last epithet in particular implies movement and activity.

Next, Los takes full command and, as a guide, points ahead to apocalypse. As a sign that the resurrection is near, his emanation Enitharmon appears to meet him:

> And Enitharmon like a faint rainbow waved before him
> Filling with Fibres from his loins which reddend with desire

> Into a Globe of blood beneath his bosom trembling in darkness
> Of Albions clouds.
> [86:50–53, E 245]

Although the two are still divided, there are portents of an impending reunion:

> And heal'd after the separation: his pains he soon forgot:
> Lured by her beauty outside of himself in shadowy grief.
> Two Wills they had; Two Intellects: & not as in times of old.
> Silent they wanderd hand in in hand like two Infants wandring,
> From Enion in the desarts, terrified at each others beauty
> Envying each other yet desiring, in all devouring Love
> [86:59–64, E 245–46]

Again we find Blake, remarkably, echoing the last two lines of *Paradise Lost:* "They hand in hand with wand'ring steps and slow, / Through Eden took their solitary way" (XII 648–49). But while Milton concludes his poem with the expulsion from Eden, Blake continues *Jerusalem* towards apocalypse and utopia.

The most extraordinary example of gender interactivity is the intense dialogue between Los and Enitharmon in plate 88. In this plate we find Los working with his hammer to promote the "mutual interchange" of the Brotherhood of Four-fold Humanity. Since it is still a fallen world Enitharmon answers him in a hostile way: "[T]his is Womans World, nor need she any / Spectre to defend her from Man. I will Create secret places" (88:16–17, E 247). The hostility inevitably conjures up the negative side of Los, the Spectre, who is well aware that he is to blame for the division of Los and Enitharmon. Thus he scornfully replies:

> The Man who respects Woman shall be despised by Woman
> And deadly cunning & mean abjectness only, shall enjoy them
> ....
> While you are under the dominion of a jealous Female
> Unpermanent for ever because of love & jealousy.
> You shall want all the Minute Particulars of Life
> [88:37–38; 41–43, E 247]

Unfortunately, this passage has been misinterpreted by most commentators and used as "evidence" for Blake's misogyny. On the contrary, I believe this dialogue between the positive and negative aspects of love is an important step towards the gender utopia that Blake visualizes in Eden. An indication of this is Blake's usage in this negated passage where certain key-words of the Spectre are spelt with an introductory lower-case letter: "love," "jealousy." In Blake's three epics it is crucial to identify the speaker of every line, and whether the voice belongs to a fallen or a redeemed character. The two negative characters here, Enitharmon and the Spectre, are rejoicing over the fallen state of love which has brought about the gender division. Los, positive thoughout the poem, "stood at his Anvil in wrath the victim of their love" (88:46, E 247). Although his work so far is in vain, he continues his labour:

> The blow of his Hammer is Justice. the swing of his Hammer: Mercy.
> The force of Los's Hammer is eternal Forgiveness; but
> His rage or his mildness were vain, she scatterd his love on the wind
> ....
> Loud howl
> The Furnaces of Los! loud roll the Wheels of Enitharmon
> The Four Zoa's in all their faded majesty burst out in fury
> And fire.
> [88:49–51, 53–56, E 247]

What is striking to notice here is the great importance of the four zoas as basic characters in the structure of Blake's mythological system.

That the poem is moving closer to apocalypse may be understood further on when Enitharmon announces her abandonment of the negatively charged female looms: "My Looms will be no more & I annihilate vanish for ever / Then thou wilt Create another Female according to thy Will" (92:11–12, E 252). This plate together with plate 93 provides another example of gender interactivity, and the conversation between Los and Enitharmon resembles the dialogue in plate 88. It is obvious here, though, that the apocalypse has drawn nearer, as Enitharmon proclaims that "The Poets Song draws to its period & Enitharmon is no more" (92:8, E 252). That mankind's period in a fallen world will soon be over is even clearer as "Los answerd swift as the shuttle of gold. Sexes must vanish & cease / To be, when Albion arises from his dread repose O lovely Enitharmon" (92:13–14, E 252).

The climax of *Jerusalem* occurs the moment the male-female reunion is completed: "As the Sun & Moon lead forward the Visions of Heaven & Earth / England who is Brittannia enterd Albions bosom rejoicing" (95:21–22, E 255). The obvious passage to compare with here is not only *Milton* 15: 47–49 when Milton descends into Blake's left foot, but also the other fusions in that poem between Bard, Los and Blake. Notably the reunion of Albion and Jerusalem is emphasized through repetition of these lines at the beginning of the following plates. As in *The Four Zoas*, this image works metonymically. Remarkably, the metonymy is reversed here, with the whole, Albion and Jerusalem, representing the parts, the individual characters. It is significant that the final five plates of *Jerusalem* have a metonymic function. The workings of the apocalypse embrace everyone and everything.

The vision is finally fourfold when Albion, mankind, seizes his bow: "[T]hen Albion stretchd his hand into Infinitude. / And took his Bow. Fourfold the Vision" (97:6–7, E 256). The vision now realized, the bow is of both sexes simultaneously. Significantly, the four zoas reappear and male and female are united in mutual Love:

> And the Bow is a Male & Female & the Quiver of the Arrows of
>   Love,
> Are the Children of this Bow: a Bow of Mercy & Loving-
>   kindness: laying
> Open the hidden Heart in Wars of mutual Benevolence Wars of
>   Love
> And the Hand of Man grasps firm between the Male & Female
>   Loves
> And he Clothed himself in Bow & Arrows in awful state
>   Fourfold
>   [97:12–16, E 256]

As a token of the mutual Love of the two sexes, the Arrows of desire are both male and female. Thus, in the apocalypse, Albion has reached his ultimate representation as androgynous man. In fourfold state, then, man is "[r]ejoicing in Unity / In the Four Senses" (98:21–22, E 257).

In the utopia at the conclusion of *Jerusalem*, Blake has erased all gender differentiation, and it is in this poem he writes that in Eden,

> Man cannot unite with Man but by their Emanations
> Which stand both Male & Female at the Gates of each
>   Humanity.
>   [88:10–11, E 246]

The emanation is traditionally a female symbol in Blake's poetry, but here on the threshold of apocalypse the emanations appropriately are of both sexes simultaneously. Thus Blake indicates the status of gender relations, or rather the complete absence of gender, in his utopia of Eden.

Conclusion: The Utopia of Jerusalem

There might therefore be some relevance in calling *Jerusalem* a humanist utopia, but since gender interactivity is the way to reach the human level it is first and foremost a gender utopia. In a condensed form Blake connects gender interactivity, reunion, togetherness and utopian humanism. While *The Four Zoas* as a whole is a chaotic poem, *Jerusalem* is harmonious. This is one of the reasons why it must be considered as Blake's greatest poetic achievement and concluding point, something which most Blake commentators agree upon, and also as his most positive and optimistic poem. It is in *Jerusalem* that the ultimate expression of mutual feelings, of love, is described as "Embraces are Comminglings: from the Head even to the Feet" (69:43, E 223).

An even greater achievement it becomes as we realize that the humanist theme of *Jerusalem* is indeed valid and needed today. Provided that we can interpret its refined symbolism it is still a crucial poem, maybe more important today with a society screaming out for improved understanding between races, classes and sexes. It is no big surprise that a highly perceptive philosopher like Jacques Derrida talks about "forgiveness or the unforgivable, a sort of eternity or transcendence, the apocalyptic horizon of a final judgement" ("On Forgiveness" 33).

But it is difficult to pick out specific textual details that demonstrate clearly that *Jerusalem* is a more harmonious poem than *The Four Zoas*. Rather, to fully comprehend this aspect the respective poems must be read as one whole unit. Similarly, any valid interpretation of Blake must attempt to encompass his whole poetic oeuvre. However, it is possible to indicate certain narratological features which show that Blake is a more confident writer in *Jerusalem* than in *The Four Zoas*, infusing the poem with a greater sense of harmony. One obvious feature is the absolutely synchronous division of the poem into four equally long chapters all consisting of 25 plates. Each chapter is directed towards a well-defined audience: "To the Public," "To the Jews," "To the Deists" and "To the Christians." This narratological device creates a greater distance between the author Blake and the text of *Jerusalem* than we find in the text of *The Four Zoas*. The Blake who writes *Jerusalem* is a more detached, near aloof, reassured and omniscient narrator—a Prospero calming the tempestuous seas, conducting his final Book.

We recall the conclusion of *The Four Zoas,* where only one of four couples reaches the highest level of utopian togetherness and thus enters Eden. The final chord of *Jerusalem* is one of as complete a harmony as can possibly be represented in the pure and simple words of poetry. While Blake's first tentative epic has a more complex mythological structure with four zoas and four emanations, in *Jerusalem* there is, ultimately, only one character to represent the male part of all mankind, Albion, and only one character to represent the female part, Jerusalem. In a reversed metonymical trope Blake accomplishes his final goal, the consummate expression of male-female reunion:

> All Human Forms identified even Tree Metal Earth & Stone. all
> Human Forms identified, living going forth & returning wearied
> Into the Planetary lives of Years Months Days & Hours reposing
> And then Awaking into his Bosom in the Life of Immortality.
> And I heard the Name of their Emanations they are named
>   Jerusalem
>
>   [99:1–5, E 258–59]

As Albion is mankind, the emanations of all men are Jerusalem. Blake's poetic oeuvre is completed.

Afterword

On his recent 2004 CD recording, Leonard Cohen sings, in the words of Frank Scott, that we can build a commonwealth again, if we search our hearts, whatever bitterness they may contain. Through that searching, we must have faith in a new beginning, so that we may rise to something greater ("Villanelle for Our Time," *Dear Heather* 8). In a world with collapsing towers, war, natural disasters, and, most recently, multiple bomb attacks at the London public transport system, terribly emphasizing the need of constant terror-alert, we surely need to search our hearts for something greater to aim at. Significantly, in another song on the same record Cohen sings about the fatal destruction one September morning in New York ("On That Day," *Dear Heather* 7). The global situation with all this put together, and in its separate parts, calls for another mode, a new way of thinking.

In his lecture "On Forgiveness" Jacques Derrida claims that "[s]ometimes, forgiveness (given by God, or inspired by divine prescription) must be a gracious gift, without exchange and without condition" (44). This extreme position, which seems to have found inspiration in the ideas advocated by Marcel Mauss in his classical study *The Gift*, is underpinned by allusion to Hegel, who Derrida elsewhere calls "the great thinker of 'forgiveness' and 'reconciliation'" (34), and his concept "the Spirit of Christianity" against which crimes are unpardonable (47). Jesus' Brotherhood of Man, with the forgiveness of sins as the guiding star, is one of the two major components of the poem *Jerusalem*, and of the eponymous eternal city. The other is a complete equality between man and woman and everything else, for "Everything that Lives is Holy" ("Song of Liberty," *Marriage* 25; *Visions* 8:10; *America* 8:13). It would be comforting in the present situation of the world to interpret "commonwealth" as a utopian state including all this, predicted by Blake two centuries ago.

In the new program for the Blake Society we can read about the London project "BlakeSpace," which is described as "an attempt to manifest Blake's principles in the way we live our lives. BlakeSpace will integrate craft and enterprise, art and artisanship in a programme to re-engage young people in danger of exclusion from our society" (Program leaflet 3). It is striking to understand that most of the issues of Blake's *Jerusalem* are still of highly topical value today: "Many of the issues Blake confronted still face us in London today, including the pervasive poverty that threatens half of our inner city children and the disappearance of traditional artisan livelihood's despite London's rapidly evolving creative sector" (Program 3). The fallen everyday reality of Blake's London is certainly still there, but the spiritual glory of the eternal city Jerusalem is more distant than any time before in the history of mankind. But obviously the legacy of Blake, and what he warns against, pervades society today, mainly being a comfort to us. For better or for worse, Blake's poetry appears more urgent now than ever.

The announcements from Cohen and Derrida above are contemporary, reassuring reactions to a world in crisis. Things might in fact have changed rather drastically only in a few years, with an overall need for comfort and positive anticipation of some kind, as a result of several traumatic global events. Through this sense people in general appear more ready to embrace the utopian ideals of Blake's prophetic poetry than only a while ago. But just some ten years back, Leonard Cohen, in a pessimistic true visionary Blakean manner, predicted the position where we now stand. As if the words were taken directly from the Book of Revelation, he envisions that the order of the soul will be overturned by a blizzard, which will make things so unstable that nothing can be measured any longer ("The Future" *The Future* 3). Close at hand here, obviously, are the biblical apocalypses, and then particularly the horrifying images from the Revelation. Just as much as this Bible book, Cohen, on behalf of the people of the earth, is dauntlessly staring damnation and destruction in the eye. And with Indonesia's devastating earthquake and tsunami flood-wave of December 2004 in fresh memory, it is as if the words of his song have already come true. Still, in the midst of this utter fictive darkness, Cohen in the same song throws out a faint glimmer of hope by proclaiming that we have only one means of survival, and that is love.

Himself an acclaimed poet, who could be a better judge of our times than Leonard Cohen? Praying and meditating with monks for a number of years presumably gives you an enhanced sense of, and closer access to, a realm of spirituality and compassion. At least in these two visionary submissions, ten years apart, he appears to have hit the prevalent feeling of the Western world.

It is striking how close Cohen comes to what Blake indicated in his visionary poems, though be it with a shorter scope of time. The songs and poems on *The Future* belong to the same category as Blake's apocalypse and damnation, rather than to his utopia with forgiveness and equality, if we see these phenomena as two opposed sides; good and bad, as it were. In this kind of writing both Blake and Cohen bring urgent warnings to mankind at crucial points of time. If we do a parallel reading of these two prophets, we notice that we can place the slightly earlier Cohen of *The Future* at the same point where Blake was when composing *The Four Zoas*, or even before that poem. Clearly then, the serene and comforting humanist qualities of Cohen's prophecies on *Dear Heather* "equal" the full-fledged confident and complete prophet Blake is in *Jerusalem*. Perhaps, if one conducts such a detailed analysis, also the respective political and social situations correspond between the two centuries somehow.

In his prophecies Blake seeks to alert mankind to the need for a new way of thinking. As Saree Makdisi has defined it: "[A] new form of art presupposes a new way of sharing, of loving, of living, of being, *in common*" (263). Maybe that is what makes Blake's apocalypse different from the biblical ones: that he envisions a positive future post-apocalypse, in contrast to the terrifying pain offered in the Bible. Damnation is present in Blake's great prophecies, but is never a realistic option.

As has been my greatest task in this book to bring to the fore: Blake's message to mankind is utterly positive, compassionate and humane. I believe, nay hope, that this is a fact that there is consensus about, in spite of those, often somewhat ignorant and not enough initiated, commentators who have considered Blake a madman, a mysticist, even an alchemist. I hope we can agree that the forgiveness of sins is the Christian, in the right sense of that word, outcome of *Jerusalem*, and thus is positive.

What regards the other major component and intent of *Jerusalem*, and of the three great prophecies in unison, gender equality, the issue is not that clear-cut, and there is definitely no consensus. Putting this concept—and its inevitable ally, Blake's view and portrayal of the female—under scrutiny, the balance rather slides in the other direction. Anne Mellor and Alicia Ostriker must of course be allowed to see Blake's female characters as negative and, astonishingly, to believe the poet himself to be a sexist, but really; on what grounds? It has of course been argued by a number of Blake critics that Blake's general view of the female grows more pessimistic over the years. But contradicting this negative critical view is the fact that the two characters Jerusalem, in the poem of that name, and Ololon in *Milton* are more positive than any of the four main female characters in *The Four Zoas*. Both Ololon and Jerusalem indicate clear developments in Blake's technical skill at drawing richer characters. They are improvements on the rather sketchy caricatures in *The Four Zoas*. While the picture of the female as an individual in *Jerusalem* may be seen as more negative, the overall impression of the poem is still positive. This is particularly manifested in the post-apocalyptic finale when male and female have regained paradise and together enter the utopia of Eden, if one views the poem as a single entity from its concluding chord.

But hopefully Blake scholarship is now on the right track. In the last ten years or so it has evidently taken a more healthy direction. Scholars and commentators like Helen Bruder, Jon Mee, Saree Makdisi and Nicholas Williams have all done a great job to bring back common sense into Blake criticism. Most all of us fanatics and lovers of Blake are indebted to the grand task David Worrall and Keri Davies have taken on their shoulders. Under Worrall's indefatigable leadership and scholarly enthusiasm Davies and Worrall himself have been able to unearth sensational new findings, in an AHRB sponsored project. Worrall's new interpretations of Blake's connections with Swedenborgians, the slave-trade, and most importantly the two Swedes Carl Bernard Wadström and Augustus Nordenskjöld and their *Plan for a Free Community in Sierra Leone* have given us invaluable new insight in several crucial issues: slavery quite naturally, but also religion, dissent, feminism and all gender issues. Davies's discovery of new letters and documents indicating a greater readership, to a great extent female, and a higher commercial value of Blake's diverse work through easy access in Joseph Johnson's print shop in the 1780s and 90s is no less significant. But without the slightest doubt, it is the latter's laborious Los-like unearthing of the Moravian archives that will change the direction of Blake studies forever. By proving the identity and birthplace of Blake's mother, Davies has finally given Blake scholarship solid ground enough to at least put one foot down to stand steadier on, for the first time since the death of our great poet and prophet. We Blakeans cannot find words enough to express our gratitude and scholarly debt to Keri.

The recent world events may be interpreted as a form of apocalyptic upheaval. With these in mind, are we today maybe better prepared to listen to visionary messages like Blake's, and others of a similar kind? If we are to take the shift in Cohen's artistic expression as an indicative thermometer of the times, then surely we are on to something new; a new mode, a new way of thinking. But it should not have to take a Cohen, a Derrida, a George Harrison, a Bob Dylan or a William Blake to somehow grasp the acutely perilous position we are all in today. We have no choice but to take in and take heed of the warnings of the great prophets.

Hopefully, we may see something positive emanating from the last few heavy trials on mankind, and a new spiritual awareness and awakening will arise among people in common. Hopefully, we may clinch the straw and embrace humanitarian ideals similar to Blake's forgiveness of sins in *Jerusalem*, or what Derrida points the finger at in his lecture. Hopefully then, we are all a step closer to Blake's utopia.

Bibliography

Ackland, Michael. "The Embattled Sexes: Blake's Debt to Wollstonecraft in *The Four Zoas*." *Blake/An Illustrated Quarterly* Winter (1982–83): 172–83.
Alexander, T. Desmond, and Brian S. Rosner, eds. *New Dictionary of Biblical Theology*. Leicester and Downers Grove, Ill.: Inter-Varsity Press, 2000.
Aune, David E. Introduction to the Revelation to John (Apocalypse). *Harper Collins Study Bible*. 2307–09.
Beer, John. *Blake's Humanism*. Manchester: Massachusetts University Press, 1968.
Bentley, G. E., Jr. *Blake Records*. Oxford: Oxford University Press, 1969.
———. *The Stranger from Paradise: A Biography of William Blake*. New Haven and London: Yale University Press, 2001.
Bergmann, Helena. "'A Thing, ugly & petticoated': Coleridge and the Radical Discourse of Mary Hays." Unpublished conference paper. Coleridge Summer Conf., July 2002, Cannington University College.
Billigheimer, Rachel. "Conflict and Conquest: Creation, Emanation and the Female in William Blake's Mythology." *Modern Language Studies* 30:1 (2000): 93–120.
Blake, William. "America: A Prophecy." In *Blake's "America: A Prophecy" and "Europe: A Prophecy."* New York: Dover, 1983.
———. "Auguries of Innocence." In *Complete Poetry and Prose*. 490–93.
———. *The Complete Poetry and Prose*. Ed. David V. Erdman, commentary by Harold Bloom. Berkeley and Los Angeles: University of California Press, 1982.
———. *Complete Writings*. Ed. Geoffrey Keynes. (1957). Oxford: Oxford University Press, 1985.
———. *The Early Illuminated Books*. Vol. 3. (*All Religions Are One, There Is No Natural Religion, The Book of Thel, The Marriage of Heaven and Hell, Visions of the Daughters of Albion*). Ed. Morris Eaves, Robert N. Essick, and Joseph Viscomi. London: Tate Gallery Publ., 1993.
———. *The First Book of Urizen*. *The Urizen Books*.
———. *The Four Zoas*. A Photographic Facsimile of the Manuscript with Commentary on the Illuminations. Ed. and commentary Cettina Tramontano

Magno and David V. Erdman. London and Toronto: Associated University Press, 1987.

———. *The Four Zoas. The Torments in Love and Jealousy in the Death and Judgment of Albion the Ancient Man*. Ed. Landon Dowdey. Chicago: The Swallow Press, 1983.

———. *The Four Zoas*. In *Vala; or, The Four Zoas. A Facsimile of the Manuscript, a Transcript of the Poem, and a Study of Its Growth and Significance*. Ed. G. E. Bentley, Jr. Oxford: Clarendon Press, 1963.

———. *The Four Zoas*. (1797). Brit. Mus. Additional MS. 39764. British Lib., London.

———. *Jerusalem*. Vol. 1. Ed. Morton D. Paley. London: Tate Gallery, 1993.

———. "Laocoön." In *Complete Poetry and Prose*. 273–75.

———. *The Marriage of Heaven and Hell*. Commentary Geoffrey Keynes. Oxford: Oxford University Press, 1986.

———. *Milton*. Vol. 5. Ed. Robert N. Essick and Joseph Viscomi. London: Tate Gallery, 1993.

———. *Songs of Experience*. New York: Dover, 1984.

———. *Songs of Innocence*. New York: Dover, 1971.

———. *The Urizen Books*. Vol. 6. (*The First Book of Urizen, The Book of Ahania, The Book of Los*.) Ed. David Worrall. London: Tate Gallery, 1995.

———. *Visions of the Daughters of Albion. The Early Illuminated Books*.

Blake Society Programme Leaflet. London, Winter/Spring 2005.

Bloom, Harold. *Blake's Apocalypse: A Study in Poetic Argument*. Garden City, NY: Doubleday, 1963.

———. Commentary in Blake. *Complete Poetry and Prose*.

Bruder, Helen. *William Blake and the Daughters of Albion*. Basingstoke and London: Macmillan, 1997.

Butler, Judith. *Bodies That Matter: On the Discursive Limits of "Sex."* New York and London: Routledge, 1993.

———. *Gender Trouble: Feminism and the Subversion of Identity*. New York and London: Routledge, 1990.

Clark, Anna. *The Struggle for the Breeches: Gender and the Making of the British Working Class*. Berkeley: University of California Press, 1995.

Clark, Steve, and David Worrall, eds. *Blake in the Nineties*. Basingstoke: Macmillan, 1999.

Cohen, Leonard. *Dear Heather*. Columbia, 2004. (compact disk recording.)

———. *The Future*. Columbia, 1992. (compact disk recording.)

Colebrook, Claire. "The Standard Historical Picture of Feminism." 18 March 2003<http://www.ed.ac.uk/englit/studying/undergrd/english_lit_1/Handouts/cc_feminism.htm>.

Coleridge, Samuel Taylor. *Biographia Literaria*. (1817). In *Poems and Prose*. 159–224.

———. *Poems and Prose*. Ed. Kathleen Raine. Harmondsworth: Penguin, 1957.

Coleridge, Samuel Taylor, and William Wordsworth. *Lyrical Ballads*. 1798. Plymouth: Northcote House, 1987.

Damon, S. Foster. *A Blake Dictionary: The Ideas and Symbols of William Blake*. Providence, Rhode Island: Brown University Press, 1965.

Damrosch, Leopold. *Symbol and Truth in Blake's Myth.* Princeton: Princeton University Press, 1980.
Dante Alighieri. *The Divine Comedy.* Trans. C. H. Sisson. Oxford: Oxford University Press, 1998.
Davies, Keri. "Mrs. Bliss: A Blake Collector of 1794." In Clark and Worrall, eds., *Blake in the Nineties.* 212–30.
———. Rev. of *The Stranger from Paradise: A Biography of William Blake*, by G. E. Bentley, Jr. *The Blake Journal* 7 (2002): 62–70.
———. *William Blake in Contexts: Family, Friendships, and Some Intellectual Microcultures of Eighteenth- and Nineteenth-Century England.* Unpub. diss. St. Mary's College, Strawberry Hill, Twickenham, 2003.
Derrida, Jacques. *Of Grammatology.* Trans. Gayatri Chakravorty Spivak. Baltimore: Johns Hopkins University Press, 1974.
———. "On Forgiveness." *On Cosmopolitanism and Forgiveness.* London and New York: Routledge, 2001. 25–60.
Doskow, Minna. *William Blake's* Jerusalem: *Structure and Meaning in Poetry and Picture.* Madison, NJ: Fairleigh Dickinson University Press, 1982.
Eaves, Morris, Robert N. Essick and Joseph Viscomi. Introduction. In Blake, *The Early Illuminated Books*, Vol. 3. 9–15.
Erdman, David V. *Blake: Prophet Against Empire: A Poet's Interpretation of the History of His Own Times.* Princeton: Princeton University Press, 1969.
Essick, Robert N., and Viscomi, Joseph. *Blake Archive.* 28 March 2003. <http://www.blakearchive.org.uk /cgi-bin/>.
———. Introduction. In Blake, *Milton.* 9–41.
Felski, Rita. *Beyond Feminist Aesthetics: Feminist Literature and Social Change.* London: Hutchinson Radius, 1989.
Fox, Susan. "The Female as Metaphor in William Blake's Poetry." *Critical Inquiry* 3 (1977): 507–19.
———. *Poetic Form in Blake's* Milton. Princeton: Princeton University Press, 1976.
Freeman, Kathryn S. *Blake's Nostos: Fragmentation and Nondualism in* The Four Zoas. Albany, NY: State University of New York Press, 1997.
———. "Narrative Fragmentation and Undifferentiated Consciousness in Blake's *The Four Zoas.*" *European Romantic Review* 5:2 (1995): 178–192.
Frye, Northrop. *Fearful Symmetry: A Study of William Blake.* Princeton: Princeton University Press, 1947.
Furniss, Tom. "Nasty Tricks and Tropes: Sexuality and Language in Mary Wollstonecraft's *Rights of Woman.*" *Studies in Romanticism* 32:2 (1993): 177–209.
Gilchrist, Alexander. 1863. *The Life of William Blake.* Ed. Ruthven Todd. London: Dent, 1982.
Gilman, Charlotte Perkins. *Herland.* (1915). New York: Pantheon, 1979.
Godwin, William. *Enquiry Concerning Political Justice, and Its Influence on Modern Morals and Happiness.* (1793). Ed. Isaac Kramnick. Harmondsworth: Penguin, 1976.
Haigney, Catherine. "Vala's Garden in Night the Ninth: Paradise Regained or Woman Bound?" *Blake/An Illustrated Quarterly* Spring (1987): 116–124.
Hamlyn, Robin, and Michael Philips. *William Blake.* London: Tate Gallery, 2000.

The Harper Collins Study Bible: New Revised Standard Version. Gen. ed. Wayne A. Meeks. London: HarperCollins, 1989.

Hays, Mary. *The Memoirs of Emma Courtney.* (1796). London: Pandora Press, 1987.

———. *The Victim of Prejudice.* (1799). Peterborough: Broadview Press, 1996.

Hill, Christopher. *Milton and the English Revolution.* London: Faber and Faber, 1977.

Hinrichs, Kimberly M. "Distinguishably One: Envisioning a Confluence of Swedenborgian and Feminist Theology." *Studia Swedenborgiana* Vol. 13: 1 (2003): 1–34.

The Holy Bible. The Authorized King James Version 1611. Cambridge: Cambridge University Press, 2001.

Hume, David. *A Treatise of Human Nature.* 1739–40. Ed. L. A. Selby-Bigge and P. H. Nidditch. Oxford: Oxford University Press, 1982.

Hume George, Diana. *Blake and Freud.* Ithaca: Cornell University Press, 1980.

Irigaray, Luce. *This Sex Which Is Not One.* Trans. Catherine Porter. Ithaca: Cornell University Press, 1985.

———. *Speculum of the Other Woman.* Trans Gillian C. Gill. Ithaca: Cornell University Press, 1985.

Jacobus, Mary. "Traces of an Accusing Spirit. Mary Hays and the Vehicular State." *Psychoanalysis and the Scene of Reading.* Oxford: Oxford University Press, 1999. 202–34.

Keats, John. *Poetical Works.* Oxford and New York: Oxford University Press, 1987.

Kelly, Gary. Introduction. In Wollstonecraft, *Mary and the Wrongs of Woman.* vii–xxi.

Kumar, Krishan. *Utopia and Anti-Utopia in Modern Times.* Oxford and New York: Blackwell, 1987.

———. *Utopianism.* Milton Keynes: Open University Press, 1991.

Leask, Nigel. "Pantisocracy." *Oxford Romantic Companion.* 635.

Liljegren, S. B. *Studies on the Origin and Early Tradition of English Utopian Fiction.* Uppsala, Lundequistska and Copenhagen: Ejnar Munksgaard, 1961.

Lincoln, Andrew. *Spiritual History: A Reading of William Blake's Vala, or The Four Zoas.* Oxford: Oxford University Press, 1995.

Makdisi, Saree. *William Blake and the Impossible History of the 1790s.* Chicago and London: University of Chicago Press, 2003.

Mauss, Marcel. *The Gift: The Form and Reason for Exchange in Archaic Societies.* Trans. W. D. Halls. New York: W.W. Norton, 2000.

McCalman, Iain. "Corresponding Societies." In McCalman, ed., *Oxford Companion to the Romantic Age.* 467–8.

———, ed. *An Oxford Companion to the Romantic Age: British Culture 1776–1832.* Oxford: Oxford University Press, 1999.

McKusick, James C. "'Wisely Forgetful': Coleridge and the Politics of Pantisocracy." In Fulford, Tim, and Peter J. Kitson, eds. *Romanticism and Colonialism: Writing and Empire, 1780–1830.* Cambridge: Cambridge University Press, 1998. 107–128.

McGann, Jerome J. "Poetry." In McCalman, eds., *Oxford Romantic Companion to the Romantic Age.* 270–79.

McQuail, Josephine A. "Passion and Mysticism in William Blake." *Modern Language Studies* 30: 1 (2000): 121–31.
Mee, Jon. *Dangerous Enthusiasm: William Blake and the Culture of Radicalism in the 1790s*. Oxford: Oxford University Press, 1992.
Mellor, Anne K. "Blake's Portrayal of Women." *Blake/An Illustrated Quarterly* Winter (1982–83): 148–55.
———. "On Romanticism and Feminism." *Romanticism and Feminism*, 3–9. Bloomington and Indianapolis: Indiana University Press, 1988.
———. *Romanticism & Gender*. New York and London: Routledge, 1993.
———. "Sex, Violence, and Slavery: Blake and Wollstonecraft." *Huntington Library Quarterly* 58:3 (1997): 345–370.
Metzger, Bruce M., and Michael D. Coogan, eds. *The Oxford Companion to the Bible*. New York and Oxford: Oxford University Press, 1993.
Middleton Murry, John. *William Blake*. London: Jonathan Cape, 1933.
Milne, Pamela J. Introduction to the Book of Daniel. *HarperCollins Study Bible*.
Milton, John. *Paradise Lost*. (1667). Ed. Christopher Ricks. London: Penguin, 1989.
Moi, Toril. *Sexual/Textual Politics: Feminist Literary Theory*. London and New York: Routledge, 1985.
More, Thomas. *Utopia*. (1516). Ed. Robert M. Adams. 2nd ed. New York and London: Norton, 1992.
Morson, Gary Saul. *The Boundaries of Genre: Dostoevsky's Diary of a Writer and the Traditions of Literary Utopia*. Austin: University of Texas Press, 1981.
Morton, A. L. *The English Utopia*. (1952). London: Lawrence and Wishart, 1969.
Murphy, Karleen Middleton. "'All the Lovely Sex': Blake and the Woman Question." In Bogan, James, and Fred Goss, eds. *Sparks of Fire: Blake in a New Age*. Richmond, CA: North Atlantic Books, 1982. 272–75.
New Dictionary of Biblical Theology. Ed. T. Desmond Alexander and Brian S. Rosner. Leicester and Downers Grove, Ill.: Inter-Varsity Press, 2000.
O'Meara, John. Introduction to St. Augustine, *City of God*.
Ostriker, Alicia. "Desire Gratified and Ungratified: William Blake and Sexuality." *Blake/An Illustrated Quarterly* Winter (1982–83): 156–65.
Paley, Morton D. *Apocalypse and Millennium in English Romantic Poetry*. Oxford: Oxford University Press, 1999.
———. *The Continuing City*. Oxford: Oxford University Press, 1983.
———. Introduction. In Blake, *Jerusalem* 9–16.
———. "A New Heaven Is Begun: William Blake and Swedenborgianism." *Blake/An Illustrated Quarterly* 13 (1979): 64–90.
Parker, William Riley. *Milton: A Biography*. London: Oxford University Press, 1968.
Pierce, John Benjamin. *Flexible Design: Revisionary Poetics in Blake's* Vala *or* The Four Zoas. Montreal and Kingston: McGill-Queen's University Press, 1998.
Piercy, Marge. *A Woman on the Edge of Time*. London: The Women's Press, 2001.
Rajan, Tilottama. "Autonarration and Genotext in Mary Hays' *Memoirs of Emma Cortney*." *Studies of Romanticism* 32/2 (1993): 149–76.
Rose, E. J. "Blake's *Milton:* The Poet as Poem." *Blake Studies* 1 (Fall 1968): 16–38.

Rousseau, Jean-Jacques. *La Nouvelle Heloïse*.1761. State College: Pennsylvania State University Press, 1989.
Russell, D. S. "Apocalyptic Literature." In Metzger and Coogan, eds., *Oxford Companion to the Bible.* 34–6.
St. Augustine. *City of God.* (1467). Trans. Henry Bettenson. London: Penguin, 1984.
Sambrook, James. *The Eighteenth Century: The Intellectual and Cultural Context of English Literature, 1700–1789.* London and New York: Longman, 1986.
Shanley, Mary Lyndon. "Mary Wollstonecraft on Sensibility, Women's Rights, and Patriarchal Power." In Smith, *Women Writers*, 148–67.
Sherman, Sandra. "The Feminization of 'Reason' in Hays' *The Victim of Prejudice.*" *Centennial Review* 41:1 (1997): 143–73.
Smith, Hilda L., ed. *Women Writers and the Early Modern British Political Tradition.* Cambridge: Cambridge University Press, 1998.
Sutherland, John H. "Blake's *Milton:* The Bard's Song." *Colby Library Quarterly* 19:4 (1983): 142–57.
Swedenborg, Emanuel. *The Delights of Wisdom Concerning Conjugial Love, After Which Follows the Pleasures of Insanity Concerning Scortatory Love.* (1768). London: Swedenborg Society, 1953.
———. *A Treatie Concerning Heaven and Hell, Containing a Relation of Many Wonderful Things Therein, as Heard and Seen by the Author.* London: James Phillips, 1778.
Tannenbaum, Les. "Coleridge and Southey: Fathers of Pantisocracy." *Path to Utopia: Pantisocracy.* 24 June 2003. <http://www.cohums.ohio-state.edu/English/People/Tannenbaum.1/studentwebs/01wi08>.
Thompson, E. P. *Witness Against the Beast: William Blake and the Moral Law.* Cambridge: Cambridge University Press, 1993.
Tuveson, Ernest Lee. *Redeemer Nation: The Idea of America's Millennial Role.* Chicago: Chicago University Press, 1968.
Ty, Eleanor. Editor's Introduction. In Hays, *The Victim of Prejudice.* VII–XXXI.
———. *Unsex'd Revolutionaries: Five Women Novelists of the 1790s.* Toronto: University of Toronto Press, 1993.
Verma, K. D. "The Woman Figure in Blake and the Idea of Shakti in Indian Thought." *Comparative Literature Studies* 27:3 (1990): 193–210.
Wadström, Carl Bernard. *Plan for a Free Community Upon the Coast of Africa.* London: R. Hindmarsh, 1789.
Wake, Wilma. "Swedenborgian Feminism: The Next Steps." *Studia Swedenborgiana* Vol. 13: 2 (2003): 17–27.
Watson, J. R. *English Poetry of the Romantic Period, 1789–1830.* London and New York: Longman, 1992.
Webb, R. K. "Religion." In McCalman, ed., *Oxford Companion to the Romantic Age.* 93–101.
Webster, Brenda S. *Blake's Prophetic Psychology.* London: Macmillan, 1983.
Wicksteed, Joseph. *William Blake's Jerusalem.* London: Trianon Press, 1954.
Wilkie, Brian, and Mary Lynn Johnson. *Blake's Four Zoas: The Design of a Dream.* Cambridge, Mass.: Harvard University Press, 1978.
Williams, Nicholas. *Ideology and Utopia in the Poetry of William Blake.* Cambridge: Cambridge University Press, 1998.

Willey, Basil. *The Eighteenth Century Background: Studies on the Idea of Nature in the Thought of the Period.* Harmondsworth: Penguin, 1972.
Wollstonecraft, Mary. *Collected Letters.* Ed. by Ralph M. Wardle. Ithaca and London: Cornell University Press, 1979.
_____. *Mary and the Wrongs of Woman.* (1798). Oxford and New York: Oxford University Press, 1987. 71–204.
_____. *A Vindication of the Rights of Woman.* (1792). Ed. Miriam Brody. London and Harmondsworth: Penguin, 1988.
Woolf, Virginia. *A Room of One's Own.* (1928). London: Penguin, 2002.
Wordsworth, William. "Preface." (1800). In Coleridge and Wordsworth, *Lyrical Ballads.*
Worrall, David. "Blake and 1790s Plebeian Radical Culture." *Blake in the Nineties.* 194–211.
_____. *Radical Culture: Discourse, Resistance and Surveillance, 1790–1820.* Hemel Hempstead: Harvester Wheatsheaf, 1992.
_____. "Thel in Africa." Unpublished conference paper. Oriental Blake Conference, Nov. 2003, University of Kyoto.

Index

Absence 21, 71, 101, 108, 118, 137, 163, 189
Ackland, Michael 55
Ackroyd, Peter 52, 161
Ahania 12-13, 66, 68, 70-71, 75, 79, 80-84, 93, 98-99, 113, 116-17, 120, 127, 137
Albion/universal man 2-5, 10, 12, 26-7, 34, 48, 52, 55-56, 60-63, 64, 71, 73, 85, 101-2, 103, 110, 122, 127-28, 132-33, 140, 146, 149-53, 159-60, 162-63, 165-67, 170-74, 177, 178-80, 181-83, 186-88,190
America 21, 40, 49
America: A Prophecy 12-13, 60, 107, 191
Androgyne/-ous 27, 149-51, 163, 183, 188
Apocalypse 1-3, 6-7, 9-13, 14-18, 19, 23, 30, 33, 35-36, 45, 68-69, 71, 77, 79, 83, 85, 90, 94, 99, 102, 103-15, 119-20, 123, 128-29, 135, 137-39, 145, 147-50, 151-54, 155-59, 162, 164, 166, 170, 174, 176-78, 180-84, 185-88, 192-93
Augustine, St. 32-34, 172

Barbauld, Anna Leatitia 52, 58
Beer, John 41
Bentley, G. E., Jr. 42-43, 46, 173
Bergmann, Helena 57-58
Beulah 12, 17-18, 24-25, 29-35, 71, 73, 107-9, 131, 133-35, 139, 141, 145, 149, 153-54, 164, 174, 177

Billigheimer, Rachel V. 38
Blake, Catherine 134
Blake, James 42
Blake Harmitage, Catherine 42
Bloom, Harold 27-28, 34
Bluestockings 58
Boehme, Jacob 24, 27
The Book of Ahania 12-13, 66
The Book of Los 12, 66
The Book of Thel 5, 51, 61-62
Bromion 6, 63-65
Brotherhood of man 14, 33, 47, 136, 141, 153, 159, 164-65, 177, 182, 186, 191
Bruder, Helen 1, 4, 23, 38, 55-56, 62, 194
Burney, Francis 58
Butler, Judith 21-24, 70, 128, 155-56

Caine, Barbara 54-55
Catalyst 19-20, 22, 131
Chaos 23, 88, 93, 100, 116, 135, 162, 165, 167, 179, 189
Christ 12, 14-15, 44, 77, 104-6, 108, 159, 164
Christian 14, 19, 32, 41, 47-48, 66, 74, 97, 106, 182, 191, 193
City 17-18, 30, 32-34, 77, 84, 106, 143, 167, 171-73, 176-77
City of God 32-34, 77, 172
Cixous, Hélène 21
Clark, Anna 54
Cock 144
Cohen 191-93, 195

Coleridge, Samuel Taylor 41, 49-50
Conjugial Love 44, 48, 50-51
Contrary/-ies 11, 25-26, 28-30, 45, 56, 61, 91, 141, 154-55, 175, 186
Creation 6, 18, 20, 27-28, 34, 38, 41, 44, 62, 67, 76, 104, 129, 135, 176, 180
Cunt 144

Damnation 10, 14, 113, 192-93
Damon, S. Foster 32, 71, 85, 140
Damrosch, Leopold 21-22, 24, 26-27, 32-33, 35, 37, 85, 91, 118, 132, 138, 150
Daniel 10, 14-17, 106
Dante 28
Daughters of Albion 12, 48, 52, 55-56, 60-65, 132-33, 159-60, 166, 170-72, 182
Davies, Keri 42, 45-46, 48, 52-54, 143, 194-95
Derrida, Jacques 182, 189, 191-92, 195
Desire 1, 7, 14, 30-31, 35, 50, 56, 58-59, 61, 63, 66-67, 73-75, 78, 87-88, 135, 168, 171, 176, 185, 188
Dissent 7, 40-41, 42-48, 56-57, 194
The Divine Comedy 28
Doskow, Minna 34
Douce, Francis 53-54
Dualism 10-11, 21, 26, 33, 43-45, 97, 115, 126-27, 133, 141, 171, 175

Eaves, Morris 60
L'écriture feminine 21
Eden 2, 9, 11-14, 17, 19, 22, 24-27, 29-35, 37, 67, 69, 72, 77-78, 82, 84, 88, 91, 99, 108-10, 115, 117, 119-21, 123, 126, 129, 131, 133-35, 140-41, 143, 145, 150-51, 153-54, 157, 161, 164-65, 169, 178, 184, 186-90, 194
Emanation 3, 13, 17, 26-29, 33, 35, 38, 57, 66, 68-74, 78, 80-81, 83-89, 91, 96-103, 113, 115-18, 120, 122-23, 126-27, 130-31, 133, 135, 137-43, 146-50, 152, 156, 159-60, 162-66, 170, 172, 174-76, 178, 183, 185, 188, 190
Enion 2, 13, 68-69, 71, 75, 78-79-80, 83, 86-88, 90, 92-93, 102, 105, 108-9, 113, 118-20, 127, 137, 160, 186
Enitharmon 13, 25-31, 60, 66-69, 71, 72-77, 81, 86, 89, 91-98, 103, 105, 114-120, 126, 127-29, 133-34, 137, 139, 144-45, 153-54, 156, 159-61, 168-69, 175-76, 178, 185-87
Enlightenment 4, 41, 47, 49, 57

Epic 1-7, 9-14, 16, 19, 24, 26, 32, 35-36, 39-40, 59, 66, 96, 103-4, 107, 109, 115, 121, 123, 125, 137, 142, 144, 151, 153, 156, 158, 160-61, 163, 174-76, 178, 183-85, 187, 190
Erdman, David V. 6, 78, 87
Essick, Robert N. 60, 141, 155
Eternity 10-11, 13, 27-30, 33-34, 38, 73, 82, 92, 97, 99, 103, 105, 110, 120, 134, 144-46, 149, 153-55, 159-61, 165, 169, 171, 174, 181-85, 189
Europe 4, 49, 166
Exile 70, 78, 80
Exodus 148
Experience 5, 11, 19, 30, 62, 64, 72, 78, 80, 83, 95, 99, 144
Ezekiel 10, 14-16, 18, 26, 85, 103, 172

The Fall 3, 7, 10-11, 14, 19-20, 22, 25-32, 334-36, 40-41, 45, 56, 61-62, 64, 66-68, 70-78, 8-88, 91-93, 97-101, 103, 105-6, 109, 111, 113-115, 117, 119, 125, 130-31, 133, 136, 138-40, 142, 145, 147-48, 150-51, 153-56, 158-59, 161, 163-66, 168-70, 173-74, 176-81, 186-87, 192
Felpham 122-24, 132, 134, 143, 150, 153, 160
Felski, Rita 21, 135
Female activity 2-4, 26, 36, 67, 113, 116-18, 124-27, 131, 148, 154, 178
Female character 1-5, 15, 19-21, 26-28, 36-39, 59-63, 66-70, 72, 74, 84-86, 104, 118, 124-33, 135, 137, 142-43, 146, 160, 162-63, 170, 172-75, 194
Female metaphor/symbol 1, 4, 21, 37-38, 113, 162, 188
The Female will 26-29, 68-69, 72, 85, 116, 130, 137, 148, 159, 168, 170, 175
Feminine 11, 29-30, 36, 45, 71, 83, 130, 135, 142, 150, 155-56, 164, 173
Feminism 1-2, 4-5, 20-22, 27, 37-38, 40, 44-45, 52-53, 55-58, 60-61, 66, 135
The First Book of Urizen 12-13, 18, 66
Forgiveness of sins 7, 14, 33, 131-32, 164, 182, 184, 191, 193, 195
Four zoas 85, 111, 120, 166-67, 177, 182-83, 187-88, 190
The Four Zoas 1-3, 6-7, 10-11, 13-16, 18, 23, 25-26, 28-29, 33-35, 52, 60-121, 122-30, 133, 135-40, 142, 149, 151-63,

167–68, 170, 172, 174–75, 179–82, 184–85, 188–90, 193–94
Fox, Susan 4, 11, 38, 40, 125–26, 128
"Free" love 25, 62, 145, 171
Freeman, Kathryn 10
The French Revolution 17, 56, 59, 118
Frye, Northrop 19, 24, 27, 29, 85, 97, 100
Fuseli, Henry 52

Gender 2–7, 9, 11–14, 19–23, 25, 27–28, 30, 34–42, 48, 50, 52, 54–57, 60–62, 64–69, 75–76, 78, 80–81, 92, 102, 106, 114–15, 117, 119, 121–29, 131–32, 134, 136–38, 147–52, 154–58, 160–62, 164–66, 168–69, 175, 178, 181, 184–90, 193–94
Gender equality 2–7, 9, 14, 19–20, 23, 30, 34–35, 37, 39, 44, 48, 56–58, 61–63, 65, 67, 121, 131, 160–62
Gender interactivity 3, 25, 35–36, 67, 69, 78, 101, 125–29, 134, 150–51, 154–56, 160, 162, 168, 175, 181, 184–87, 189
Gender utopia 2–4, 7, 12–14, 26, 35–36, 39–41, 52, 60–61, 65–66, 68, 76, 122–23, 125–27, 129, 131–32, 134, 136–37, 149, 154–58, 160–61, 165, 169, 187, 189
Generation 17, 24–25, 29, 32, 71–72, 82, 97, 100, 111, 116, 123, 126, 137, 140–41, 143, 176
Genesis 14, 19–20, 30–31, 45, 176
Genitals 35, 69, 143, 145
Gilchrist, Alexander 43
Godwin, William 49
Golgonooza 143–44, 172, 177, 185

Haigney, Catherine 4
Hayley, William 132, 142
Hays, Mary 1, 4–5, 55, 57–59, 65–66, 133
Hegel, G. W. F. 191
The Hermaphrodite 149–51, 165, 171
Holistic 39, 124
Humanism 40–42, 132, 165, 181, 189, 193
Hume, David 41, 57
Hume George, Diana 4, 20

Illuminated writing 5, 43, 52–53, 61, 158, 160
Imagination 24, 26, 41, 43, 96
Innocence 11, 30, 62, 70, 72, 75–76, 80, 82, 87–88, 90–91, 95, 101–2, 105, 108–9, 111–13, 115, 119, 137, 161, 173, 178, 178, 183–84
Irigaray, Luce 21–22, 33
Isaiah 10, 14–16, 103, 106–7, 112

Jacobins 7, 48–54
Jealousy 2, 5, 31, 66, 75–76, 78, 81, 86, 92, 94–97, 122, 130, 132–33, 140–41, 143, 147, 151, 159, 165, 168, 186–87
Jerusalem 17–18, 25, 27, 34, 69, 73, 77, 84, 86, 104–6, 133, 142–44, 159–60, 162–66, 171, 172–74, 176–77, 179–80, 183–85, 188, 190, 192
Jerusalem 1–3, 6–7, 11, 13–14, 16–17, 23–25, 28, 33–35, 37, 39, 47, 57, 76, 85, 94, 97, 101, 107, 114–15, 121–24, 127, 131, 135, 137, 141–42, 149–51, 153–57, 158–90, 191–95
Jesus 7, 18, 47, 106, 133, 168, 178, 182, 191
Johnson, Joseph 5, 41, 51–55, 61, 133, 194

Kabbalah 27
Keats, John 86
Kristeva, Julia 21

The last judgement 91, 103
Leutha 60, 64, 126–27, 129–31, 132–33, 139
Locke, John 54
London 5, 40–41, 45, 47–48, 51, 53, 57, 66, 122–23, 136–37, 153, 162, 166, 171–73, 177, 179, 192
London Corresponding Society 48
Loom 77, 113, 120, 127–28, 179, 185, 187
Los 12–13, 17, 30, 35, 66, 68, 70, 72–77, 81, 88–90, 91–96, 97–98, 100–1, 103–7, 114–15, 120, 122, 126–29, 134, 135–37, 138–39, 141, 143–44, 146, 152–54, 156, 160, 162–63, 166, 168–71, 174–78, 182, 184–88, 194
Love 2, 25, 27–28, 30, 32, 34–35, 43–44, 47–48, 50–51, 61–64, 66, 71–72, 74–76, 78–79, 86–87, 93, 95–96, 98, 104–5, 111, 113, 115–17, 130–31, 140–41, 143–45, 159, 161, 163–65, 167–71, 173, 176, 181–82, 185–89, 194
Luvah 10, 13, 18, 26, 30–31, 68–71, 75–76, 82, 86, 99–102, 108, 110, 112–13, 117, 120, 127, 139–40, 162–63, 165–67, 182

Makdisi, Saree 15, 49, 193–94
Male activity 2, 36, 65, 84, 148

Male character 1, 3, 36, 60, 68–69, 72, 78, 84, 104, 123–27, 139, 143, 156, 160, 162, 171, 178
Marriage 22, 34, 42–44, 46–47, 51, 63, 73, 92
The Marriage of Heaven and Hell 11, 14, 43–44, 76, 116, 142, 175, 191
Masculine 11, 83, 130, 155–56, 164
Masculinist signifying economy 21, 70, 128
Matthew 15, 34
Mauss, Marcel 191
McQuail, Josephine A. 38
Mee, Jon 42, 53, 194
Mellor, Anne 1, 4, 21, 36–37, 55, 135, 194
Messiah 11, 15
Millennium 7, 9, 11–12, 14–15, 104, 136
Milton 1, 3, 17, 35, 122–27, 129, 133–36, 138–39, 142–43, 145, 146–49, 150–56, 160, 172, 188
Milton 1–3, 6–7, 11, 13–14, 17–18, 29–30, 35, 60, 76, 96, 115, 121, 122–57, 158–60, 163, 165–66, 170–72, 174, 179, 184, 188, 194
Milton, John 24, 123–26, 135, 138–39, 146–47, 150, 172, 184, 186
Misogynist 1, 37–38, 83
The Moment 4, 11, 14, 22, 25, 41, 56, 72, 76, 120, 123, 125, 129, 132–35, 140, 145, 149, 151–54, 156, 158–59, 169, 181, 184–85, 187
More, Hannah 58
More, Sir Thomas 12
Morton, A. L. 2, 12, 35
Muggletonians 42, 44–46
Murphy, Karleen Middleton 37
Mysticism 38
Mythology 5, 13, 24–26, 38, 66, 73, 109, 165

Negation 5, 10, 13, 19, 25–26, 28, 34, 45, 64, 66–67, 70, 76–7, 80, 85, 87, 92–93, 96, 105, 109, 111, 113, 115, 119, 138–39, 147–51, 154–55, 159, 164, 168–71, 173–75, 184
Nordenskjöld, August 50–51, 194

Ololon 1, 3, 122–27, 129, 133–35, 142–43, 146–52, 154–55, 156, 160, 172, 194
O'Meara, John 32
Oothoon 5–6, 60, 62–65, 132–33, 137, 153, 160

Ostriker, Alicia 1, 4, 68–69, 72, 77, 86, 130, 194

Paine, Thomas 18, 52–53
Paley, Morton 9, 12, 15, 18, 43, 104, 123, 162, 181
Pantisocracy 49–50
Paradise 11, 19, 29–32, 46–49, 53, 61, 69, 75, 87, 105, 109, 119, 173, 183, 194
Paradise Lost 100, 129–30, 138–39, 186
Passion 26, 38, 47, 57–59, 64, 66, 88, 167, 181
Patriarchy 4, 20–24, 25, 33, 36, 44–45, 48, 54, 56, 58–59, 62, 64–65, 83–84, 96, 167
Penis 47, 144
Phallocentric symbolic: order/phallogocentric language 21–22
The Pickering MS 52
Pierce, John, B. 6, 25
Piercy, Marge 135
Plato 14, 27
Post-apocalyptic 13, 19, 23, 29, 32–33, 71–72, 84, 193–94
Post-lapsarian 3, 14, 70, 97, 150
Post-structuralism 22
Pre-apocalypse 36, 123, 137, 151–54, 155–56
Pre-lapsarian 11, 19, 67, 72–73, 115, 173
Presence 45, 47, 71, 76, 87, 106, 137
Priestley, Joseph 5, 49, 52
Prophecy 1–2, 5, 9–17, 35, 45, 51, 57, 60 66–67, 76, 91, 97, 115, 123, 131, 134, 136, 146, 150, 156, 161, 170–71, 178, 192–93, 195
Prostitution 22, 66

Radical 1, 5–7, 19, 22, 24, 40–42, 45, 48–50, 52–53, 56–58, 60, 62–64, 66–67, 87, 115, 128
Rajan, Tillotama 58
Reason 18, 24, 26, 45, 47, 49, 56–59, 67, 70, 72, 96–97, 101, 137, 141, 146, 154, 165, 174
Reconciliation 3–4, 59, 108, 120, 149–50, 182, 191
Redemption 10, 14, 104, 109, 136, 145, 164, 182
Religion 5, 14, 16, 22, 41, 45, 106, 115, 136, 170, 194
Resurrection 12, 14, 16, 34, 77, 104, 113, 147, 153, 167, 185

Reunion 3, 11, 15, 35, 38, 49, 67, 71–72, 84, 108, 115–20, 123–24, 126, 128, 137–38, 148–52, 154–55, 162, 166, 178, 183, 186–90
Revelation 10–12, 14–18, 25–26, 45, 80, 85, 103–4, 106, 172, 192
Revolution 13, 25, 40, 42, 47–48, 52, 56, 61, 63, 65, 94, 107, 139, 178, 181
Revolution, American 40, 107
Revolution, French 13, 40, 52, 61, 107
Romanticism 9, 41–42, 45, 58
Rousseau, Jean-Jacques 58, 62
Russell, D. S. 15–16

Satan 45, 96–97, 100, 129–32, 134, 137–39, 142–43, 149–50, 179
Scapegoat 80–81, 129
Scott, Frank 191
The Second Coming 11, 15, 79, 84, 94, 105, 138
The Serpent 6, 20, 31, 84, 98, 130–31, 184
Sexist 1, 20–21, 37, 75, 194
Sexuality 2–5, 19–23, 30–31, 33–36, 39, 40, 44–45, 47–51, 54–58, 60–67, 70–71, 73, 75, 77, 93, 96, 98, 100, 108, 110, 115–16, 125, 128, 130, 132–33, 135, 140–46, 150, 155, 161, 163–66, 170–71, 176, 184, 187–89
The Shadowy female 28, 61, 70–71, 126–27, 137, 139–40, 152
Shelley, Percy Bysshe 27, 41
Sherman, Sandra 57
Sin 7, 11, 14, 19–20, 33, 71, 75, 81, 87, 92, 99, 108, 110, 113, 129–32, 139, 164, 171, 180, 182, 184, 191, 193, 195
Slavery 55, 63, 194
The Song of Los 12, 66
Songs of Experience 11
Songs of Innocence 11, 111–12
Songs of Innocence and of Experience 11, 95
Southey, Robert 49–50, 173
The Spectre 6, 25–26, 68, 72, 76–77, 85, 87–88, 91, 95, 99, 104–5, 115, 138–39, 154, 166, 168, 175–76, 186–87
Spiritual utopia 14–18, 79
Sublation 11
Swedenborg, Emmanuel 43–46, 48, 50–51, 194

Tannenbaum, Les 49–50

Tayler, Irene 4
Tharmas 13, 25, 68–69, 75–78, 80, 85, 86–91, 92, 94, 97, 100–2, 108–9, 111, 113, 118–20, 127, 159, 162, 166–67, 182
Theotormon 63–65, 144
Thompson, E. P. 42, 44–46
Thrale Piozzi, Hester 58
Togetherness 3, 11, 24, 34–35, 37, 57, 71–72, 77, 84, 113, 115–20, 121, 123, 128, 156–57, 161–62, 182–83, 184–89, 190
Transcendence 107, 115, 127, 189
Twiss 53–54
Ty, Eleanor 60

Ulro 17, 24–25, 29, 101, 104, 133, 141, 147–48, 150–51, 155, 159
Unity 11, 16–17, 28, 34–35, 38–39, 48, 51, 59, 68, 72, 77, 125–26, 128, 136–38, 143, 146–47, 149–52, 155, 159, 169–71, 173, 178, 182, 188
Urizen 12–13, 18, 26, 66, 68, 70–71, 74–75, 80–85, 89–94, 96–99, 100–2, 109–11, 113, 116–17, 119–20, 127, 133, 137–39, 140, 162–63, 166–67, 182
Urthona 13, 25, 68, 72, 76, 85, 88–89, 91–96, 98, 100, 102, 113–15, 117, 120, 162, 166, 175, 182
Utopia 1–4, 6–7, 9, 11, 12–18, 19, 22–23, 25–37, 39–41, 49–50, 52, 56–57, 60–63, 65–68, 72, 76, 80–84, 87–89, 104, 108–11, 114–15, 120–27, 129, 131–33, 135–37, 140, 148–50, 153–58, 160–61, 165, 169, 172–74, 176–77, 180–82, 184–90, 192–95

Vagina 144–45
Vala 13, 28, 30–31, 34, 61, 67–68, 69–72, 77, 80, 83, 90, 97–102, 108–9, 113, 117–20, 127, 140, 142, 150, 160, 163–67, 170, 173–74
Vala 6, 18, 26
Vala's Garden 30, 80, 102, 108–9, 117–19
Verma, K. D. 38–39
Vindication of the Rights of Woman 4, 52, 56, 62–64
Viscomi, Joseph 60, 141, 155
Vision 2, 7, 9–11, 13–18, 20, 32–35, 38–39, 41, 43–45, 49, 70, 74, 79, 82–84, 90, 92, 99, 104, 106, 108–9, 114–15, 118–19, 121–22, 124, 126–27, 131–33, 146, 153–55, 159–60, 162, 164, 169,

172–74, 177, 180, 182–85, 187–88, 192–93, 195
Visions of the Daughters of Albion 5–6, 12, 47–48, 52, 56, 60–61, 62–65, 66, 160, 191

Wadström, Carl Bernard 50–51, 194
Webster, Brenda 4, 37–38
Williams, Nicholas 2, 4, 12, 36, 56, 62, 194
Wollstonecraft, Mary 1, 4–5, 40, 47, 49, 52–53, 55–58, 61–64, 66, 133, 145
Woman 1, 3–5, 11, 17–22, 28, 31–32, 34–41, 45, 49–52, 54–58, 60, 62–64, 66, 67, 75–77, 81, 86–88, 97–98, 110–11, 114–18, 120, 123, 131, 133, 135, 141–42, 146–49, 166, 168–69, 171–72
Woolf, Virginia 58
Wordsworth, William 41
Worrall, David 18, 43, 48, 51, 53, 194–95

Zoa 11–3, 6–7, 10–11, 13, 15–18, 23, 25–30, 33–35, 52, 60–62, 65–73, 75–78, 80–82, 84–87, 90–91, 93–94, 96–100, 103–4, 107–9, 111, 113–17, 119–31, 133, 135–40, 142, 149, 151–68, 170, 172–75, 177, 179–85, 187–90, 193–94

www.ingramcontent.com/pod-product-compliance
Lightning Source LLC
Chambersburg PA
CBHW032055300426
44116CB00007B/753